Djuna Barnes and Theology

NEW DIRECTIONS IN RELIGION AND LITERATURE

This series aims to showcase new work at the forefront of religion and literature through short studies written by leading and rising scholars in the field. Books will pursue a variety of theoretical approaches as they engage with writing from different religious and literary traditions. Collectively, the series will offer a timely critical intervention to the interdisciplinary crossover between religion and literature, speaking to wider contemporary interests and mapping out new directions for the field in the early twenty-first century.

Series editors: Emma Mason and Mark Knight

ALSO AVAILABLE IN THE SERIES:
The New Atheist Novel, Arthur Bradley and Andrew Tate
Blake. Wordsworth. Religion, Jonathan Roberts
Do the Gods Wear Capes?, Ben Saunders
England's Secular Scripture, Jo Carruthers
Victorian Parables, Susan E. Colón
The Late Walter Benjamin, John Schad
Dante and the Sense of Transgression, William Franke
The Glyph and the Gramophone, Luke Ferretter
John Cage and Buddhist Ecopoetics, Peter Jaeger
Rewriting the Old Testament in Anglo-Saxon Verse, Samantha Zacher
Forgiveness in Victorian Literature, Richard Hughes Gibson
The Gospel According to the Novelist, Magdalena Mączyńska
Jewish Feeling, Richa Dwor
Beyond the Willing Suspension of Disbelief, Michael Tomko
The Gospel According to David Foster Wallace, Adam S. Miller
Pentecostal Modernism, Stephen Shapiro and Philip Barnard
The Bible in the American Short Story, Lesleigh Cushing Stahlberg and Peter S. Hawkins
Faith in Poetry, Michael D. Hurley
Jeanette Winterson and Religion, Emily McAvan
Religion and American Literature since the 1950s, Mark Eaton
Esoteric Islam in Modern French Thought, Ziad Elmarsafy
The Rhetoric of Conversion in English Puritan Writing, David Parry

FORTHCOMING:
Marilynne Robinson's Wordly Gospel, Ryan S. Kemp and Jordan M. Rodgers
Weird Faith in 19th Century Literature, Mark Knight and Emma Mason

Djuna Barnes and Theology

Melancholy, Body, Theodicy

Zhao Ng

BLOOMSBURY ACADEMIC
LONDON • NEW YORK • OXFORD • NEW DELHI • SYDNEY

BLOOMSBURY ACADEMIC
Bloomsbury Publishing Plc
50 Bedford Square, London, WC1B 3DP, UK
1385 Broadway, New York, NY 10018, USA
29 Earlsfort Terrace, Dublin 2, Ireland

BLOOMSBURY, BLOOMSBURY ACADEMIC and the Diana logo
are trademarks of Bloomsbury Publishing Plc

First published in Great Britain 2022
This paperback edition published 2023

Copyright © Zhao Ng, 2022

Zhao Ng has asserted their right under the Copyright, Designs and
Patents Act, 1988, to be identified as Author of this work.

For legal purposes the Acknowledgments on pp. vii–viii constitute
an extension of this copyright page.

Cover design by Eleanor Rose
Cover image: The Authors League Fund and St. Bride's Church, as joint literary executors of
the Estate of Djuna Barnes.

All rights reserved. No part of this publication may be reproduced or transmitted
in any form or by any means, electronic or mechanical, including photocopying,
recording, or any information storage or retrieval system, without prior
permission in writing from the publishers.

Bloomsbury Publishing Plc does not have any control over, or responsibility for, any
third-party websites referred to or in this book. All internet addresses given in this
book were correct at the time of going to press. The author and publisher regret any
inconvenience caused if addresses have changed or sites have ceased to exist,
but can accept no responsibility for any such changes.

A catalogue record for this book is available from the British Library.

A catalog record for this book is available from the Library of Congress.

ISBN: HB: 978-1-3502-5602-6
PB: 978-1-3502-5606-4
ePDF: 978-1-3502-5603-3
eBook: 978-1-3502-5604-0

Series: New Directions in Religion and Literature

Typeset by Integra Software Services Pvt. Ltd.

To find out more about our authors and books visit www.bloomsbury.com
and sign up for our newsletters.

Contents

List of Figures		vi
Acknowledgments		vii
Preface: Theology and the Queer Body		ix
Introduction: A Dialectic of Melancholy and Theodicy		1
Melancholy and Ontology		1
The Question of Theodicy		10
Weak Theodicy		16
The Judgment of Art		21
Moods, Modes, and the Ontology of the Work of Art		26
1	Melancholy and the Fall	33
	Laughing and Crying	38
	Hybrid Bodies: The Problem of Corporeal Assumption	45
2	Comedy I: *Ladies Almanack* and the Lesbian Sensorium	53
	"Girls! Girls!"—or Utopia	58
	Becoming-Lesbian	67
3	Comedy II: *Ryder*, Rape, and Recurrence	83
	Humor, Satire, Irony	87
	To Spit or Swallow?	103
4	Tragedy I: *Nightwood* and the Eschatological Body	117
	The Resurrection of the Body	119
	Of Beasts Blond and Damned	128
5	Tragedy II: *The Antiphon* and the Refusal of History	149
	Sublimation and Its Discontents	157
	Play and Repining	169
Conclusion: Life or Death?		177
Bibliography		182
Index		197

Figures

1.1 Djuna Barnes, "All Because of Wendell!" *Ryder*. © The Authors League Fund and St. Bride's Church, as joint literary executors of the Estate of Djuna Barnes — 37

1.2 Albrecht Dürer, *Elk*, 1504, drawing. London, British Museum. © The Trustees of the British Museum — 47

1.3 Thelma Wood, *Bushbuck Among Bamboo Trees*, 1928. © The Authors League Fund and St. Bride's Church, as joint literary executors of the Estate of Djuna Barnes — 48

1.4 Albrecht Dürer, *Adam and Eve*, 1504, engraving. New York, Metropolitan Museum of Art — 49

2.1 Djuna Barnes, "Sweet May," *Ladies Almanack*. © The Authors League Fund and St. Bride's Church, as joint literary executors of the Estate of Djuna Barnes — 61

3.1 Djuna Barnes, "The Joke in the Tragedy," 1913. © The Authors League Fund and St. Bride's Church, as joint literary executors of the Estate of Djuna Barnes — 94

4.1 Joseph Ottinger, *Crucifixion*, c. 1750–1800. © The Authors League Fund and St. Bride's Church, as joint literary executors of the Estate of Djuna Barnes — 141

4.2 Albrecht Dürer, print from *Apocalypse*, 1497–8, woodcut. New York, Metropolitan Museum of Art — 147

5.1 Emily Coleman, drawing from "Book of Drawings," undated. MSS 105, Emily Holmes Coleman papers, Special Collections, University of Delaware Library. Newark, Delaware. © by Estate of Emily Holmes Coleman — 154

5.2 Emily Coleman, drawing from "Book of Drawings," undated. MSS 105, Emily Holmes Coleman papers, Special Collections, University of Delaware Library. Newark, Delaware. © by Estate of Emily Holmes Coleman — 155

Acknowledgments

This book has been made possible thanks to the support of many. My gratitude is due to David Dwan, from the first for taking my project on at Oxford, and for seeing it through to completion. His critical attention has been indispensable, and has been one source of continuity over these past years of discontinuities. I thank him for taming the melancholy in my own writing of melancholy, and for—as he likes to put it—being 'on my side.'

Others who have offered me invaluable academic guidance at Oxford include Marina Mackay, Ankhi Mukherjee, and Jeri Johnson. Laura Marcus and Sanja Bahun have read a version of this book in its entirety, for which I am deeply grateful. Their keen advice and continued efforts in supporting my research have been a moving source of encouragement. Harry Daniels, Daniel Abdalla, and Yaron Wolf have all read portions of the book as it took shape; Anna Espínola Lynn has lent a much appreciated art-historical eye in support of my apprehensive inclusion of visual material; and Cathryn Setz most crucially furnished me with a copy of her co-edited volume on Barnes when it was still inaccessible. I am thankful furthermore to the editors at Bloomsbury, Ben Doyle and Laura Cope, and the series editors for *New Directions in Religion and Literature*, Emma Mason and Mark Knight, for taking on this project—as well as to the anonymous readers for Bloomsbury for their heartening and insightful reviews.

Much of the archive work undertaken in the writing of this book has also been facilitated by the help of others. I owe my thanks to the staff at the Djuna Barnes Archive, and, in particular, Amber Marie Kohl at the University of Maryland, for presenting me with the scans of some crucial material; as well as to Isabel Howe, at The Authors League Fund, who has been wondrously kind, meticulous, and supportive throughout in her assistance with copyright and permissions clearance; Paul Cougnard at the Fonds Jacques Doucet, a thoroughly accommodating presence during my time spent there; Curtis Small, for his swift work in hunting down the two sketches from the Emily Holmes Coleman Papers; and Joseph Geraci, for going through the trouble of clearing a number of copyright hurdles on my behalf.

I am also thankful for the varieties of research, financial, and institutional support from Wadham College, Oxford, and the Rothermere American

Institute, where this project was seen through—and most of all to the Wadham 1610 Society, without whose generosity, in the form of a full scholarship, this book would never have materialized. My deepest gratitude is due, furthermore, to Torkel Mattesson, for being the first to confront me with the problem of theodicy—and Kjølv Egeland, for first intimating an answer. Finally, I have to return here in a few meager words all that has been given to me by my most forbearing friends, who have stood by me through a number of dark—seemingly unending—years, and who have reminded me on more than one occasion that to dwell permanently among the dead was to bring death too to those yet living. You know who you are.

The last word I reserve here for the "damned" and the "disqualified" of history. It is for you after all that this was written. We do not know your names, but we try not to forget.

Preface: Theology and the Queer Body

Perhaps all women are really obscene, for they make love to death in their hearts. So did Swann.

(Barnes 1939e)

I think I am taking on to myself Thelma's wish to murder me, doing it myself, so it wont [sic] be suicide after all, when it happens (how many suicides <u>are</u> suicide and how many proxy murders?)

(Barnes 1938g)

We all bring ourselves to the grave but the artist like two people is one who pushes and who is pushed.

(Barnes 1940b)

Following Freud's canonical formulations in "Mourning and Melancholia" (1917) and *The Ego and the Id* (1923), it has often been suggested that human bodies assume their forms via a constitutive division: the pre-melancholic self, suffering loss, is broken in two. This lost love is set up again in the chambers of the self, where it lives in tension with its developing—or in less congenial cases—atrophied host. Melancholy thus signals the organism's division into the ego and the superego, which becomes the productive or parasitical scion of a lost love. Such a superego, grown out of this lost love, can be nurturing or suffocating. Either way, it shapes the emergent subject by coding self and world with systems of value and meaning, conditioning development with a mixture of critique and affection. With the loved one internalized, subject and body inherit significance. A net of positive and negative affects, of beauty and its others, moral systems and meanings made manifest, is thrown over the world. This is particularly so in the case of individuation from one's parental figures in early life: weaning is also the acquisition of meaning. In certain cases of debilitating melancholia, however, this turns into a covenant with Death, a devotion to an internalized persecutory fury that directs one not toward any developmental telos, but the termination of one's own existence. The citations here from Barnes's letters demonstrate this morbid turn: the Dance of Death that afflicts the multitude ("we all bring ourselves to the grave") is re-choreographed into a *pas de deux* by the divided parts of the "artist," given over now to a fatefully coordinated pulse of action (pushing) and submission (pushed).

We might say then, that in contrast to the general melancholy of modern subjectivity, the acute melancholy of Barnes's artist, singled out thus, stands for a form of mourning gone awry—gone, indeed, *queer*. With particular urgency, queerness would appear to raise the question of the relation between the many shapes of the self melancholic subjects come to assume in the *historical* world, and the horizon of the self's own end—that is, its *eschatological* orientation. It is precisely this question that Sarah Coakley raises in response to Judith Butler's seminal readings of melancholic gender (Coakley 2000). If bodies come to assume their queer shapes through a constitutive internalization of love and death, is it possible to think these historical selves, rooted in melancholy, in tension with the horizon of their overcoming? Coakley hence points to an "eschatological horizon which will give mortal flesh final significance, a horizon in which the restless, fluid post-modern 'body' can find some sense of completion without losing its mystery, without succumbing again to 'appropriate' or restrictive gender roles" (2000, 70). We might in fact ask after Barnes: in turning against itself, is the geminated body, engaged in self-consumption, re-oriented toward that radical finitude signaled in Heidegger's "being-toward-death," or toward that anticipated renewal that Ricoeur finds "in the light of the Resurrection"? (Ricoeur 1974, 409–10). Having escaped Europe in the throes of the Second World War, Barnes at one point references Job 1:21-22 and questions this possibility of a new beginning:

> What I have now is a new, almost new life, lean and full of memories; because of losing everything, those memories are dead memories; not lost, but different: the finishing cut was made in this country. Now I can begin again "naked as I came into this world"… an aged birth. It is in the Bible so. I am laid in the skeleton instead of the cradle.
>
> (1941a)

If a rebirth from melancholia is suggested here, it remains, however, paradoxically an "aged birth" *into* death. Having superseded death, she returns once more re-oriented toward it, "laid in the skeleton instead of the cradle." Is one reborn—or locked merely into an eternal repetition of death?

Recognizing the intimate link between the psychosomatic aporia of the human subject and queer embodiment, a number of theologians have sought to emphasize the queerness of the body of Christ himself. In Graham Ward's "theological account of sexual difference," the foundational role of "relation" ensures that "[e]mbodiment maintains its excess, maintains its transcorporeality in and through its congress with the mysteries of other bodies" (Loughlin 2007, 84). For Elizabeth Stuart, the melancholic incorporation of Christ's body in his followers—most notably in the partaking of the "sacramental flesh"—binds these both to death and its supersession before "the throne of grace":

> Queer flesh is sacramental flesh nudging the queer performer towards the Christian eschatological horizon, and sacramental flesh is queer flesh nudging the Christian towards the realisation that in Christ maleness and femaleness and gay and straight are categories that dissolve before the throne of grace where only the garment of baptism remains.
>
> (Loughlin 2007, 75)[1]

The queerness of Christ's body, "permeable, transcorporeal and transpositional," prompts Stuart to the claim, not without a trace of Christian exceptionalism, that "the church is the only community under a mandate to be queer" (Loughlin 2007, 65-6). For Barnes too, a God who is above all, through all, and in all (Ephesians 4:6), it would seem, must be queer. As a notebook jotting dating probably from November 1917 has it: "Even God could not keep straight the things he had planned in a line—" (cited in Miller 1999, 243).

The readings of Barnes this book proposes target the queer body in its "excess embodiment," in relation to the horizon of its end—an end that is suspended in indecision, however, and interrogated by the artist. As will be seen, in bracketing out the eschatological destination of subjects sunk within the interim zone of melancholic existence, the questions of life or death, salvation or damnation, surface urgently once more. If for Stuart, "it is only within the church that queer theory reaches its *telos*, with the melancholia of gender replaced by the joy born of the death and resurrection of Christ," then the question has to be raised: where does that leave the non-Christian, or non-believer? (Loughlin 2007, 75). We will have occasion over the course of this book to see how Barnes's avoidance of any firm religious commitment refers these forms of historical embodiment to a variety of ends, including those of profane or "obscene" import, converting the subject into a devotee of mortal finitude—as with the women who "make love to death in their hearts." It is not my intention to endorse any of the comic or tragic worlds set up across the Barnes corpus in the following

---

[1] The reference here, of course, is to Galatians 3:28, that in baptism: "There is neither Jew nor Greek, there is neither bond nor free, there is neither male nor female: for ye are all one in Christ Jesus." For a compelling reading of Saint Paul's theological anthropology and modern philosophy, see Dunning 2014.

pages, but merely to present the aesthetic and theological imagination of one of modernism's most singular, cryptic minds, and to offer an analytic record of the sufferings of melancholy, ranging from the universal (laughing and crying) to the idiosyncratic and queer (sex- and species-indifference), and indeed to expose the hidden logic that relates them, next to their imagined—or tragically denied—horizon of overcoming.

Introduction: A Dialectic of Melancholy and Theodicy

Melancholy and Ontology

Ay, in the very temple of Delight
Veil'd Melancholy has her sovran shrine,
Though seen of none save him whose strenuous tongue
Can burst Joy's grape against his palate fine.
(John Keats, "Ode on Melancholy," l.25–8)

All other joyes to this are folly,
None so sweet as Melancholy.
[…]
All my griefes to this are jolly,
None so damn'd as Melancholy.
(Robert Burton, The Anatomy of Melancholy, 1989–2000, 1:lxx)

Melancholia, melancholia, it rides me like a bucking mare
(Barnes 1938a)

In the spring of 1940, confined in a sanatorium on Lake George against her will, the 48-year-old Djuna Barnes finds herself sparring with one "German Jew of a psychiatrist," who, like some psychoanalytic daimon, would "reappear" intermittently, "a burr on a horses [sic] rump" (Barnes 1940b). The diagnoses regarding her state of mind, emerging in reports for more than a year now through her letters to her friend, Emily Coleman, amount however to a potpourri of medicine and invention. These exhaust the resources of endocrinology ("general melancholia with an hemmorhage for a menstruation […] funny—all from lack of thyroid and ovarian hormones!"—1939c), otorhinolaryngology and gynecology ("melancholia up the gorge," and her "private quarters shoved at with rubber gloves"—1939d), horology ("It is now my melancholy hour (one of them) four o'clock in the afternoon"—1939b), and neuropsychology ("The trouble with me is awful nerves, melancholia (change of life, dear) and madness"—1939h). If, in these collisions of suffering and caprice, something of the quality of a psychosomatic pastiche comes through, this might not be surprising to a reader familiar with *Nightwood*'s "mystic" mountebank, Matthew-Mighty-grain-of-salt-Dante-O'Connor (*Nightwood*, 28). Voracious in their assimilative tendency, prolific, regurgitative, and capricious in turn, these variations on the theme of melancholy seem to be as much a result of *passive* subjection to pain as well as an *active*, imaginative response to it. To return to the psychomachia in the sanatorium, having fended off the first Freudian epigone, Barnes finds herself facing a second "Dempsey of the sub-conscious"—Dempsey, being the American professional boxer Barnes interviewed in 1921 (Barnes 1940b; *Interviews*, 283–7). Parrying both with her "great sense of humour," she refuses to "turn [her] belly out," and dodges with disquisitions on "Goethe, Bauer, Bachaus, Memling, Mozart, Beethoven and Proust!"—effectively vaulting the pit of depth psychology, "refusing to talk about anything personal," to cover everything from German Romantic literature and music, contemporary musicianship and politics,[1] Early Netherlandish painting, French literary modernism, to post-Hegelian philosophy and theology.[2] The proliferation of sources is matched by an assimilative strategy. When, for instance, she writes, "This sanatorium has put the final iron into my soul"—melancholic refrains from Keats are sounded,[3] even as she dons the mask of "Alice in Wonderland" and weaves in citations from Plato and Shakespeare, spinning forth ever-expanding intertextual arabesques that, inevitably, return to the one mythic scene evoked in all of her major works—that of *the Fall*: "You know, I could tear the world apart and spill the rotten seeds, and slap it back together again, and it might start all over again and be endurable until Eve once more bit into that apple … or whatever it was!" (1940b).

Melancholy, as it manifests itself in Barnes's work, may appear at first sight to be a particularly difficult motif to pin down. Yet, this wandering, profligate encroachment of melancholic discourse on the resources of literary, theological, medical, and art history is not in fact peculiar to Barnes. By the time of her birth

---

[1] Wilhelm Backhaus, a German pianist, was awarded a professorship by Hitler in 1936.
[2] Bruno Bauer was a German philosopher and theologian and a student of Hegel.
[3] "My heart seems now made of iron […] You see how I go on—like so many strokes of a Hammer." The latter half of this quotation is marked out in Barnes's copy of *The Letters of John Keats* (1935, 370).

in 1892 to Elizabeth and Wald Barnes, in a log cabin on Storm King Mountain, New York, "melancholy" was already an oversaturated term, owing much to a variety of ideas of diverse provenance across history. Despite this, the aim of this book is to reveal how Barnes's numerous deployments and redeployments of melancholy in her art and writings are nonetheless imaginative, somatic, and aesthetic responses to a precise existential predicament—that is, a specific mode of being situated, or *thrown*—affectively, bodily, and psychically, in the world, which the myth of the Fall enshrines. A structural consistency, in other words, persists across most of its heterogeneous manifestations, holding forth against the intractability of its changing symptoms: from its embedment in the corporeal pathologies of Galen and Galenic science, the theological articulations of Burton and Saint Theresa, its affiliation with genius by Aristotle and Ficino, through the poetic formulations of Keats and Baudelaire into the modern world of psychoanalysis from Freud to Kristeva, "melancholy" has exhibited a concern with a specific *structure of existence*.[4] Following Ilit Ferber's work on *Philosophy and Melancholy*, my approach to melancholy here considers "the diversity of its internal configuration" across history to retain at a basic level "the structure of its innermost form": such a "structural view of melancholy" addresses "the different ways in which the melancholic state of mind determines the relationship between a subject and the world" (Ferber 2013, 10). Melancholy, as such, pertains to how the subject–object interface is configured. The lineaments of this ontological structure, I hope to show, may be traced in this primal scene of the Fall.

While recent scholarship on melancholy has moved toward reincorporating its productive, performative, and even manic side against a hermeneutic tradition that has seen mainly attenuation, defeat, and paralysis, my book, in jointly articulating the themes of melancholy, the body, and theodicy in Barnes's writings, seeks to address three co-implicated themes that have remained submerged thus far: (i) the elements of *both* laughter and tears as embodied correlates to melancholy, conjugating hence its two seemingly oppositional poles (as suggested in the "bucking mare" rhythm); (ii) the theological, in addition to ontological, coordinates that structure melancholic existence; and (iii) the various crises in embodiment melancholy entails, often projecting the body against the image of its end, whether in the finality of death or the infinitude of its resurrection.

---

[4] For a historical overview of the various configurations of "melancholy," see the anthology *The Nature of Melancholy* (Radden 2002).

Deploying different critical apparatuses, recent publications by Sanja Bahun, Jennifer Rushworth, Drew Daniel, and Jonathan Flatley have sought to locate the import of Robert Burton's usage of "melancholize" as a verb in its active dimension. Understood variously in terms of the "symptom" (Bahun 2013, 5), "semi-mourning [*demi-deuil*]" (Rushworth 2016, 8), "assemblage" (Daniel 2013, 7–17), or "a mobile machine of self-estrangement" (Flatley 2008, 7), melancholy encodes both suffering and, *with qualifications*, suffering's supersession. Melancholy, in all these cases, is understood against the horizon of its own overcoming, incorporating the aesthetic and political practices that, even as they retain the very traces of the melancholy that prompts them, take a minimal turn away from passive immersion. It is hence conceived in a state of dialectical tension between a condition of woundedness and its aftermath. Thus, for Bahun, the "melancholic symptom" is both a mark of trauma and its partial "cure," sedimented in the formal properties of the artwork itself (2013, 9, 33), just as for Rushworth, "half-mourning" preserves the stain of loss even as it strives to overcome it in textual practice. A similar structure of melancholic overcoming is proposed by Daniel and Flatley even if a Deleuzian terminology is given preference to over a Freudian one. Daniel's "melancholy assemblage," in "joining structure to fluidity," both charts and *produces* the "ongoing, fragile, and reversible correlations between bodies and languages," compounding passive record and active reaction (2013, 11). Along similar lines, Flatley's machinery of "self-estrangement"—a kind of "aesthetic technology"—dredges out the hitherto submerged and convoluted relations of history and politics to make these cognitively available, and which therefore, as a strategy of "affective mapping," enables the modulation from depoliticized depression to reengagement—or, in terms sourced from Baudelaire, from world-withdrawn *ennui* to, as it were, *woke* and enraged *spleen* (2008, 4–6). A dovetailing of vocabulary in these accounts is thus occasionally observable. The modulation from the structure of melancholic existence to a neighboring or even oppositional one that bears its trace even as it is altered, minimally or drastically, is conceived as a kind of turn, resistance, or diversion—in short, a *differential repetition*—that is captured by the morpheme "counter." If it constitutes, with, Flatley, a "counter-mood" (2008, 5), it enables, with Bahun, "mood-bending" and the practice of "countermourning" (2013, 4). A similar function may also be observed in the related modifiers of "half-," "semi-," and "mid-": Derrida's notion of "*demi-deuil*"—or "mid-"/"semi-mourning"—is thus mobilized by Rushworth in her reading of Proust's *Recherche* (2016, 91–125). Melancholy, in these accounts, is understood as a constellation of history and art, the suffering involved in temporal existence, and the aesthetic response contained in the corresponding production of specific textual worlds.

There are certain ontological implications, then, to the distribution of melancholy across these two moments of suffering and praxis that may be extended here. "Mood," or *Stimmung*, to recall, is Heidegger's term for the specific affective relation between subjectivity and world, the *interface* by which they are mutually disclosed and determined. As Giorgio Agamben explains: *Stimmung*'s position "is neither within interiority nor in the world, but at their limit. Thus being-there, insofar as it is essentially its own opening, is always already in a *Stimmung*, is always already emotively oriented […] *Stimmung*, rather than being itself in a place, is the very opening of the world, the very place of being" (1997, 92). Melancholy's involvement of both a "mood" and a "counter-mood" may hence be understood as a constellation of two distinct modes of being interfaced with the world, and hence, a rearticulation of the very relation between subjectivity and being by which both are constituted in the first place. Melancholy, as previously mentioned, thus pertains specifically to this subject–object interface. In the expanded terms of the metaphysical discourse that Barnes inherits, the "world" or "being" that is disclosed to the subject in this relation—as the totality of entities (bodies, persons, concepts, institutions) and their organizing matrices—is often referenced as *Creation* itself, along with its prosopopoeic trace, the *Creator*. This theological frame, ever present in Barnes's works, situates melancholy precisely at the relational interface between the postlapsarian subject and the Creator/Creation. That these theological premises and corollaries are never far from Barnes's depictions of melancholy suggests a particular value here in my attempt to move beyond the level of a *symptomatology* to an *ontological* analysis. Where a symptomatology would read, or even reify, a clinical condition or cause from a set of observable symptoms via a backward postulate, an ontological analysis remains attentive to the changing interface between subjectivity and being. The logic that structures these symptoms, in other words, is closely affiliated with the primordial relation that co-articulates the self and its world. As Darian Leader contends, given that preexisting 'symptom pools" and "idioms of distress" are available to the subject to draw on, configure, or extend, it is worth looking beyond "surface symptomatology" to the "structure of symptoms"—that is, the particular mode of the subject's "relation to the symptom," "how the subject speaks about their symptom," "what place" the symptom occupies rather than its "content" (2016, 27–8, 33). Critical sensitivity to ontological structures thus enables a departure from a symptomatological assessment on three counts: (i) it respects the variability in symptomatic manifestation in melancholy, without taxonomizing them according to a normative model prepared in advance and derived elsewhere—whether on the Freudian couch, in the Kristevan clinic, or out of the quantitative data of modern psychiatry; (ii) in going beyond the surface "content" of these symptoms (linguistic and psychomotor retardation or acceleration, mordant self-critique, sleep disturbances, etc.), it reads them as expressions and responses to particular modes of being interfaced with the world; (iii) it considers the variability of this interface itself, and hence does not predetermine melancholy's "counter-mood."

This book proposes accordingly a neo-ontological account of melancholy that sets up a critical relation between life and art, bringing the *existential mood* of suffering into dialectical apposition with the *aesthetic mood* in the work of art. Melancholy names this relational joint between an initial mood we are thrown into, and the counter-mood enclosed in the work of art. The manner in which the two are disclosed and constelled, as will be seen, is where and how the literary and religious imagination mediates experience and response, figuring the process by which the *reception* of life—along with its entire phenomenology of suffering—incites a creative *return*, as spiritual riposte and aesthetic craft, in the artwork itself. The premise of such an ontological analytic of melancholy is that the existential data of pain and joy, the irruptions into laughter and tears, the vicissitudes of embodiment, and myriad invasion of affects, are all rooted first and foremost in the structures of the self, its world, and their specific modes of relation. The entire symptomatic galaxy of the melancholic—the changing cope of its surface phenomenology—emerges from the shifting interface between self and world. Disclosing the phenomenology of fallen existence, and with it the spiritual response enclosed in the work of art, thus leads us toward an analysis of the forms of *relational ontology* in life and art, and how these are modulated from the passivity of existence to aesthetic activity.

The terms of this discussion will be developed in greater detail throughout this introduction. This preliminary outline of the task proposed here, however, already suggests a contribution to a theoretical understanding of theological approaches to literature, and indeed a study of the relations across the domains of life, literature, and theology. This book orientates itself according to its two primary ends. First, it offers a focused reading of the Barnes oeuvre, resituating it within the context of religious experience and theological motifs to bring a new legibility to a body of works which has never been satisfactorily illuminated outside this context. Second, it brings together theology and theory to conceptualize broader questions in the field of religion and literature, most notably those pertaining to the ontological analysis of existence and the work of art. The wager here is that it is precisely at the level of ontology that literature, theology, and existence are able to encounter each another most meaningfully, beyond mere analogizing or the subsumption of one domain into another. Such temptations account for many a transposition of "melancholy" or "tragedy" from the theoretical elsewhere of psychoanalysis or theology to frame the literary text, instead of allowing the literature itself to stand its ground as a fully formed "world" in its own right. It is thus no longer quite a matter of laying my theoretical cards on the table to say that this book presents a synthesis of psychoanalysis, theological anthropology, aesthetic theory, and literary close reading. These analytic perspectives are certainly brought into conjunction throughout. But the clou of the critical method here is rather—to adapt Walter Benjamin's famous formulation—that these analytic chess pieces are determined in their movements ultimately by the *structure of worlds* they refer us back to (see Benjamin 2003, 390). Otherwise put, it is where these ontic investigations disclose specific ontological premises that meaningful comparisons and contrasts present themselves. How—in diverse ways—the interface between self and world is configured at various points in these analytic domains forms the field of our focus. Ontology, as the study of the relations that coordinate self and world, reveals both the conditioning ground of melancholy and the work of art created in its wake. Ontology, in other words, will take us to the wings of the theaters of the worlds of melancholic existence and melancholic art, where the stage is set each time anew for the unfolding of a particular image of history. As we will see, how these worlds are structured, and set up, has much to say about the nature of the comic and the tragic.

In developing the theoretical groundwork for an ontological analysis of melancholy and art, this book nonetheless centers its material on the Barnes corpus and its context of a modernism of religious experience, at the intersection of French Decadence, post-Romantic Symbolism and Surrealism, and the modernist novel.[5] Such a relocation of Barnes's works within the framework of theology proposes to bring to light the still undisclosed significance of her art in terms of the vastness of its theological anthropological vision and the deeper spiritual premises of melancholic suffering. Reading one of modernism's queer icons on theological grounds may occasion some resistance. It is worth clarifying, however, that I do not intend to reproduce a certain gesture of disavowal that Barnes herself was increasingly disposed to in her later years—disaffiliating

---

[5] For representative studies, see Hanson (1997), Pinkerton (2017), Lewis (2010), and Biles and Brintnall (2015).

herself adamantly from the queer and avant-gardist lens trained on her writings and, indeed, her life, which she repudiated as reductive encroachments[6]—but to read, precisely, the logic within the aesthetic and libidinal configurations of her work at the very level where her theological ruminations, speculations, experimentations, and profanations operate. As will be seen, this is motivated by the insight that, for Barnes, the phenomenology of affect and embodiment is indissociable from the larger ontological structures that condition it. If, then, a greater theoretical consciousness, with changing emphases, has been brought to bear on Barnes scholarship over the decades—from queer and trans theory (Boone 1998; Herring 2007; Glavey 2016; Heaney 2017), psychoanalysis (Carlston 1998; Sanchez-Párdo 2003; Rupprecht 2006), post-humanism (Goody 2007), critical theory (Miller 1999), feminism and gender (Broe 1991; Scott 1995), to intertextuality (Caselli 2009), and affect theory (Nieland 2008; Taylor 2012)—a key aim of my study here is to retrieve the theological frame that nonetheless remains largely unarticulated, and in resituating the insights of previous scholarship within this perspective, modify, extend, and redirect their import.

Indeed, apart from Steve Pinkerton's recent work on *Blasphemous Modernism*,[7] the theological mediations through which Barnes's aesthetic takes shape have hardly been addressed by scholarship in the last few decades, having fallen out of favor after early critical appraisals, including those by T. S. Eliot, Kenneth Burke, and Emily Coleman.[8] The absence of any theological paradigm in Diane Warren's chapter-length review of the history of Barnes scholarship is perhaps symptomatic in this regard (2008, 1–22), registering a critical tendency that, more than a decade later, has seen little redress in the collection of essays on Barnes published in the edited volume *Shattered Objects* (2019). Bar Cathryn Setz's relocation of Barnes's late poetry within the metaphysical tradition, the cursory references to religion are often unsustained, its imaginative logic not quite unraveled (Pender and Setz 2019, 130–46). Much of the theological lexicon that motivates Barnes's aesthetic—unstintingly infixed across her entire corpus—remains unread. This book proposes a corrective in this direction.

---

[6] See, for example, her letter to Christine Koschel: "I am not a 'modern' after all! Which sound [*sic*] strange for one who is considered avant guard [*sic*]!" (1969b). Later, to Silas Glossop, she adds: "Nor am I a 'Surrealist' or [Hippy?] or Dada etc" (1978).
[7] Another notable exception is an article on "Sacra/Mentality" by Elizabeth Freeman (2014).
[8] Even Suzanne Hobson's work in *Angels of Modernism* ends up collapsing Barnes's theological imagination into the sexological discourses of the period, in one instance nearly tempting her into a hypercorrection of *Nightwood*'s "uninhabited angel" to an "uninhibited angel," slipping in some of the sexological typecasting of trans persons as promiscuous (2011, 134).

Doing so will also take us back to the Barnes archive, where ample evidence of Barnes's engagement with a wide range of religious literature remains held—from Augustine and Aquinas to the neo-Thomists in France (Jacques and Raïssa Maritain, acquaintances of Coleman and admiring correspondents of Barnes)[9] and Germany (Josef Pieper, "that remarkable Catholic writer"—Barnes 1961), Protestant thinking from Luther to Paul Tillich, Martin Buber's Judaism,[10] and varieties of French mysticism medieval and modern, including Marguerite Porete and Simone Weil. The material is extensive, but this book will center its focus on the nature of melancholy and its dialectical relation to the question of theodicy—that is, the vindication of God the Creator given the manifest evidence of suffering and evil in the created world.

Barnes's own references to this motif in systematic theology are numerous, even if they do not always explicitly raise the name of God, or indeed the word "theodicy" itself. Some words are due, however, on the relation between a classical account of theodicy as the vindication of God to a version of *weak* theodicy articulated here as the vindication of life, understood nonetheless by Barnes in terms of Creation, the work of the Creator. As will be seen, the evidence of suffering and evil in melancholic existence provokes the postlapsarian subject to stand before the question: is life even worth living? Interpellated from the place of such suffering, the judgment of the melancholic subject finds expression in the work of art. My introduction moves on next to address how a meaningful account of theodicy in relation to Barnes, who never explicitly deploys the term, may be developed by unfolding the notion of a *theodistical unconscious*, one that encrypts a response to the question of suffering and evil in Creation, its transcendental implications (i.e., what this says about the Creator), and, ultimately, the very value of life itself, in the form and content of the work of art. The theodistical unconscious of the work of art, in short, encodes a response to the experience of suffering and evil. The trauma encountered in historical existence throws us before such questions as: why do suffering and evil abound in Creation, and how does this square with a Creator, supposedly omnipotent, omniscient, and omnibenevolent? Is God justified given all this? Is life itself—given its premise of a world *like this*, a God *like this*—justified at all? *Is life, in*

---

[9] The Maritains are occasionally mentioned in the Barnes-Coleman correspondence. Jacques Maritain includes an extract from *Nightwood* in his A. W. Mellon Lectures in the Fine Arts (1953), of which Barnes held a copy. See also their brief exchange on *The Antiphon*, in which Maritain records his "deep interest and admiration" (Maritain 1958).
[10] On being included in Bo Beskow's book on Dag Hammarskjöld with Saint-John Perse and Martin Buber, Barnes writes: "isn't this glory enough [...] I mean the mere mention of us within a volume on so good a man" (1969a).

fact, worth living? In articulating melancholy dialectically with the question of theodicy, two worlds are thus netted in a constellation: the suffering encountered in history, and the artwork that encodes its response to such suffering. The mode and presentation of this capture, as will be seen, determines the aesthetic judgment on the question of theodicy.

The Question of Theodicy

The question of theodicy is often understood as the vindication of God in the face of evil and suffering.[11] If the historical emergence of the term itself—a combination of the Greek *theós* (God) and *díkē* (justice)—may be credited to Leibniz in the early eighteenth or late seventeenth century,[12] the themes it broaches find sustained accounts already in Augustine, Aquinas, and the Hellenistic Fathers, and continue to be grappled with in the context of the Enlightenment, Romanticism, and the modern world, through writers as diverse as Alexander Pope, Keats, Blake, and Hegel, to Dostoevsky and William James.[13] As John Hick's historical overview of the various theodicies proposed in Western thought suggests, however, most of these attempts at confronting the problem of evil fall under the rubric of an Augustinian or an Irenaean "type." The former is premised more emphatically on the notion of the Fall and is hence more retrospective in its orientation toward perfection: born perfect, we lapse into the *status corruptionis* of existence via original sin, and return, finally, to perfection. As Paul Fiddes notes, this effectively proposes a "U-shaped divine comedy" (1991, 47–52). The Irenaean variety, however, privileges an eschatological approach in which humanity is created imperfect *ab initio* in order to develop, over time, toward perfection (2000, 262–5). Divinization (*theosis*), here, is often brought into analogy with the child's maturational process. Ontologically incomplete at birth, she or he grows from the image (*imago*) of God—an imperfect prefiguration—to His perfected likeness (*eikōn*). Fiddes similarly explains: "as Irenaeus perceived early in Christian theology, the Old Testament does not portray a perfect, but

---

[11] Ricoeur offers an effective summary: a theodicy is the affirmation, without contradiction, of "three propositions" that are on the surface incompatible—that is, (i) God is all-powerful; (ii) God is absolutely good; (iii) evil exists (2004, 20).

[12] For an account of the genesis of Leibniz's theory of "the best of all possible worlds" in the historical context of the Enlightenment, see Nadler 2010, 78–107.

[13] For an anthology of the historical attempts to grapple with the "problem of evil" in the West, from pre-Christian to post-Auschwitz thinkers, see Larrimore 2001. See also Neiman 2015.

an immature, original state of human life" (2000, 19). Divinization occurs only through a teleological development oriented toward the likeness of God.

Throughout her life, Barnes encountered the works of some of the thinkers raised in Hick's study, though, as with a number of them, the term "theodicy" itself is not raised explicitly. The problem of evil is nonetheless quite clearly formulated on many occasions, and provisional theodicies are often tentatively suggested, refuted, or asserted, as in her January 10, 1936, letter to Coleman:

> We condemn God, saying why has he planted evil in the world, if he is all powerful and all perfection, but what do we know of his design, it is His, and for that we should be a little reverent.
>
> (Cited in Herring 1995, 305)

In this one instance at least, a possible reconciliation with "evil" is intimated, with the "design" here, withdrawn from human knowledge, functioning as a reference to God's management of the world in the Divine Economy. More detail concerning this "design" emerges in a later letter, as the lineaments of a divine "plan" are conjured up, and simultaneously questioned. Barnes writes to Coleman in 1938:

> Why angels were made men that they should grow is a mystery to me, does the long falling down make them better? It shouldn't, but perhaps in heaven (?) angels are to that place what babies are to our world, they must grow up, for tho [sic] children are pretty dreadful (they are not those n[i]ce pink bottomed little angels that people like to make out, they squash flies and tear dragons [sic] wings off, and occasionally drown their brothers and sisters in a frenzy of childish experiment and amusement) but they are not learned, is learning the whole plan?
>
> (1938g)

A more concrete outline of a theodicy emerges here. Elements from the Augustinian and Irenaean traditions are conflated in a speculative account that locates imperfection or incompleteness at birth within a lapsarian structure (a "long falling down"). Furthermore, a synchronization of salvational and ontogenetic histories may be observed: divine creation and human procreation form the departure gates from which angels and babies make their passage into mortal beings via the Fall. Natural evil is also suggestively embedded in these fallen children in their early years, who—while initially gratuitously violent and infanticides in their own right—are to develop, or "grow up," according to the "whole plan." "[L]earning," in the sense of a *Geistesbildung*, accounts for the formative process by which the imperfect self achieves divinization. Creation, flawed as it is, is nevertheless located within a teleological frame as a region compounded of good and evil for the sake of the divinization of humanity.

In his attempt to unfold a "theodicy for today," informed by the Irenaean tradition, Hick in fact takes over the terms deployed by Keats's well-known letter of 1819 that Barnes herself would have come across in the latter half of thirties when her own letter to Coleman was written. What Keats formulates in this letter is an account of the development of the soul out of the trials of existence: "this world," he writes, is perhaps not so much that "'vale of tears' from which we are to be redeemed by a certain arbitrary interposition of God and taken to Heaven," but rather, "The vale of Soul-making" (Keats 1935, 334–5; Hick 2010, 295). This world, in other words, comprises the tribulations by which individuals are "school[ed]" into souls: "Do you not see how necessary a World of Pains and troubles is to school an Intelligence and make it a Soul?" (Keats 1935, 334–5). The contours of an Irenaean theodicy thus emerge here: born imperfect, we pass through the "vale of Soul-making" in this world toward divinization. Suffering, framed within a teleology of soul-making, becomes a necessary evil.

Barnes's interrogative suspension of the claims made in her letter, however, suggests that the mystery of evil is not fully exhausted by such a teleological theodicy. As will be seen, where neither the Augustinian nor Irenaean solutions suffice, the question of theodicy is re-posed alongside the testament of pain, each time with yet another provisional response enclosed in the work of art. Far from a systematic account of evil's place in the world, Barnes's responses to the question of theodicy do not just fall short of any consistent theoretical elaboration, but also vacillate from joyous affirmation of the Creator/Creation to total condemnation of the same. Suspending the note of finality in the various solutions to the problem of evil in systematic theodicies thus leaves the question open for the melancholic artist. Evil and suffering themselves appear less like logical conundrums to be "solved" by reason, and lean closer to existential, phenomenological, and affective impediments to the flourishing of life. Drawing on Gabriel Marcel's *Philosophy of Existence,* Hick thus observes a possible contrast between conceiving of evil as a "problem" and evil as "mystery": "evil is not a problem to be solved, but a mystery to be encountered and lived through" (Hick 2010, 9–10). Even if "there is no hope of establishing an exact frontier between problem and mystery," it is nonetheless possible, even crucial, to resist the reduction of the "mystery of evil" to an "intellectual problem" to be reasoned away (2010, 9). Barnes's interrogative suspension of her own theodistical inventions suggests that such responses remain inadequate. Evil, exceeding containment within theory, is thrown back into the region of "mystery": "Why angels were made men that they should grow is a mystery to me, does the long falling down make them better?" Such myths attempt to explain, but do not exhaust, the protest against and provocation faced in the encounter with evil and suffering. The place of "heaven" itself, in fact, is suspended with a "(?)."

Barnes's dissatisfaction with any systematic theodicy, and her consequent move toward the inventions of aesthetic response, is not an isolated occurrence in modernity after the Nietzschean proclamation—God is dead. In his study of *Religious Experience and the Modernist Novel* (2010), Pericles Lewis notes:

> Around the turn of the twentieth century, a generation of social thinkers who had been trained in nineteenth-century positivist social science, including William James, Émile Durkheim, Sigmund Freud, and Max Weber, sought new means to describe and study religious inclinations without necessarily deciding the question of whether or not there is a God. They were concerned more with the structure of faith than with its truth content.
>
> (2010, 19–20)

More than this suspension of the "truth content" regarding God's existence, however, are the extensive negations of previous theological solutions to the questions that continue to be provoked despite the increasing retrenchment of religious faith—otherwise known as the "process of secularization" leading into the modern world (Lewis 2010, 19). Steve Pinkerton's recognition of the spiritual work of blasphemy thus relates the active negation of prevailing religious forms and doctrines on the part of a number of modernist artists, including Barnes, to "a commitment to playful and critical reworkings of orthodoxy, coupled with a respect and even reverence, not for God, or scripture, or the church, but for *religious faith itself* and its enduring cultural sway" (2017, 5). Referencing one of Barnes's influences in religious matters, Lewis similarly observes:

> Without submitting to the institutional religion of church or synagogue, the modernists found methods to describe through fiction what came to be known, after William James, as "religious experience," the basic consciousness supposedly at the root of all religions but isolated from any institutionalization in a theology or a church. [...] The attempts of all of the modernists to describe forms of experience that would traditionally have been called 'religious" reflects a blurring of the lines between the sacred and the profane.
>
> (2010, 20)

The claims put forward by Pinkerton and Lewis thus indicate that a negation of the existing creeds and structures of religion ends up leading into the afterlife of religion, which permeates emergent cultural and aesthetic forms once more in a kind of dialectical supersession: "If God died in the nineteenth century, he had an active afterlife in the twentieth" (Lewis 2010, 25).[14]

Lewis's concerns are centered on the persistence of "transcendent experiences" and their displacement from more conventional theological representation into the very "structure of the novel," tasked now, through formal innovation, to bear witness to that portion of life that has now erupted from its institutional containment (2010, 19). Though he does not quite explain the nature of such "transcendent experiences," it is nonetheless possible to raise a more general point from this. For many in the modern world, religious solutions have been eroded by a process of secularization, leaving religious experiences and questions exposed to be re-encountered anew on an existential, phenomenological level. The "basic consciousness" said to be at the source of religious institutions is thus laid bare, and emerges in many ways in an interrogative, provocative mode. With regard to the question of theodicy in particular, the erosion of its systematic responses may be said to leave the provocations of evil and suffering all the more acute against the soul of the melancholic. Theodicy, traditionally a systematic answer to the presence of evil in Creation, now becomes a *question*. It is specifically in this tension between one's interpellation by suffering and the absence of a solution that melancholy may be located. "Religious melancholy," spoken of already by Robert Burton, is thus characterized by James as a suffocating confrontation with evil: "A mystery is concealed, and a metaphysical solution must exist"—*must*, here, standing out more as protest than claim (James 1982, 152). Speaking of "the sick soul," or "those persons who cannot so swiftly throw off the burden of the consciousness of evil," James writes: "Not the conception or intellectual perception of evil, but the grisly blood-freezing heart palsying sensation of it close upon one, and no other conception or sensation able to live for a moment in its presence" (1982, 133, 162).

In the absence of any systematic theodicy, then, the afterlife of theodicy may be traced within the works of art themselves as responses to melancholy. Critical scholarship has in fact identified theodicy as mode of thought specific to the eighteenth century (Geyer 1992, 47; Späth 2004, 261). In the context of the Enlightenment, it would seem that the drive toward a systematic rationalization of evil would find its home around the turn of the century, with the meditations of Leibniz, Malebranche, and Antoine Arnauld entering into heated debate in the public sphere (Nadler 2010). For Gerhard Fitzthum, however, it is precisely in the context of a nascent secularization in the eighteenth century that inherited

---

[14] See also Matthew Mutter's work on modernism's "religious inheritance" in *Restless Secularism* (2017).

ideas of God began to be increasingly measured against the testimony of everyday experience (Fitzthum 1992, 14). As Eberhard Späth notes, a certain brand of reverse judgment is built into the process:

> Theodicists undertake to acquit the omnipotent of the charges resulting from the state of the world; it is particularly in the 18th century that they propose to answer, as his attorneys in the 'Court of Reason,' the accusation of injustice brought against him. This endeavour implied a fundamental change of Mankind's position in relation to God: Man no longer considers himself solely as a being observed from above, but also as looking at God, as it were, eye to eye. Typically, theodicy is imagined in legal terms, as a kind of plea in court, in which arguments for either the Divine or the human side are weighed.
>
> (2004, 262)

Moving into the twentieth century, however, the negation of these modes of systematic reckoning suggests a certain falling away of the question of theodicy itself. What does in fact appear to occur, however, is once again the dismantling of the structures of reason erected to contain the evidence of evil, alongside the displacement of the form and manner of response from a ratiocinative balancing of accounts, to the level of the existential, literary, and aesthetic. While Späth is skeptical about the possibility of "subconscious theodicists" in modernity, we will have occasion to observe how a form of theodistical unconscious remains in the very ontological premises of life and art (2004, 276).

This non-systematic approach to theology is in keeping with Barnes's own method and her skepticism regarding the capacities of existing, organizational responses to confront the mysteries of life. Barnes's allusions to theological motifs and sources are notably wide-ranging, unrestricted by denominational affiliation or any professed faith, leading Pinkerton to speak of her "lack of any clear religious identification" (2017, 112). As she herself writes to a convert Coleman on September 24, 1942: "If you become a Roman Catholic what do you have to do? I wish I were one, or at least a Church of England like my people." When the publication of *The Antiphon* in 1958 draws attention and praise from a number within the Catholic community, she is moved to write to Elémire Zolla on April 23, 1968: "I am afraid I shall have to disappoint you. I am not Roman Catholic. If I followed the family, I would be, on my mother's side, Episcopllian [sic], on my fathers [sic], Protestant (he was 'nothing')—I am head-first for the Mysteries."[15]

---

[15] She reports, however, in a February 17, 1940, letter to Emily Coleman, of having recently discovered that her "mother's people (French Hugonauts [sic]) were Calvinists"—adding, "this accounts for everything!"

An indication of Barnes's relation to theology may be suggested further by the evidence of her letters: on the one hand, her avowed interest in only three topics in life—"beauty, art and religion" (cited in Herring 1995, 221)—and on the other, her non-sectarian, non-orthodox, and hence critically imaginative relation to the tradition. While she continues to refuse any religious identification throughout her life, she is nonetheless not averse to putting her signature down in 1971 for a petition against the "'disposal' of the Gregorian—Latin—rites" in response to a plea from her Italian translator Christina Campo to "save the Catholic Mass": "what atrocious audacity"—she adds (Barnes 1971a). This conflicting relation to Catholicism in particular is also voiced in an October 30, 1938, letter to Coleman, in which she acknowledges: "Catholicism is the D.T.'s (probably) of the best souls."

When it comes to the Jewish tradition, a similarly complex attitude has managed to elicit, on the one hand, a pathos of identification from an Argentinian-Jewish writer ("I think that Djuna is jewish or if she is not, she must have loved for many years someone who was"),[16] without preventing her on the other hand from lapsing into rhetorical tropes that have been deemed anti-Semitic (Trubowitz 2005). These contradictions serve to emphasize Barnes's unorthodox, blasphemous, possibly offensive, relation to a variety of religious traditions. Instead of expecting a systematic theodicy to emerge from such religious ambivalence, it would appear that an initial theoretical "weakening" may be a more profitable move in seeking to understand the intervention of art in response to melancholic existence.

Weak Theodicy

If theodistical thinking has been rejected by a number of writers, this is quite often due to its perceived alliance with a ratiocinative disavowal of evil. William James's diatribe against "the systematic theologians," their "logical machines," along with the rationalist theodicies of Hegel and Leibniz, are in fact repeated in Ricoeur's more recent assessment (James 1982, 446). Theodicy, for Ricoeur, is "a combat in favour of coherence," and, as such, a systematizing enterprise within an "argumentative framework" and an "onto-theological mode of thought" (2004, 65, 20–1). Its "first summit," is thus Leibniz's notorious theory of the "best of all possible worlds," the target of many Voltairean vituperations after the Lisbon earthquake of 1755; and

---

[16] Campo forwards this letter to Barnes in November 1969.

its "second," that of Hegel's "totalizing dialectic," which, with "a rational *hybris*," reads history as a long series of fracture and meliorative repair, in effect positing "a vision of the world where pan-tragism is ceaselessly recuperated into pan-logicism" (2004, 50, 48). Against these ontotheological attempts to conceptualize suffering, both James and Ricoeur insist on rethinking the existence of a form "radical evil." The inability of theodistical thought to encounter "the enigma of real suffering, of *irreducible* suffering" thus leads Ricoeur to propose, via Karl Barth's notion of a radical negativity irreconcilable with God and Creation ("*das Nichtige*"), a renewed negotiation with a world indissociably linked to evil and suffering, through "thought, action, and sentiment" (2004, 51–65).[17]

This takes Ricoeur close to Fiddes's account of the three interrelated approaches to suffering in modern theological thought: the "'theoretical,' 'practical,' and 'aesthetic'" (2013, 169). As Fiddes notes, however, their coordinated response may nonetheless constitute a "fragmentary 'theory'" and a "modest theodicy" (2013, 188). Theodicy, in its *weak* sense, that is, aside from Ricoeur's rendering *stricto sensu*, names a persevering engagement with a world in which "*irreducible* suffering" not only persists, but cannot be explained away. Whether explicitly stated or implicitly coded, the response to such a fallen world, where minimally affirmed, records a positive—*if qualified*—judgment on Creation and the Creator, and where refused, repudiates these in a negative judgment making impossible or illusory, any and all "theoretical," "practical," or "aesthetic approaches." A weak theodicy, in this sense, names a basic reconciliation with existence, a positive judgment on life in spite of evil and pain—even if in the minimal sense of a deferral of final court. On the other hand, falling below this minimal threshold, an anti-theodistical vision may be said to be implicated in a negative judgment that *decides on* the worthlessness, falsity, even evil, of Creation and the Creator. In situating melancholy before the theodistical question, this book reads Barnes's individual works as aesthetic responses to life that incorporate in them, both formally and thematically, a *judgment* on the value of existence, whether positive and reconciliatory, or negative and non-reconciliatory.

A weak theodicy, as such, marks the minimal threshold of life's value, and functions as the implicit prerequisite—the unconscious condition of

---

[17] Barnes would have been aware of such a distinction between an Augustinian conception of evil as a mere absence of good (*privatio boni*) rather than a radical otherness in its own right as Ricoeur and James seem to suggest. She relays a conversation on the theme with Thelma Wood to Coleman in November 1935: "Thelma […] said she did not like William James' *Variety of Religious Experience* [sic] as it was superficial and proved him ignorant, even of his quotations from St. Augustine; St. Augustine believing that evil was not a substance, but a swerving from truth, that James thought good and evil two substances, etc, etc" (Guirl-Stearley 1999, 116).

possibility—of a continued engagement with the world on any practical, aesthetic, or theoretical level. As the marker of *existential consent*, it enables the continued acceptance— however grudging this be—of the on-going gift of life, binding the melancholic creature to the donation of Creation even if only in the aggravated mode of desiring to radically re-face it, or in the attenuated mode of drifting through the time that remains. So long as the heart beats, the lungs open to air, and the body receives the food of the earth, a minimal consent to life is transcendentally implicated. So long as one continues to act, think, and create— indeed, *live*—one continues to posit a minimal theodicy in each moment that elapses in one's existence. There remains, of course, below the threshold of such a weak theodicy, the choice to *refuse life*.

The weakness of a "weak theodicy" proposed here thus takes on two aspects: (i) its displacement from systematic rationalization toward practical, aesthetic, and provisional theoretical responses; and (ii) its proposal of a modest, indeed *minimal*, threshold for the vindication of life, existentially evidenced in acquiescing to a continued sojourn in the time that remains. My account here may be set beside the recent consolidation of critical trends in "Weak Theory, Weak Modernism" by Paul Saint-Amour. The turn away from the systematizing impulse in the history of theodistical thought in modernity charted above is matched by Saint-Amour's contextualization of modernism's emergence at a time when strong metaphysical paradigms were increasingly retrenched: "a post-Nietzschean weakening in the philosophies of history and aesthetics was a condition of modernism's emergence, at least in the European context, as a cultural phenomenon. Modernism, by these lights, is made both necessary and possible in the west by theory's weakening" (2018, 440). Saint-Amour also notes, however, that this "theoretical weakening" has at times been "partially written over"—indeed, overcompensated for—by modernism itself, or at least the strands of "energetic masculinism" that have defined it in its early critical formulation. The loss of strong metahistories—not just of the "Hegelo-Marxian" variety that Saint-Amour pinpoints, but more crucially of the salvation history of Christianity itself—becomes the grain of wheat that dies in bringing forth the many fruits of modernist aesthetics. Modernism, as a result, has at one time come to be figured as "the zenith of myth or of its future-oriented counterpart, metanarrative" (2018, 440–1).

Saint-Amour offers his weak advocacy of weak theory through Gianni Vattimo and Eve Sedgwick, conceding that not all will consider it "worth the sacrifice of analytical certitude, reach, force, and occupancy" (2018, 442). In delineating the threshold of a weak theodicy here, my own purpose is not primarily advocacy; rather, the initial intention is to conceptually reconstruct the status of theodistical thought in modernity, against which Barnes's art may be measured. Indeed, as will be seen, this book proposes a variety of aesthetic responses to the question of theodicy across the Barnes corpus, including the *strongly* affirmative (Chapter 2), the *weakly* affirmative (Chapter 3), the *weakly* tragic (Chapter 4), and the *strongly* tragic (Chapter 5). The retrenchment of the rationalist edifice of classical theodicies interpellates the melancholic subject before a court of judgment on the value of life, where she stakes her own claims. In this light, Saint-Amour's repeated references to Nietzsche expose a paradoxical element to weakness that remains unaccounted for, but is relevant here: the death of the ontotheological God and His cognates of History, Reason, perhaps even Art, goes hand in hand with the rise of the Overman—called forth to stand in the shoes of his predecessor—who is made to decide on life itself, its meaning or absence of meaning, its direction or cyclical return, and the possibility or impossibility of affirming—even *loving*—it. The point here is not to carry over Nietzsche's own strong response to the weakness of modernity, but to relay the question over to Barnes herself.

Whether life is ultimately worth living or not is a question that Barnes often returns to, vacillating from histrionic assertion to witty suspensions of judgment. "Having life is the greatest horror," she writes to her mother, Elizabeth Chappell Barnes, on February 19, 1923: "I cannot think of it as a 'merry, gay & joyous thing, just to be alive'—it seems to me monstrous, obscene & still with the most obscene trick at the end" (cited in Parsons 2003, 1). Four years earlier, before her departure for Paris, she pronounces in a 1919 interview for *Pearson's Magazine* by the New York editor Guido Bruno: "We live and suffer and strive, envious and envied. We love, we hate, we work, we admire, we despise ... Why? And we die, and no one will ever know that we are born ... Joy? I have had none in my twenty-six years" (*Interviews*, 386). If something of the attitudinal comes through in these declamations, suggesting a form of self-fashioning along the lines of an aristocracy of suffering—a "blacker-than-thou" brand of tragic *hauteur*—this is partly due to their citational quality. The "Wisdom of Silenus," as it is often called, dating from the time of Theognis and referenced in studies on tragedy from Schopenhauer to Nietzsche, is also cited in James's *The Varieties of Religious Experience* (1902), which Barnes read: "Best of all for all things upon earth is it not to be born nor to behold the splendors of the Sun; next best to traverse as soon as possible the gates of Hades" (James 1982, 142). On the surface of things at least, these assertions all enclose a negative judgment on life, summarily dismissing its value. Neat as they are, it is hard to accept them as Barnes's final word. As a matter of fact, her penchant for the epigram often leaves things hanging in the balance, as indicated in one of her late ones that has made its way onto the cover of Hank O'Neal's informal memoir: "*Life is painful, nasty and short ....In my case it has only been painful and nasty*" (1990). Here, the Hobbesian dictum against life is reversed in a joke that ends up shifting the scales once more.

In Barnes's own life, these shifting judgments find a corollary in at least two recorded suicide attempts. In February 1939, in the grip of alcoholism, Barnes swallows eighteen Veronal tablets in a London hotel, provoking a "nervous crisis" and several hospital visits (Herring 1995, 246). The latter attempt is handed down to us with an insinuation of farce. In March 1981, having survived a number of surgical procedures, and just one year before she dies, Barnes empties her numerous bottles of medicine into a paper bag and swallows two handfuls of them. She rings O'Neal, saying, when he arrives: "They always told me I could do it with what I had at hand and I tried, but it didn't work." For his part, O'Neal, whose growing incomprehension and intolerance of Barnes's ways are amply evidenced in his "informal memoir" of her last years, reports: "she'd failed to empty two or three of the bottles into the bag; one that was still intact contained the sleeping pills. I said nothing" (O'Neal 1990, 187–8). Both in art and in life, Barnes's responses to the value of existence in the face of suffering are, on numerous occasions, seemingly brought to a decisive judgment, then overturned. At times, these judgments undermine themselves at the get-go in ironic statement. So it seems, a weak attachment to life preserves her from the decisive turn to death.

Even so, the purpose of this book is to consider the question of theodicy primarily in the realm of aesthetics rather than the existential decisions of practical life. It thus remains to us to elaborate an account of the *aesthetic judgment*, and how it is enclosed in the work of art. As will be seen, while joy and pain may form the woof and warp of Barnes's wit, her individual works tend toward the enclosure of a specific presentation of the world as, *in the last instance*, commensurable or non-commensurable to human existence. In this sense, what I am proposing here may be considered in some aspects a *strong* theory in Saint-Amour's formulation, with certain caveats: "Strong theory is *decryptive*, bent on decoding or unmasking a vast array of phenomena [...] Weak theory is *descriptive*, seeking to know but not necessarily to know better than its object" (2018, 444). In seeking to disclose the ontological premises of each work of art, my project is founded on a decryptive reading of the conscious or unconscious decision to set up the terms of the world of the artwork, and to read this as, in the last instance, an acceptance or refusal of life: *either/or*. In Barnes's case, this is not necessarily to "know better than the object" but to read the object's own manifest judgment—to let it speak for itself—as we will see in the following chapters. This accounts for the importance attached to literary close reading in this study, language being the medium in which the world of the artwork discloses itself. This book is divided accordingly into two halves, pivoting on the issue of *reconciliation*, and Barnes's various takes on it. Each production of a textual world exhibits a specific relation to the extra-textual world, and may hence be said to encrypt a particular ontology, which, like an existential "mood," presents a specific manner of being situated in the world. Whether as love, hatred, patience, or aggression, the affective interface between self and world is always co-implicated with a specific ontological structure. The two basic configurations that I take up here, based on a *final judgment* on the question of theodicy, are thus the comic and the tragic. Where a comic judgment on life names, at the very least, a minimal vindication of Creation and the Creator in spite of evil and suffering, and hence enshrines, however weak, a rudimentary—if non-systematic—theodicy, a tragic judgment summarily repudiates the value of existence, rendering all further practical, theoretical, and aesthetic responses worthless, perhaps even complicit in evil by continuing with life. A tragic response to suffering is thus an *anti-theodistical* one. The question is now raised: how does a work of art, as a response to melancholic existence, encrypt its judgment on the question of theodicy?

The Judgment of Art

In her February 4, 1939, letter to Coleman, Barnes quotes two long passages from the last volume of Proust's *À la recherche du temps perdu*, including the following lines on the "interior book of unknown signs":

> art is the most real of all things, the sternest school in life and truly the Last Judgment. This book, the most difficult of all to decipher, is also the only one dictated to us by reality, the only one the 'imprinting' of which on our consciousness was done by reality itself. [...] The book written in symbolic characters not traced by us is our only book.[18]

The chaff of love, politics, and society winnowed from his life by this point in *Le Temps retrouvé*, Proust's narrator isolates "art" as the ultimate "real." As the "Last

[18] See also Proust 1990, 186.

Judgment," it presents life from the perspective of the end. Eschatologically reconsidered, existence is purified into the "book" in the hand of "reality itself," "imprint[ed]" into "our consciousness." "Reality," in this sense, having inscribed itself into the subjective vessel of the mind, returns to itself via a hermeneutic detour, reading off the "trace[ry]" of "symbolic characters" and "unknown signs" in a process of exegetical repetition: we read ourselves as written. Writing and reading are collapsed here into the book of the self, which, as a book that is both already written and to be written, is produced—later passages clarify—as a *"transcription"* or even *"tradu[ction]"*—that is, a form of textual repetition from a hieroglyphic script of the real (*"livre intérieur de signes inconnus"*) to that laid out in legible signifiers before us (Proust 1990, 203, 351). The exact nature of this "repetition," however, proves to be a recurrent point of vacillation in Proust: it is both a matter of "deciphering [*déchiffrer*]" and *"un acte de création,"* both passive and productive. Suggestively, both are compressed in the further proposition of art as a kind retrograde or crabwise motion, a *"marche en sens contraire"* that reads the phenomenal world against the grain (*"les apparences qu'on observe [...] traduites et [...] lues à rebours"*—1990, 186, 203). Proust, in fact, comes through in Barnes's quotations to be more disposed toward a notion of "re-writing" as a conservative repetition of a preexisting script: "we are not at all free in the presence of the work of art to be created, that we do not do it as we ourselves please, but that it existed prior to us and we should seek to discover it as we would a natural law because it is both necessary and hidden" (Barnes 1939b; Proust 1990, 186). For Barnes, on the other hand, art as the eschatological repetition of life leans rather toward the side of a *differential* retake—a *creative reconstruction* rather than decryption. Otherwise put, it is the productive repetition of existence in the light of the end itself, within a textual body that reconfigures, reorganizes, and revaluates. As with Ricoeur and Frank Kermode, for whom art "refigures time," or alternatively, brings it into significance by restructuring sequence (*chronos*) in view of a critical moment (*kairos*), art rewrites life from eschatological "vantage ground" (Ricoeur 1985, 27; Kermode 2000, 45–7).[19] That which has been lived *in time* is reviewed in an aesthetic last judgment *at the end of time.*

This perspective on art as a judgment on existence, already theologically inflected in Proust, is directed more specifically toward theodistical concerns in Barnes's portrayal of Joyce as, among his other quirks and kinks—including

---

[19] Some of Barnes's notes to her memoirs of Paris are collected under the heading, "Vantage Ground" (*Collected Poems*, 235–42).

his penchant for "anis-pernodsuze et fine—[the strongest concoction known to man]," "opopanax," "iron finger rings," "pointless jokes," and, it seems, pointless excursions to the brothel[20]—the literary descendent of not only Proust (said to be "[h]is literary father"—*Collected Poems*, 244) but also Job and Dostoevsky:

> Joyce was as poor as Job [...] Tall and thin, with an ancient dignity, a flat back head that ran scrupulously into the line of his neck, a patch over one eye, a fine nose, a small, martyred, satirical, and stubborn mouth. There you have Joyce, the Grand Inquisitor come to judge himself and his generation. To question him was to receive a cold, terrible gaze. Joyce alone could question Joyce.
> (*Collected Poems*, 238)

If the question of theodicy often returns to the Book of Job, this is because, as Ricoeur points out, it unfolds a "lamentation become plaint, and plaint brought to the level of contestation" (2004, 31-2). Job, simultaneously just *and* suffering, punished beyond sense, weighs down on the economy of salvation to the point of fracture. G. K. Chesterton thus remarks on "the riddle of the book of Job":

> Everywhere else, then, the Old Testament positively rejoices in the obliteration of man in comparison with the divine purpose. The book of Job stands definitely alone because the book of Job definitely asks,
> "But what is the purpose of God? Is it worth the sacrifice even of our miserable humanity? Of course, it is easy enough to wipe out our own paltry wills for the sake of a will that is grander and kinder. But is it grander and kinder? Let God use His tools; let God break His tools. But what is He doing, and what are they being broken for?"
> (Cited in Žižek 2009, 52)

Job's lamentation, brought to the pitch of a "contestation," verges on an audacious counter-judgment on the Lord Himself, who, feathers ruffled, demands in the wild lines of the concluding theophany: "Wilt thou also disannul my judgment? wilt thou condemn me, that thou mayest be righteous?" (Job 40:8). The exegetical history of the book of Job need not detain us here; the main takeaway for us is Barnes's portrayal of Joyce as martyr and judge—as he who suffers in life and judges in writing, who returns to the Creator, in artistic form, his take on Creation.

---

[20] "He carried the calendar of saints wherever he went, even into the red light district, where he often talked to the madame of the beauty of Greek art, pushing the girls off his knees with the stern reprimand, 'Je suis un prêtre'" (*Collected Poems*, 251).

As with Job, the parable of "The Grand Inquisitor" in Dostoevsky's *The Brothers Karamazov* which Ivan presents to his brother, Alyosha, effectively brings the gavel down against God. "I hasten to return my ticket"—that is, to freedom and existence—Ivan claims, repudiating all visions of a world in which suffering could be erased in a "higher harmony": "It is not worth one little tear of even that one tormented child [...] with her unredeemed tears! [...] I want to remain with unrequited suffering [...] *even if I am wrong*" (Dostoevsky 2004, 244–5, 246–64).[21] In Barnes's last play, *The Antiphon*, this inquisitorial role is handed over to Miranda, artist and daughter, in a settling of accounts with her predecessors above and here below. In a moment of exasperation, her mother, Augusta, responds to her judgment with the exclamation: "To think I have a daughter for Inquisitor!" (*Selected Works*, 195).

What Barnes's association of artist and judge points to is a notion of the artwork itself as a *response* to life and its theological corollaries, the Creator and Creation: it is, in the title of her late play, the *antiphon*. This takes my observations close to discussions in narrative and aesthetic theory regarding the "antitype" and the writing of history. The typological relation that structures Biblical narrative informs Northrop Frye's studies on the "theory of modes," unfolded into the two primary forms of the "comic" and "tragic" (1990, 33–70). Frye's concerns lead him to a similar discussion of "repetition," divisible into its *conservative* and *creative* aspects, broken down here into Platonic and Kierkegaardian strains. While Platonic repetition nostalgically recapitulates static ideas in their purity through a process of *anamnesis* or "recollection," a Kierkegaardian brand of "repetition forwards" enables "not the simple repeating of an experience, but the recreating of it which redeems or awakens it to life, the end of the process [...] being the apocalyptic promise: 'Behold, I make all things new'" (1990, 345). Frye's focus is thus on the properly historical dimension that "typological thinking" enables, which is "revolutionary" insofar as it departs from a cosmology of eidetic stasis, all of whose phenomenal mutations are essentially, *sub specie aeternitatis*, void: the "typological structure and shape of the Bible" makes "its mythology diachronic" (Frye 1983, 82–3). Existence, brought to fulfilment in the "antitype," is thus reconfigured according to patterns of meaning, bringing the past into historical relation with the present. Hayden White considers this a form of "reverse causation" by which current consciousness rearticulates that which it has succeeded chronologically according to its concerns and obligations, contributing hence toward a "'construal' of a relationship between a

---

[21] See also Fiddes's reading (2013, 177–8).

past and a present" (White 2010b, 270–1). That Frye is able to relate the "mode of thought" encrypted within the typological relation to the kind of awakening that Joyce's Stephen Dedalus seeks suggests that this "theory of history" is precisely one that is predicated simultaneously on a kind of *counter-history*, one that runs in reverse, against the flow of time, in order to re-center life in relation to a particular end-point, magnetizing it into a field structured round specific *eschata*—that is, the "last things" at the end of time (Frye 1933, 80–1). To wake up from the nightmare of history is to re-envision it against its inexorable sequence from the "vantage ground" of a now-point. Repeating forwards thus names a retrospective consideration of the past within the coordinates of a new constellation, an aesthetic reckoning that, as such, is not only *creative* in the content it selects, in the medium of its presentation, and its formal articulation into patterns of causation and significance, but also, in this very process itself, constitutive of a *judgment* on the value and meaning of the past.

In Agamben's reading of the Pauline typological relation, he identifies it as the historical bracket of "messianic time," an "area of tension" that "clasps together and transforms past and future, *typos* and *antitypos*, in an inseparable constellation." This constitutes a "conversive movement," by way of the de-completion of the supposedly complete past and repletion of the incomplete present, leading him to propose: "Messianic time is a summary recapitulation of the past, even according to the meaning of the adjective in the judicial expression 'summary judgment'" (Agamben 2005, 74–6). Writing, in this sense, by typologically relating past and present, functions as an aesthetic "last judgment." Barnes's antiphon, considered in this light, is a return in reverse to the sending of the Creator, which, in sounding out the lacunae of the created world, recalls past time in a summative repetition, via a literary act that runs against the grain of the book of life. The world, traversed by its joys and sorrows, is thus siphoned off via a final either/or into damnation or grace, as spelt, ultimately, on the sibylline leaves of the artist. "For earth […] her dapple is at an end," it might be said after Gerard Manley Hopkins: "Lét life, wáned, ah lét life wind/ Off hér once skéined stained véined varíety | upon áll on twó spools […] black, white; | right, wrong" ("Spelt from Sibyl's Leaves," l.5, 10–12).[22] In sum, each work of art may be observed to encrypt an aesthetic judgment that decides on the question of theodicy, providing a determinate response to melancholic existence in setting up its own aesthetic world, within which is enshrined its "counter-mood" of *either* comedy *or* tragedy. In turning now to a theory of

---

[22] The Barnes Archive holds two editions of Hopkins's works.

"literary worlds," I propose to bring the foregoing discussion on "moods" and "modes" into critical conjunction.

Moods, Modes, and the Ontology of the Work of Art

Melancholy, as I have suggested, may be understood as a dialectical constellation of two worlds: of *life* as it is lived in fallen existential time, and of *art*, which, in enclosing a portion of this life according to its own creative principles, encrypts an aesthetic judgment on the value of the former. What, then, is meant by the ontology of the work of art? On a basic level, this means quite simply, as Heidegger writes: "To be a work is to set up a world" (2001a, 43). The production of a work of art creates its world, comprising its own internal laws, affects, and meaning. In Ruth Ronen's account in *Possible Worlds in Literary Theory*, a fictional world is "constructed as a world having its own distinct ontological position, and as a world presenting a self-sufficient system of structures and relations" (1994, 8). The artwork, in other words, encloses its particular world by abstracting itself from the wider world: *history*, understood as lived time, is thus contained and differentially repeated in the *counter-history* cordoned off in the work of art. As Eric Hayot explains: "The work and the world name a self-enclosing, self-organizing, self-grounding process" (2012, 24). This process, and the close association it bears with the posited world, is thus set in relief by Heidegger's term "worlding." The becoming-world of the world itself is hence often represented by the catchy—if irritating—polyptoton: "The *world worlds*" (Heidegger 2001a, 43). Such a world is primordial in the sense that it is the premise of beings, and opens onto the space of Being, the arena in which inner-worldly entities exist in relation to the whole:

> The *world worlds*, and is more fully in being than the tangible and perceptible realm in which we believe ourselves to be at home. World is never an object that stands before us and can be seen. World is the ever-nonobjective to which we are subject as long as the paths of birth and death, blessing and curse keep us transported into Being.
>
> (2001a, 43)

The "world," understood in these terms, refers us to the invisible ground of the artwork, and indeed life itself, as that which discloses, determines, and structures its very emergence. It is possible to represent it in other terms: as that which supports the emergence of the work but which remains behind the scenes, such a "world" may also be referenced as the "unconscious" of the work of art. So Hayot writes: "Worldedness emerges as the unconscious of the work, as the establishing framework for the unmentioned rules that constitute the work as a total whole (that is, as a work at all)" (2012, 54). What is meant by "aesthetic world," therefore, is "the *diegetic totality* constituted by the sum of all aspects of a single work or work-part, constellated into a structure or a system that amounts to a whole" (Hayot 2012, 44).

To summarize then, in the process of its "worlding," the artwork sets up a world. In detaching itself from its embedment within life, it enacts a differential repetition from historical existence to aesthetic summation. A specific turn is thus achieved from the lifeworld to the aesthetic world. This turn is precisely where the interface between subject and world is reconfigured. The dialectical constellation of suffering in life and response in art may thus also be represented as a dialectical constellation of two differentially repeated worlds. It is in this turn itself that the judgment of art is encoded. The process of "worlding" names the action of an encrypted—or unconscious—summation of life, one that structures and governs the nature of the artwork but which itself often remains unthematized. The "world" of the work of art, in other words, names the place of its transcendental, the "unmentioned rules" and determinants of its emergence. Hayot writes:

> Aesthetic worlds, no matter how they form themselves, are among other things always a relation to and theory of the lived world, whether as a largely preconscious normative construct, a rearticulation, or even an active refusal of the world-norms of their age. [...] Aesthetic worldedness is the form of the relation a work establishes between the world inside and the world outside the work.
>
> (2012, 45)

It is precisely in this "form of relation"—the articulating joint between life and art—where the unconscious of the work of art encodes its response to melancholic existence. While it is true, as Hayot notes, that the aesthetic world is measured against the "frame of judgment" of the external world, my focus here is on the inverse judgment that also takes place, *on* the external lifeworld, *by* the work of art (2012, 45). "To world is to enclose, but also to exclude"—and indeed what is included and what is excluded, together with the unthematized principles that guide this process of "worlding," constitute, in the last instance, an aesthetic judgment on life (2012, 40).

If the world names the hidden premise of life and art, the term may also be developed by the descriptors, "mood" and "mode." Where a mood refers to the hidden premise of affects, mode refers to the hidden premise of the artwork's genre. Heidegger's moods may be usefully read in conjunction with Frye's theory of modes, insofar as they both refer back to the unconscious determinants of life and art. Understood in the Heideggerian sense, moods name the manner in which *Dasein* is situated in a particular world and coordinated existentially with it, determining—or "attuning"—the way in which the world is disclosed to us. As Heidegger writes: "[w]hat we indicate *ontologically* with the term *attunement* [*Befindlichkeit*] is *ontically* what is most familiar and an everyday kind of thing: our mood [*die Stimmung*], being in a mood [*das Gestimmtheit*; lit. 'moodedness']" (2001b, §29). As the manner in which we are interfaced with the world, mood opens up and structures the very coordinates of our existence, into which we are, as it were, *thrown*. In Flatley's account of melancholy, projecting ourselves from a melancholic mood into its counter-mood maps out the relation between the first world into which we are thrown, and the second world into which we are "re-thrown" (Flatley 2008, 82). In like manner, Frye's modes refer us to the primordial structures of the world, in particular, the world of the artwork. White's observation is thus on point: Frye's modes are not reducible to "genre" (2010a, 251). The emphasis, Frye himself notes, is on the "pregeneric elements of literature" beyond the various generic conventions of a specific literary form: "If we are told that what we are about to read is tragic or comic, we expect a certain kind of structure and mood but not necessarily a certain genre" (Frye 1990, 162). Modes, therefore, name the manner in which portions of life are encapsulated within a specific textual world, and, to this degree, wrenching them from their historical location into the reformulated body of the artwork itself, with its own "structure and mood."

The work of art, then, enclosing as it does the movement of history with a counter-historical vision, produces a textual world that depends, in its very production, on a basic ontological determination [*Bestimmtheit*] and attunement [*Gestimmtheit*]—that is, a structuration in terms of *mode* and *mood*. In the thematic and formal properties of the artwork, articulated the way they are, a basic judgment on existence may thus be found: an either/or of *comedy* or *tragedy*—that is, a *yes* or *no* to the Creator and Creation. Every work of art, premised on its specific mood and mode, encrypts its specific relation to the life it differentially repeats and contains. The dialectical constellation in melancholy of lifeworld and art-world is thus, like the typological relation, a way of construing a "form of relationship" between the problem of suffering in existence, and a summary judgment from the vantage ground of the end.

In the context of Barnes's work, such a typological relation is irreducible to a comic resolution, whether in terms of a more orthodox Christian account of the redemption of the elect in the Last Judgment, or even the *weaker* comic ontologies presupposed by Bahun, Rushworth, and Flatley. Leaving the typological relation open to the aesthetic configuration of the artist avoids the prospect of ontotheology that Ricoeur, as much as Heidegger, finds limiting. If, for Heidegger, the threat of ontotheology consists in an overdetermined response to the question of Being, effectively "forgetting" Being with a hubristic and totalizing configuration of history, the aesthetic judgment on the other hand encloses *a* world—rather than *the* world—within an artwork that does not have to stand in as the final antiphon to existence in general. Such an attempt has in fact been classed by Frye as a fallacy of "existential projection"—that is, an unwarranted extension of the mood/mode enclosed in the artwork to the world at large (1990, 63). While written, therefore, from an eschatological vantage point, each work of art is ultimately an isolated end that history once again reopens with time. Instead of a *general* or even *fundamental ontology*, I am proposing here an account of *regional* or *particular ontologies* of the comic and the tragic, each of which may be ruptured once again with the re-emergence of the question of Being—or, more specifically in the context of Barnes's works, the question of theodicy. Where a general ontology purports to determine the nature of the cosmos *in toto—qua* World of worlds—a regional ontology of the individual artwork indicates merely the structural determinants of a single, isolated aesthetic world. What I hope to avoid here is the tendency to carry over prior metaphysical commitments into the discussion of these literary modes. To dispense with the supporting, though often hidden, ontologies that shape previous critics's accounts of modernist art, melancholic art, or even art itself *tout court*, enables the critical retrieval of the aesthetic judgments on the question of theodicy in Barnes's works themselves. These, after all, do not consistently fall into a comic or a tragic mode.

It is arguable, for example, that no strong theory of tragedy emerges in Rowan Williams's discussion of *The Tragic Imagination*. Embedded as it is within the general comedy of Christian salvation history, it rounds up with the strained concession: "The awkward conclusion [...] is that the tragic imagination is always framed and informed by the comic" (2016, 154). For Williams, what the resurrection of Jesus signifies is the inauguration of "the new world," that is, "the final phase of the history of God's relation with his people": "God and the world are now [...] settled in the full and final shape of their relationship. [...] The end has begun" (2017, 62–3). To articulate the consequences of this in the terms that have guided our discussion so far, post-Resurrection history is, for Williams, locked into its final ontological coordinates: the "new world" is also a "last world," and, as the ultimate answer to the question of Being, constitutes a quintessentially ontotheological claim. The interface between self and world, creature and Creator—"God's relation with his people"—has also come into its final configuration in this version of the end-of-history thesis, final in "shape" if not in content: it is, as it were, "decisive[ly] fix[ed]" (2017, 64). The final mood and mode of the world is settled: it is comic. In the same vein, insofar as Bahun's notion of "countermourning," Rushworth's "semi-mourning," and Flatley's "aesthetic shudder" are founded on a minimal investment in futurity, "melancholy," for them, is ultimately reabsorbed into the comic mode.

On the flip side, George Steiner, with his understanding of tragedy as the final negation of all salvational possibilities—"redemption," "social melioration," or "messianic intervention"—ends up paralyzing the interface between self and world into a "dialectic of enmity" (2008, 32, 35). His reconsideration of his earlier work in *The Death of Tragedy*—which Barnes read—thus leads him to the awkward conclusion: "Desiderated: an adequate theory of comedy, of the riddles of grief, singular to man" (2008, 44). For Steiner, tragedy's "*Ur-grund*"—a form of fundamental attunement, or *Grundbefindlichkeit*, as it were—is that of "original sin": "the necessary and sufficient premise, the axiomatic constant in tragedy is that of ontological homelessness" (2008, 30). As I go on to show in my first chapter with a reading of Baudelaire, however, Steiner's words here also read like a good definition of comedy. "Ontological homelessness," while a premise of melancholic existence, is a necessary but *insufficient* condition of both tragedy and comedy: it is the artist's final judgment that brings this to typological fulfilment in her enclosed textual world. But she can also change her mind. In any case, we need not accord her the last word.

My approach, eschewing these metaphysical imports, seeks instead to articulate the various comic and tragic modes which are envisioned by Barnes in her various writings, without embedding them finally into a general ontotheology. Comic and tragic worlds are set up in the artwork but represent, necessarily, the limited judgment of the artist. In the avoidance of a general ontotheology of Being, the question of theodicy is continually re-posed. As Agamben points out, a possible consequence of bracketing out the end of time as a predetermined destination—be this salvation or damnation—is a suspension of history before the question of its "last judgement": "The exclusion of concrete eschatology transforms historical time into a suspended time, in which every dialectic is abolished and the Great Inquisitor watches over so that the parousia is not produced in history" (2011a, 8). Agamben's characterization of the Grand Inquisitor here as he who permanently adjourns the final court of judgment casts him as an allegorical figure of melancholy as presented above. Existence in this "suspended time"—that is, in a zone of arrest before the question of theodicy—is life bracketed out in soteriological indecision, stranded, like O'Connor in *Nightwood*, "in a melancholy that had no beginning or end" (*Nightwood*, 99). The Barnesian artist, however, vested as she is in the signature trappings of the Inquisitor, does not merely set the Creator and Creation within an interrogative frame, but also takes the further step to enclose these within a summative judgment of her own. Relocating this historically withdrawn "parousia"—a final reckoning and coming-to-presence of past time—within the artwork itself, she offers, in miniature, an aesthetically exhibited response to her predecessor. What is enclosed in each artwork is thus a provisional summation of the inherited world—as comedy or tragedy—a final account that nonetheless is available to be re-opened once more by the elapse of time itself—*if*, indeed, such time does continue to come.

Each chapter of the main body of this book thus pivots on the question of theodicy, offering, paradoxically, a "last judgment" that is not last, but capable of being overturned—perhaps once and for all, perhaps not. The affirmative response, however minimal, is recorded in the first half dedicated to Barnes's comic imagination, and the negative response, in the second half reserved for tragedy. Prior to this, however, my first chapter further unfolds the ontological structure that relates melancholic existence to the Fall, focusing on the psychosomatic division of the melancholic subject. In addressing Barnes's interpretation of the symptoms of the Fall in relation to the phenomena of laughing and crying, in addition to sex- and species-difference, this chapter also demonstrates how an analysis of the existential structures relating self and world is closely tied to a phenomenology of affect and embodiment. The ontology of the comic and tragic is thus associated with, yet distinguished from, the psychosomatic responses of laughter and tears.

Chapter 2 moves on to consider comedy as a form of maximal reconciliation by presenting Barnes's alignment of God and artist/woman in *Ladies Almanack* via the conjunction of the divine and human will—otherwise known as *synderesis*. Chapter 3 reads *Ryder* as a comic text that disables reconciliation in the present whilst projecting it into the future, retaining, thereby, a minimally affirmative judgment on existence. Finally, my last two chapters on tragedy argue against all remnants of a theodicy, emphatically refusing any reconciliation with the world as it is or as it might be. Chapter 4 recounts the weak tragedy of *Nightwood* in which hope eventually expires, while Chapter 5 reads *The Antiphon*'s totalizing enclosure of all of past time in its theater of tragedy. The tragic judgment on life concludes with the "Bad News," as it were, of a world in which Death—rather than Life, eternal or otherwise—is ascendant.

1

Melancholy and the Fall

In a letter to Emily Coleman dated October 30, 1938, Barnes returns again to the problem of evil, writing this time of Wordsworth's failure to confront its presence in the created world:

> Fleeting thoughts: Peter Bell (just re read it) we are not satisfied with it because it is not evil enough. For what are we thirsty!?! Marvellous the ass standing with hanging head over the water. Read the ode ["Intimations of Immortality"] [...] it is beautiful, almost as if he had made the trees, lakes and moon himself, nature repeated, and thats [sic] just why I cant [sic] love it as you love it, its [sic] too new and pure with the devil left out, he feels himself cross, discontent, but he does not braid the two together. He does for a minute in Peter Bell. Nothing lovelier than "the moon doth with delight, Waters on a starry night Are beautiful and fair."

The reference here is to the following lines from Wordsworth's "Immortality Ode" on the glory of Creation: "There was a time," Wordsworth writes, "when meadow, grove, and stream,/ The earth, and every common sight,/ To me did seem/ Apparelled in celestial light,/ The glory and the freshness of a dream" (l.1–5). Yet as Wordsworth also records, the experience of such beauty can lapse into an inaccessible past, draining "celestial" presence into its inoperative residue: "The things which I have seen I now can see no more. [...] But yet I know, where'er I go,/ That there hath passed away a glory from the earth" (l.9, 17–18). Such alienation from the enchanted heart of nature constitutes an "evil day" (l.42).

Despite the moral and aesthetic pathos registered in these lines, however, Barnes considers the ode inadequate in its confrontation with "evil." Like *Peter Bell* (1819), which remains "not evil enough," the "Immortality Ode" has "the devil left out." What she gleans from Wordsworth appears to be primarily the promise of redemption from this "evil day." In fact, insofar as nature's "Inmate Man" is never fully divorced "From God, who is our home," humanity's entry into

Creation presents not so much a thoroughgoing Fall into evil, but a mitigated "sleep and a forgetting":

> Our birth is but a sleep and a forgetting:
> The Soul that rises with us, our life's Star,
> Hath had elsewhere its setting,
> And cometh from afar:
> Not in entire forgetfulness,
> And not in utter nakedness,
> But trailing clouds of glory do we come
> From God, who is our home:
> Heaven lies about us in our infancy!
>
> (l.58–66)

Wordsworth suggests in these lines that we are only partially alienated ("*not in entire forgetfulness*") from our divine provenance "elsewhere," in "God [...] our home," leaving us still wrapped about with "trailing clouds of glory" in this world, infants swaddled with heaven's residue. If something of a Fall is intimated here it is not one that produces a total, irremediable division between "Heaven" and the *status corruptionis* of existence in the natural world. Evil does not quite prevail.

Barnes's reading of this major poet of English Romanticism latches onto his denial of the "devil." For her, Wordsworth's poem merely "repeat[s]" the natural world in and as the written word, returning Creation to the glory of its first days. The belated creator thus presents a restorative iteration of his predecessor: "almost as if he had made the trees, lakes and moon himself, *nature repeated*." Barnes sums up her resistance to Wordsworth's Romanticism: "Wordsworth, these nature writers, seem to me to clean nature up too much." The traces of the Fall in their poems are ultimately submerged or transformed via an idealizing aesthetic that appears to redeem Creation by means of a backward repetition. Unconvinced of the restored glories of "moon," "lakes," and "trees," Barnes anticipates their undoing: "But I sit with Judas and wonder when these will be betrayed."

In the same 1938 letter to Coleman, Barnes hence acknowledges her preference for another English Romantic, William Blake, known for marrying "the two verities, Heaven and Hell"—as she puts it elsewhere (Barnes 1939a)—as well as Emily Brontë for the "reality of Heathcliff and Cathy" in *Wuthering Heights* (1847). Their respective visions of evil will in fact later earn them a place, together with Baudelaire, de Sade, and others, in Georges Bataille's 1957 collection of essays, *Literature and Evil*. The notes gathered in Barnes's letters thus suggest a certain preoccupation with the nature of evil, and its relation to beauty, goodness, and the created world. Having discussed her dissatisfaction with Wordsworth, she considers the entanglement of good and evil with an idiosyncratic formula—the "holy imprint of the Devil hoof":

> Perhaps only direction of good and evil; you fall (the fall of Lucifer) and you are a fallen angel; you rise (the heavenly chariot,—race with Einstein) and you are: Christ—things that come down, meteors, angels, storms, we seem to think evil, things that rise, nature, trees, flowers, fire, prayers, good; no, on the other hand this wont [sic] do—there are showers of good omen, and there are uprisings of evil, its [sic] not direction then but <u>kinds</u> in direction—

This brief schematization of good and evil into rising and falling vectors only gets her so far. She concedes: "this is all insane, but I'm just putting down for fun what runs through what is called my head." In a post-Nietzschean age purportedly beyond good and evil, Barnes's continual return to evil's mystery provokes her into the role of a theological *bricoleuse*, crafting and re-crafting answers in response to an unending melancholy.

As I have suggested, the experiences of suffering and evil in life that contribute to Barnes's understanding of melancholy unfold a specific manner of being in the world, a specific existential mood into which we are thrown. Barnes's various thoughts on the nature of melancholy are often pinned to a notion of the Fall, suggesting a feature of ontological volatility in life that leaves the afflicted subject adrift with its symptoms, propelling it in various "kinds" of "direction," and even—as we will see—expelling it from its own body. This unifying theme of the Fall suggests the relevance of an ontological understanding of melancholy capable of disclosing a consistent, structural configuration beneath its variegated field of presentation. Just as Ferber's consideration of the "ontological structure" of mood and melancholy enables a "vertical rather than horizontal direction of investigation," gathering together the "history" of melancholic manifestations into various determinations of "the relationship between a subject and the world," so too might such an approach constellate the manifold Barnesian variations on the theme into a recognizable pattern (Ferber 2013, 10). The myth of the Fall, understood ontologically as the rupture from unity or harmony, finds a plethora of ontic equivalents across Barnes's writings. Otherwise put, where we are said to fall *from* and *into* is subject to numerous re-articulations. Ferber's reconstruction of the "melancholic mood" from Heidegger, Benjamin, and Freud, thus points to its "non-intentional" structure: melancholy, in a strict sense, has *no* object that can be brought into full phenomenological presentation (2003, 8, 42–50).¹ As a loss to the second degree—a *lost loss* or a "cognitively inaccessible loss" (Bahun 2013, 5)—its formulation is always based on a reconstruction. The ontological wound that the Fall names, casting the subject from union (with Nature, the Mother, God, etc.) into its divided existence may be variously thematized. The *postlapsarian* condition in Barnes thus presents a state of division from a prior wholeness: it is, by turns, *post*-Romantic (after Wordsworth); *post*-medieval, as derived from Edwin Muir's reading of Hermann Broch;² *post*-Reformation, following the "crisis of the Christian soteriological narrative" that the Lutheran interrogation of the authority of the Church and the sacraments entailed (Weber 2015, 95–9);³ *post*-war, as recorded in her memoirs of the "war of nerves" in France, when German invasion was imminent;⁴ *post*-pastoral, as depicted in her anti-pastoral with its animals left out-of-joint with time and nature;⁵ *post*-Sapphic, as in the disruption in *Ryder* of a sororal Eden by Wendell's appearance on the horizon, with "thundering male parts hung like a terrible anvil" (see the result of this in Figure 1.1—*Ryder*, 40–2); as well as, of course, *post*-nature, reiterated in the early short stories through to her late works, encapsulated none too subtly in the title of a *Vanity Fair* contribution (Barnes, "Against Nature").

Melancholy's association with an ontological wound that divides the subject from a preexisting harmony is thus, on one level, *structural*. The terms in which such a division is articulated, however, are plural and *historically* implicated. Charles Taylor's observation that modernism's aesthetic and philosophical projects reveal a symptomatic pursuit of "unmediated unity" or "merging with

---

[1] See also Freud's claim in "Mourning and Melancholia" that a "loss of a more ideal kind" is involved in melancholy, suggesting "an object-loss is withdrawn from consciousness": "the patient cannot consciously perceive what he has lost [...] he knows *whom* he has lost but not *what* he has lost in him" (*SE* XIV, 245).

[2] See also Muir's admiring assessment of Barnes in the same volume (1939, 149–50).

[3] In the Catholic Doctor O'Connor's portrayal, the Lutheran motto, *sola fide*, by personalizing the soteriological relation, effectively corrodes the external signs and measure of grace: the "Lutheran or Protestant church [...] is the girl that loves you so much that you can lie to her." Having "started something he never thought to start," Luther himself "went wild and chattered like a monkey in a tree" (*Nightwood*, 18).

[4] "I came back to it [Hotel Académie] through a Paris that I had once lived in for fifteen years, and now it stood before me like a friend who had no memory. [...] When Christ said that man must give up his worldly possessions to follow him he stated a fact. Man is now yet more desolate, for he must lose his possessions and his life with his convictions shaken" (*Collected Poems*, 265).

[5] "The lonely adder hissing in the fern,/ The lizard with its ochre eyes aburn—/ Each is before, and each behind its time" (*Collected Poems*, 82).

Figure 1.1 Djuna Barnes, "All Because of Wendell!" *Ryder*. © The Authors League Fund and St. Bride's Church, as joint literary executors of the Estate of Djuna Barnes.

the other" is given diverse instantiation by Bahun: as "a pursuit of 'oceanic feeling' (Freud), longing for the 'primal unity' of the infant-mother dyad (Klein), the homeless's search for 'undivided totality' (Lukács), and approximation of Being (Heidegger)" (Taylor 1989, 471; Bahun 2013, 21). Melancholy, in this sense, names the place of the subject's alienation from its origin and envisaged destination in "unmediated unity," between a suffering world and the redeemed world it tends toward. In situating melancholy in the liminal region between a "mood" into which one is already thrown and a "counter-mood" that the artwork produces, the emphasis is placed on the *ek-centric* predicament of the subject, withdrawn from itself, its own body, and its regular negotiations with the world, without a corresponding relocation within any immediately available soteriology. Understood ontologically in terms of the Fall, melancholy—as we now move on to observe—also entails a phenomenology of embodiment that alienates one from the immediate flesh. Its corporeal markers, registered across the Barnesian oeuvre, range from the everyday (laughing and crying), to the more extraordinary (sex- and species-hybridity).

Laughing and Crying

In the memoirs of her time spent in Paris as an American expatriate among the literary and artistic avant-garde of the 1920s, Barnes considers the appeal of the French polymath Jean Cocteau: "he set the tragic muse on the circus horse! Fratellini and Hamlet mixed; Greek legend, Christian morality, and the street fair were brought together" (*Collected Poems*, 236). Though attributed to Cocteau, neither the heady encounter of heaven and Hellenism at the carnival nor the mixing of stage clowns and tragic metaphysician is foreign to Barnes. The "circus horse," like the "bucking mare," saddles the artist with the contrary forces of the comic and tragic, rattling her back and forth from pole to pole. Among the drafts of the poetry of her later years, unpublished in her lifetime, a series collected under the header "Laughing Lamentations" suggests that her own remark regarding the "hilarious sorrow" of Dan Mahoney, the living prototype for *Nightwood*'s Matthew O'Connor, informs her thoughts on the nature of laughing and crying (Barnes 1958b). The openings of two of these drafts are a sardonic portrayal of the body transported by these buffeting affects:

> When first I practised all my eyes in tears,
> With flapping nostrils like a blowing horse,
>
> Laughter under-water bow'd her head
> Like any peasant in a praying stall.
>
> (*Collected Poems*, 221, 224)

Pushing physiology to the fore, Barnes's depictions exhibit the hidden conjunction of laughing and crying in that common moment when the body transgresses its own boundaries through its orifices, tearing, snorting, blowing, sniffling, and siffling ("O siffleur, too sinful and too jubilant"—*Collected Poems*, 221). Intimations of sin and repentance, joy and guilt, throw passing light and shade over these images, unsettling them from the contours of any fixed affect.

This presentation of the body in *ek-stasis*, out-of-joint with itself and with God, owes something to the writings of the French symbolists, including the Comte de Lautréamont, rediscovered and revered by the Surrealists in the interwar years, for whom Barnes professed admiration till the end of her life (O'Neal 1990, 48), as well as Baudelaire, in particular, his tract on laughter, *De l'essence de rire* (1855). The "physiologists of laughter," Baudelaire claims, are in "unanimous agreement" that "the comic is one of the clearest marks of Satan in man." It is, in fact, a "symptom":

human laughter is intimately connected with the accident of the ancient fall, of a physical and moral degradation. Laughter and grief express themselves through the organs that have the control and the knowledge of good and evil, the eyes and the mouth [...] the laughter of his lips is a sign of as great a state of corruption as the tears in his eyes.[6]

(Baudelaire 1981, 143–6, 150)

Laughter and tears, as symptomatic manifestations of humanity's loss of "unity," evidence the disequilibrium of the body's relation to itself, defiling the very image of God: "God, who desired to multiply his own image, did not place lion's teeth in man's mouth—but man bites with his laughter; nor did He place, in man's eyes, all the fascinating duplicity of the serpent—but man seduces with his tears" (Baudelaire 1981, 143). The body that is torn from itself, possessed by a diabolical excess to which it grants involuntary testimony in spasmodic discharge, in the form of an "emanation" or "explosion" of vapors and waters, is marked with the "sign of debility" as much as the "diabolic"—devil-ridden as much as melancholy-ridden (1981, 160, 144–6). Baudelaire, like Barnes, collapses both phenomena physiologically into "a nervous convulsion, an involuntary spasm," with the consequence that other symptomatic paroxysms are drawn into the province of Satan: a "sneeze," for example (1981, 146). Informed by similar insights, Lautréamont's exhortation in the *Chants de Maldoror* envisions the body pushed to the verge, breaching its borders in effluvial release:

> let it be then a melancholy laugh. Laugh, but weep at the same time. If you are unable to weep with your eyes, weep with your mouth. If it be still impossible, urinate[.][7]

(Lautréamont 1924, 184–5)

The various seizures of the body, its expropriation from itself and its subsequent emissions, exhibit the vicissitudes of humanity in the *status corruptionis* after the Fall. If the foci for these corporeal irruptions are the eyes and mouth for Baudelaire and Lautréamont, with occasional outposts at the nostrils and urethra, Barnes indicates Satan's residence in another of these fleshly recesses: melancholy, to recall, can be accompanied by "an hemmorhage for a menstruation." Barnes's frequent associations of the "womb" with "damnation"

---

[6] The Barnes Archive holds several editions of Baudelaire's poetry and prose.
[7] This edition is held in the Barnes Archive.

and the vulva as a "curse" in later life are in fact prefigured by an early unpublished narrative fragment, likely based on her grandmother Zadel's death, involving the expulsion of cancerous matter, posthumously, from her vagina (Herring 1995, 21–2). Melancholy, if imputable to a spiritual source, retains consequences in the flesh, as a body struck by crisis, ruptured from itself. In showing up in the psychosomatic subject, it remains rooted in the embodied dimensions of sex and species. The individual chapters of this book will examine the specific ties of melancholy to sexed embodiment. For now, however, the theological frame surrounding laughing and crying requires further specification.

Crucially, as Baudelaire notes, the self-dispossession of the body when diabolically possessed, produces symptoms that not only register affliction somatically but also tentatively re-suture the fault lines in its being. Laughing and crying, in disarticulating the subject, simultaneously initiate a rudimentary restructuration. Melancholic *ek-stasis* and return thus carve out, for Baudelaire, the narrative arc of a *felix culpa*:

> And pray observe that it is also with his tears that man washes away man's sorrows, that it is with laughter that he sometimes softens man's heart, and draws it closer; for the phenomena produced by the Fall will become the means of redemption [*les moyens du rachat*].
>
> (1981, 143)

It might be said then that for Baudelaire, a normative, even *reflexive*, practice of mourning is inscribed at the level of the body itself. Thrown into ontological exile, it restores itself through a form of repair that not only re-equilibrates the self at an individual level but also relocates the convulsive, porous, body into communion with other stricken bodies as a link in the chain of salvation history. These physiological disturbances, in the normative body, chart the reflex arc of a soteriology.

Such a theological frame surrounding laughing and crying often finds its way into Barnes's writings, and offers some explanation for a number of otherwise opaque formulations. In her 1936 novel, *Nightwood*, the mordant wit scintillating through the eloquent involutions of Doctor O'Connor's despair is registered as a "melancholy hidden beneath every jest and malediction" by the Baron Felix Volkbein, who himself suffers from a "laborious melancholy" (*Nightwood*, 35, 7). O'Connor maps out the theological dimensions here in relation to the coordinates of the Fall and redemption: "creative misery," he claims, "comes from being smacked down by the devil, and lifted up again by the angels" (*Nightwood*, 28). Having plummeted into the created world via a guffaw, O'Connor declares he intends to exit from it in like fashion, fleeing the poverty of "disqualification" to reach toward laughter's redemptive promise: "Laughing I came into Pacific Street, and laughing I'm going out of it; laughter is the pauper's money" (*Nightwood*, 29).

Barnes's characteristic move, however, is to the interrupt this soteriological arc. O'Connor's envisioned comic conclusion to existence ultimately fails to come to pass, while Nora—plagued with "some inscrutable wish for salvation"— is left suspended between the two moments of expropriation and recovery (*Nightwood*, 41). Her "sense of humor" appears to be absent, leaving her "smile" and "chuckle" bracketed out in the interim of an abstracted physiological response, self-enclosed at the level of animal "needs":

> One missed in her a sense of humor. Her smile was quick and definite, but disengaged. She chuckled now and again at a joke, but it was the amused grim chuckle of a person who looks up to discover that they have coincided with the needs in a bird.
>
> Cynicism, laughter, the second husk into which the shucked man crawls, she seemed to know little or nothing about. She was one of those deviations by which man thinks to reconstruct himself.
>
> (*Nightwood*, 48)

Where Baudelaire's account of salvific laughter effectively tears the organism from itself, leaving him a "shucked man" in order to reconstitute him anew, this "second husk" of the recuperated self is withdrawn from Nora, stranding her on the wayside of the Baudelairean soteriological arc in an animal reduction. As a "deviation" from the redemptive destiny of Christendom, she becomes a "reconstruct[ion]" of the very image of Man.

The distance Barnes takes from the salvational account of laughter may be measured precisely in the ruination of its mourning reflex—or ritual even, when considered on a communal level. The redemptive arc from fall to salvation is broken, severing Baudelaire's theological anthropology into two distinct moments, marked by—first—the uncanny stigmata of *denaturalized* laughter and tears, displaced from their normative corporeal loci—and second—the waylaying and detraction of their remedial tenor. Urination and menstruation, as melancholic symptoms, thus function as aberrations of mourning, disruptions of the normative bodily responses to the self-division that diabolic possession entails. The logic of Freudian melancholy is, in this account, corporeally embedded: the inability to mourn is an inability to laugh and cry (*SE* XIV, 244–7). Where Baudelaire's "rictus" of the "damned" falls in line "with the purest orthodoxy of laughter" (1981, 147), its distorted hieroglyph, branded on the corrupted flesh, makes its way from Lautréamont's plastered grin—a bleeding slit cut wide, "split [...] where the lips join" with "a penknife whose blade has a keen edge" (1924, 5)[8]—to that contained, and (miso-)gynecologically coded, in Barnes's grim joke in *The Antiphon*:

> Augusta: What's a woman?
> Dudley: A cow, sitting on a crumpled grin.
>
> (*Selected Works*, 140)

Existence—in particular, existence as women—names the postlapsarian corruptibility of the flesh. A vulvar grimace, perverted from the laughter and tears of redemptive history, leaves its bearer stranded in ontological exile. In *Nightwood*, too, the "grin of the dead," a "low riding mouth in an empty snarl of the groin," as Barnes's gloss to Signor Maffi makes clear, is an aborted laugh, transmigrated into a genital *rictus*, a "[c]urse against the female organ" (Barnes 1948).[9] Just as the 1958 edition of *The Antiphon* associates Augusta's "poke" with the "Hemorrhage of time," *Nightwood* turns loss into an eviscerating force on the bereft, "dragging time out of his bowels," once again locating the body as the living vessel through which the effects and affects of the fall into history are borne (*The Antiphon*, 132; *Nightwood*, 27). Here it seems, Augustine's *in tempora dissilui* finds its corporeal foci.[10]

These bodily orifices, insofar as they negotiate the transactions between self and other, may hence be considered the somatic junctions for the kind of interfacing that *Stimmung* performs as the disclosive premise between *Dasein* and its world. Laughing and crying, as O'Connor understands them, rupture rather than redeem communion:

> One cup poured into another makes different water; tears shed by one eye would blind if wept into another's eye. The breast we strike in joy is not the breast we strike in pain; any man's smile would be consternation on another's mouth.
>
> (*Nightwood*, 29)

---

[8] The motive for this act is clear: "I would have laughed like others; but that weird imitation was impossible." After this surgical intervention, however, he notes: "It was a mistake! [...] The blood which flowed abundantly from the wounds made it impossible to ascertain whether it was really the laughter of others. But after some moments of comparison, I see clearly that my laughter does not resemble that of mankind, that is to say I am not laughing." Later on, Maldoror performs a similar operation on the vagina of an "unfortunate child" with "an American knife, made up of ten or twelve blades," eviscerating her "[f]rom this enlarged hole" (1924, 5, 148).

[9] This association of the vagina with death is in fact made graphically in Memling's *Polyptych of Earthly Vanity and Divine Salvation* (c. 1485), where the cleft detail of a woman's labia in a central panel mirrors the toad attached to Death's genitalia on the left panel. See also Barnes's drawing, "The Beast" (c.1928)—reproduced as the cover image for this book—which features similarly cloven labia on a faceless, supine woman, with matching, cloven hooves.

[10] "I fall into dissolution amid the times" (Augustine 1912, XI.29.39). The Barnes Archive holds a copy of the first volume of the 1912 Loeb library edition of the *Confessions*.

Not all physiological "emanations," ocular or buccal, record a remedial reflex: *Nightwood*'s Doctor invokes not just an incommensurability of symptoms but also the inimical relations that ruin community. One man's pity is another man's pepper spray. If a certain degree of *formal* similarity is indicated in both "pain" and "joy," expressively recorded in the action of striking one's breast, the gesture nonetheless is differentially repeated as its affective components change: motor similitude dissimulates the changing affects of the body, charged with sorrow or pleasure. Suffering is as nontransferable as happiness. Whether aggravated into tears or smiles, the body here signals the formal moment of its self-expropriation, struck from somatic equilibrium, *without*, however, the corresponding salvific recovery gained in the making of the Holy Community. From one eye to the next, "different water" is pressed out, just as each smile on a "mouth" may be contorted into "consternation" on the next.

Ironic sabotage is thus found attached to O'Connor's appeal: "*Misericordioso!* Save me, Mother Mary, and never mind the other fellow!" (*Nightwood*, 28). If grace were to be had at all, it would be thieved from one's neighbor. No communion of laughing or crying mouths is established here to rescue these fallen subjects, stalled as they are in the melancholic limbo between division and recovery. As O'Connor later cries: "all suffering does *not* purify—begging everybody's pardon." Suffering may in fact be "composed wickedly," void of purpose, a testament to "pointless agony" (*Nightwood*, 124–5). The corrupted laughter of the damned, drained of salvific significance, is made explicit in a line from the drafts leading up to the publication of *Nightwood*: "Humour is supposed to be a saving grace, that is a lie, it is a tragedy" (*Nightwood: The Original Version*, 311). In the lines following this that do make it to publication, laughter is indexed again as a sign of the Fall: "every nation with a sense of humour is a lost nation, and every woman with a sense of humour is a lost woman" (*Nightwood*, 14). Scattered across the Barnesian corpus, this laughter, conjugated with sin and damnation, exhibits the melancholic dispossession of the body from itself, while, conversely, bracketing out its soteriological end. From the laughter of the Pope in *Nightwood* to that of Roger in "A Sprinkle of Comedy" (1917) and Pilate in "The Terrorists" (1917), the diabolic testament of—respectively—the "man who forgoes his angels" (*Nightwood*, 2), who reduces humanity to "expert monkeys" (*Smoke*, 89–90), or, indeed, sharpens his "melancholy" to "robust hate" (*Smoke*, 161–2), is issued forth in cacophonous peals. Dislodged from the arc of mourning, laughing and crying, in their profane vicissitudes, traverse the body to leave in their wake a symptomatic trail, spangling the flesh of the melancholic with their uncanny traces. We see these catatonically frozen as "grimaces/ of the dead" or as "discs upon [...] eyes like/ Husks of tears" in *The Book of Repulsive Women* (*Collected Poems*, 51-2). We see them rupturing elsewhere too in transmuted form, as "blood" from "the horned-toad's eye" and the "hemorrhag[ing]" nether grin in *The Antiphon*, or as the residues of "breastmilk" in the "man in tears" from a late verse fragment (*Selected Works*, 181; *Collected Poems*, 182).

At this stage, it is possible to resituate these bodily correlates of melancholy on a more theoretical level. Helmuth Plessner's philosophical anthropology, in addressing the "belonging-together of laughing and crying," identifies both as limit expressions and reactions [*Grenzreaktionen*] to a specific existential predicament (2003, 366). Both are responses to a particular disunity identified as humanity's "eccentric position in existence [*exzentrische Position im Dasein*]," inhering in the "double-role" that "corporeal existence imposes on the human": "he *is simultaneously* body and *in* i.e. *with* a body." He is hence stranded in the liminal region between "being-in and being-with [*In- und Mitsein*]," "having and being [*Sein und Haben*]" a body (2003, 372-3). "Eccentricity" names the "position of being simultaneously in the middle and at the periphery" (2003, 374). It is in situations of strain where the regular negotiations between being and having a body fall apart that the body collapses back into itself. The result is a form of self-seizure that retrieves a provisional unity from its disunity: by capitulating from the complex of "being-in and being-with" a body, it resumes, simply, the state of being-a-body. As with Baudelaire, laughter and tears both signal our self-dispossession, a "loss of self-mastery," and suture us back to ourselves, as "responses to a borderland scenario [*Grenzlage*]"—that is, the limbo where our regular negotiations between being-in and being-with a body are suspended (2003, 359, 378). As both "self-betrayal" and "self-maintenance," laughter and tears are limit responses to limit situations, a shattering of the "organized unity of spirit, soul, body" that is also nonetheless the last trick up the anthropological sleeve, demonstrating thereby a "humanity" that consists in the ability still to "cope where nothing more is to be done." If the provisionally maintained "body-soul-spirit unity" is given up in crisis, it is folded over now into that other unity of the body itself, gathering the "eccentric" subject back into the vessel of the re-centered self (2003, 363-4). The "formal" similarities of laughing and crying are thus broken down into two moments: (i) the disruption of a regular situation of embodied negotiation with the world; (ii) the recuperation of one's being-human in the collapsed unity of the shaken body (Plessner 2003, 364).

To bring the foregoing discussion to a head then, "melancholy," resulting from ontological exile, names the subject's exposure at the limit of the world. Pushed to the verge in crisis, the structured relations between self and body, subject and environment, disintegrate to throw one back onto a foundational anthropology. At the very brink of the world, melancholy also negotiates a response that is, however, not necessarily the outcome envisioned by Plessner or Baudelaire. Replacing the *reflex* arc of laughing and crying with the *mediated* response of writing—that is, in and as *comedy* and *tragedy*—interrupts the two sequential moments of rupture and repair in normative mourning. If laughing and crying indicate normative, even reflexive practices of mourning, comedy and tragedy, as literary *mediations*, present no longer a predetermined *reaction* to a limit situation, salvaging the divided self within some divine (Baudelaire) or humanistic (Plessner) economy, but an imaginatively and aesthetically inflected *response*, that is, as *judgment* and *creation*. Writing, in this sense, is situated where the soteriological arc of laughing and crying is disrupted, diverted into an aesthetic praxis that reroutes the reflexive action of the body through a cognitive detour—conscious or unconscious—emerging thence in mediated form, as comedy or tragedy. Where a *reflexive* reaction to crisis is predetermined (whether by psychomotor instinct or behavioral conditioning), a *mediated* response emerges after some degree of psychosomatic re-processing. The laughter and tears that have been displaced from their normative foci, whether to innervate other regions of the flesh, sectioning off the equilibrated body into tense aggravations, or to take a further turn toward comic and tragic writing, thus exhibit the work of melancholy as a form of interrupted mourning. As will be seen, this logic of bodily expropriation in laughing and crying similarly informs the precarious hybridity of the melancholic subject, often leaving it stranded in a state of indecision between the sexes and between species. I defer my discussion of the problem of sexual difference to O'Connor's trans-femininity in Chapter 4, and focus on the problem of species-difference for the rest of this chapter.

Hybrid Bodies: The Problem of Corporeal Assumption

To some degree, this understanding of melancholy as ontological exile helps to explain the proliferation of animals and animal-human hybrids in Barnes's writings, artwork, and even dreams. Her May 21, 1938, letter to Coleman, in which she speaks of being ridden by melancholia, passes via a stupefying *non sequitur* into an oneiric account of a "seal woman," who, as it were, "told me to feel her":

> she was almost like a human, but prickly when you touched her, and she had legs and a pelvis, but nothing else, and she said she could not talk much because she was fish, she smelled like a fish, briny, and her brothers were ferocious puppy seal animals with puppy hair, they came up out of a lake to fight me, and one of them ate my only weapon, a long brush, and my cain [sic], head and all, under the waters of the lake a red and white dog seemed to be floating, but not dead, shallow blue water, under a line of trees—how is that for a dream? Animals, always animals, its [sic] sickening, and those babies of my mother'a [sic], and now its [sic] fish.

I will not attempt to take on the role of a "Dempsey of the sub-conscious" here, but have chosen to cite this in full as an indication of how far existing scholarship on melancholy and modernism fails to make a note of, much less account for, the many conceptually rebarbative elements that are raised here and elsewhere by Barnes: species-difference, sex-difference, as well as their envisaged—and foiled—dissolution. Some of these aspects are, however, retained in the apparition of the eland in *Nightwood*—often taken to be the cynosure of the Barnesian oeuvre—which I propose to read here to round up my discussion of melancholy and its tie to ontological division. From this, the logic that binds laughing, crying, and hybridization across sex- and species-difference to the structure of melancholic existence may be derived.

On first encounter, the eland is rather out-of-the-way as a choice for an animal. Joanne Winning has, however, convincingly shown its relation to Robin's prototype, Thelma Wood, silverpoint artist and Barnes's lover. In her shimmering bestiary of lions, giraffes, and elephants, we find one prominent silverpoint drawing of a "bushbuck" (see Figure 1.3). Following a letter from Barnes to Coleman in 1936 around the time of *Nightwood*'s publication, Winning notes that Wood's silverpoint, while catalogued in the archives as a "bushbuck," is likely an eland: "I have been having the most awful dreams lately, all about animals. I'm beginning to wonder what Thelma's Eland has increased in my animal aware spirit" (Barnes 1936; cited in Winning 2013, 316). Thelma's eland succeeds another, more than four centuries ago, by Albrecht Dürer, whose depictions of the Apocalypse Barnes held copies of. As a major figure of both silverpoint art and woodcuts—a medium Barnes was particularly drawn to—Dürer's allegorical meditations on melancholy and eschatology in his 1504

Figure 1.2 Albrecht Dürer, *Elk*, 1504, drawing. London, British Museum. © The Trustees of the British Museum.

drawing (Figure 1.2) and engraving (Figure 1.4) are likely interwoven into her own.

In Paul Smith's revision of Erwin Panofsky's iconological interpretation of Dürer's elk as a "symbol of melancholy," "linguistic remotivation of animal names and of proverbial material" are incorporated to locate it within a soteriological narrative (2014, 312). Smith notes that the elk in Dürer's 1504 copper etching "The Fall of Man"—or "Adam and Eve"—is modeled on his 1504 drawing of the same animal, beneath which is written, "*heilant*," an archaic of the German word for elk, *Elendt*, which also stands for "sorrow," or *Elend*, in modern German: "the word is derived from the Old Saxon *elilendi*, which is composed of **alja* ('other') and *land* ('country'). The original meaning of the word is thus: living in another country, which is the cause of misery" (2014, 312–13). The Fall, signifying spiritual alienation, is at the same time presented in dialectical relation to Redemption: not only is the elk's hoof used in medication "to treat epilepsy, the *falling* disease— just as Christ by his body cures mankind from the evil consequences of the

Figure 1.3 Thelma Wood, *Bushbuck Among Bamboo Trees*, 1928. © The Authors League Fund and St. Bride's Church, as joint literary executors of the Estate of Djuna Barnes.

Fall," its name is homophonous with the Redeemer himself (*Heilant* being the present particle of *heilen* [to cure]) (2014, 313). Dürer's elk effectively embeds melancholy within an aesthetically exhibited theodicy. Barnes's reference to the "eland" in fact segues into a "unicorn," another dense Christological symbol of

Figure 1.4 Albrecht Dürer, *Adam and Eve*, 1504, engraving. New York, Metropolitan Museum of Art.

medieval iconography that she would have been familiar with from her visits to the Musée de Cluny where the *La Dame à la Licorne* tapestries are housed.[11] These allegorical dimensions may be taken into consideration in Robin's moment

---

[11] "Have you seen the divine unicorn tapestries at the Cluny?" (Barnes 1934).

of awakening in the Hôtel Récamier, one that consolidates mythic content to suggest species-difference as a form of ontological alienation:

> The woman who presents herself to the spectator as a 'picture' forever arranged, is, for the contemplative mind, the chiefest danger. Sometimes one meets a woman who is beast turning human. Such a person's every movement will reduce to an image of a forgotten experience; a mirage of an eternal wedding cast on the racial memory; as insupportable a joy as would be the vision of an eland coming down an aisle of trees, chapleted with orange blossoms and bridal veil, a hoof raised in the economy of fear, stepping in the trepidation of flesh that will become myth; as the unicorn is neither man nor beast deprived, but human hunger pressing its breast to its prey.
>
> (*Nightwood*, 33–4)

The state of immersion Robin is in when we first encounter her is framed with reference to two timelines, ontogenetic and phylogenetic—that is, at the level of individual and of species existence. Doctor O'Connor is called in to resuscitate her therefore from a sleep from which, not just her conscious subjectivity, but her species-being itself, is erased. The Robin roused from this particular slumber is worked into an image of her continued predicament, that of being precariously perched at the cusp of nature and culture—the point, that is, of melancholic indecision between worlds. Ek-statically located at the place of a "turn," she remains an image of the exclusion from animality, without, however, a corresponding absorption into humanity, and is lodged therefore at the interface between, on the one hand, the primal myth of "a forgotten experience" or a phylogenetic "racial memory," and on the other, the economy of salvation or Divine Economy said to govern human history. Ontologically volatile, an "image" of transition rather than a designable being, Robin, as a "mirage of an eternal wedding" is figured as an illusory copula forever straddling without quite bridging the caesura between animal and woman: she is the perennial turn of the "beast turning human," an "uncertainty"[12] broken, from one moment to the next, into a shifting holography of wings, horns, and hooves, draped equivocally with the sacral raiment of pagan and Christic devotion. Instead of a *felix culpa* that would recover her fall from immersion within the natural world into the salvation history or *Heil-geschichte* across human time, Robin, like the eland, is stranded in an "economy of fear," "a hoof raised" in limbo, bracketed out from

---

[12] Baron Volkbein hence remarks in relation to Robin: "An image is a stop the mind makes between uncertainties" (*Nightwood*, 100).

any teleological direction. Melancholy, as ontological exile, is thus allegorically presented here in an eland dressed in the spiritual ciphers of "chaplet[s]," "orange blossoms," and "bridal veil," ruptured from the coordinates of its being to find itself egressed into a zone of "trepidation," where instinctual life is lost to the enigma of the Word, *denaturalized* without being *divinized*, wedded neither to Nature nor to God, but reefed where the "flesh [...] will become myth." If the "Bride" of Revelation 21:9, the "wife of the Lamb," is invoked here, its soteriological consummation is stalled. Robin's eland, in its esoteric paraphernalia, is sundered from the somatic unity of the animal—that is, being *in* and *as* a body—toward an absconded groom. Its mythological kin is the unicorn, inscribed with ontological lack, but reducible "neither to man nor beast deprived," a symbol instead of the "human hunger" for an illegible desideratum, an unthematized "prey" that it presses close to, its "breast" returned to visual, sonic, and semantic propinquity to itself—its primal self—as "beast." This ecstasy thus provokes an "insupportable joy," channeled not into laughter or tears, but held in the rapture of an opaque anti-epiphany. It is akin to Barnes's gloss to Pierre Leyris on her aporetic description of Nora as, on the one hand, "an early Christian" who "believed in the word," yet capable of neither further ascent nor descent, but kept "in one place," a "body eternally moving downward" but "immune to her own descent," traversed by the contrary forces of "derangement" and "equilibrium" (*Nightwood*, 46):

> I think it means something like this:—the force of mystery that keeps, like a cork on a geyser, an impermiable [*sic*] body dancing on the top of that it would drown in—bliss? beatitude? The knowledge of the unknowable? (un-know-able)? In other words, state of un-gifted
>
> (Cited in *Nightwood: The Original Version*, 220–1)

"Un-gifted," with connotations of being un-graced, suggests Nora's displacement from a divine economy of salvation, having hit the spiritual ceiling, without recourse, however, to a return to the "bliss" or "beatitude" of oceanic merger: "A religious woman [..] without the joy and safety of the Catholic faith," as O'Connor describes her (*Nightwood*, 54).

That Robin, herself both a Catholic convert and one of the "disqualified,"[13] does eventually seem to sink back into nature, renders her initial "awakening"

---

[13] There is also a suggestion toward the end that Robin leaves the Church: "As she had taken the Catholic vow long before, now she came into church as one renouncing something" (*Nightwood*, 150).

all the more acute. The "insupportable joy" she inspires is much like the displaced waters of Nora's geyser, retaining the *ek-stasis* that laughter and tears, as limit reactions to limit situations, resolve. Torn from its psychosomatic self-coincidence, the melancholic being breaks out in spasms and secretions, breaching its own lineaments into the graduated spaces across sex- and species-difference. Melancholy, then, names the place of a ruptured soteriology: it is the still-point in an "economy of fear," lived out in the transitional space between "flesh" and "myth," body and signification, and, finally, the *pause* before the theodistical question. A zone of suspension thus opens up here between the mystery of suffering and evil, and a decisive response. Interrupting the two moments structuring the phenomena of laughter and tears—that is, between ecstasy and recovery, alienation and redemption—melancholy leaves its subjects stalled before an existential either/or—a "yes" or "no" to the Creator and Creation. The artist's response, as a *mediated* rather than reflexive gesture, takes laughter and tears to the second power, in the *creative judgment* on life encoded in her art, whether as comedy, or as tragedy. Each of the following chapters will thus consider the suffering of the melancholically expropriated body and the dialectical response it occasions in art, whether in comic reconciliation or tragic renunciation.

2

Comedy I: *Ladies Almanack* and the Lesbian Sensorium

In Barnes's 1934 edition of Proust's *Recherche*, the following passage in the second volume, *Within a Budding Grove*, in which the narrator comments on Odette's altered appearance, is marked out:

> But another reason for this change lay in the fact that, having reached the turning-point of life, Odette had at length discovered, or invented, a physiognomy of her own, an unalterable "character," a "style of beauty," and on her incoherent features—which for so long, exposed to every hazard, every weakness of the flesh, borrowing for a moment, at the slightest fatigue, from the years to come, a sort of flickering shadow of ability, had furnished her well or ill, with a countenance dishevelled, inconstant, formless and attractive—had now set this fixed type, as it were an immortal youthfulness.
> (Proust 1934, I.271; cited in Caselli 2009, 14–15)[1]

Two forces beset the body here, one of dispersal and another of cohesion. These are accompanied by two temporal registers—namely, the organic time of age ("weakness of the flesh"), resisted in turn by an aesthetic stasis ("immortal youthfulness"). The contingencies of mortality that plague the body assume a certain prominence at this "turning-point of life," as "expos[ure]," "hazard," and "weakness" come to accentuate Odette's "incoherent features [*traits décousus*]," exerting a deconstituting pressure over her countenance, now "dishevelled, inconstant, formless and attractive." Countering the thousand natural shocks that the flesh is heir to, however, are the composure and stability that the assumption of the self's image enables. Form becomes flesh as Odette achieves "a physiognomy of her own," associated with an aestheticized timelessness. Having set in place "this fixed type," her body is consolidated into "an unalterable

---

[1] See also Proust, 1973, 186.

'character,' a 'style of beauty.'" A crucial hesitation on the narrator's part, however, on whether this acquired physiognomy is "discovered" or "invented" will prove to be symptomatic of an ontological indecision regarding the form of the body in which the flesh is said to be contained or even constituted. Is this body-image already embedded in the organism, amenable to "discovery" through the eye of fashion, or is it created—"invented"—in the course of one's existence?

One specific manifestation of this ambivalence is recorded in Mina Loy's 1919 advertising pamphlet, *Auto-Facial-Construction*, which, as Christina Walter suggests, seems to have developed out of Bess M. Mensendieck's system of functional movement exercises. This project, characterized by Mensendieck as a "sculpt[ing] in flesh," is in Loy's pamphlet energized by a rhetoric of authenticity or original selfhood—and hence, to rehash Proust's terms, less "invention" than "discovery" (cited in Walter 2014, 134). Fashion and even civic duty are cast here as antagonists to "the original form of the face (intrinsic symbol of personality)":

> Different systems of beauty culture have compromised with our inherent right, not only to "be ourselves" but to "look like ourselves," by producing a facial contour in middle age, which does duty as a "well preserved appearance."
> (Loy 1997, 165)

Yet, if the autotelic dimension of a self returning to itself in auto-facial-construction is emphasized by the iteration of such phrases as "the basic principle of facial integrity," "the original form of the face," and "the original facial contours," a marked note of dissonance is struck when Loy, cashing in on her "specialised interest in physiognomy as an artist," speaks not just of the "conservation" of the face, but, crucially, its "reconstruction." The interval that opens up between the "facial-construction" of the title to the augmented term "*re*construction" signals a discrepancy—an indecision even—that is covered over by what Walter terms "a sleight-of-hand substitution" (2014, 136). For Walter, Loy "emphasizes that through her production process one manifests, paradoxically, a 'constant and natural resource' of beauty, a kind of raw material rather than a manufactured good" (2014, 136–7). The unity of self and body that is staged in this pamphlet as a return to facial origins thus takes a detour through an alienating process of self-fashioning. The self is rescued by (re)constructing an "origin" that it comes to assume against the contingency of the untrained flesh, subjected to "the ravages of time" (Loy 1997, 166). "Discovery" and "invention" become one and the same process.

In this chapter, I set out to unfold how Barnes's *Ladies Almanack* (1928) presents an intervention into the status of the body that escapes this synthetic dialectic of flesh and form, living substance and transformative art. In mobilizing an anti-representational aesthetic, Barnes's *Almanack* departs from the imagistic or muscular synthesis of the self—whether "invented" or "discovered," "constructed" or "reconstructed"—to reach toward the drives, forces, and affects that circulate beneath and beyond the body's integrated form. Barnes's response to her contemporaries is both textually and paratextually indicated. In her 1972 foreword for the Harper and Row edition, a jocular challenge to Proust is suggested in her claim that her slim little almanac, an anachronistic return of a medieval genre, forms nothing less than the "Neap-tide to the Proustian chronicle"—that is, the equal or near-equal to his seven-volume literary Gargantua (*Ladies Almanack*, 87). Loy may be seen as another target here with her appearance in the almanac as Patience Scalpel, the only heterosexual of the text, who laments the neglect of posterity within a Sapphic enclave where reproductive obligations are traded for immediate pleasure:

> they love the striking Hour, nor would breed the Moments that go to it. Sluts! [...] Are good Mothers to supply them with Luxuries in the next Generation; for they themselves will have no Shes, unless some Her puts them forth! Well I'm not the Woman for it! They well [will?] have to pluck where they may. My Daughters shall go amarrying!
>
> (*Ladies Almanack*, 13)

Barnes sketches her friend in satirical lines here. Loy's own claims in her "Feminist Manifesto," drafted in November 1914, belabor the "right to maternity" of "[e]very woman" and indeed "her race-responsibility." (Loy 1977, 155) These were unlikely to appeal to Barnes, who presents her journalistic self in a 1916 article as "[o]ne of the birth controllers" (Barnes, "Becoming Intimate with the Bohemians").[2] Loy's call in this manifesto for "the <u>unconditional surgical destruction of virginity</u> through-out the female population at puberty" may be behind her "Scalpel" and "Patient" monikers and for Dame Evangeline Musset's own surgical misadventure, when as "a Child of ten," she was "deflowered by the Hand of a Surgeon!" (*Ladies Almanack*, 24).

Ladies Almanack takes some distance from the body chronicled in Proust and promulgated at times by Loy. The attachment to the organism at the level of its "naturalness" or of its coherence and "integrity" present in these writers under

---

[2] Barnes is less restrained in her June 6, 1941, letter to Emily Coleman regarding Kay Boyle's "bloody fecundity": "revolting. She should have been born a rabbit and have written in lettuce. The trouble with that girl is, she's got condor blood, and looks it. There is really something wrong with her ... her stuffing comes out in so many places that one wonders where she is bound."

the guise of rediscovery and reconstruction is done away with in Barnes's text. There are certain libidinal implications in this move, which will be charted here. As Leo Bersani has argued, the formation of the bounded subject set apart from the objective world inaugurates a condition of self-mastery while simultaneously isolating that self in an alienated existence. "Psychoanalysis," in particular, "has been the most authoritative modern reformulation of the Cartesian and the Hegelian opposition [...] between Nature and Spirit or between the *res extensa* and thought" (2010, 140). By undoing the psychic structure that sets up the alienated relation between self and world, however, the subject–object interface, as will be seen, may be eroded: melancholic division is thereby reconfigured into the reconciled world of comedy. The strategy of reconciliation in *Ladies Almanack* consists in articulating desire beyond the terms of the bounded ego, eluding hence the theatre of alienation between the desiring subject and the perennially receding horizon of its fulfilment.

Barnes's *Almanack* encloses a comic world founded on ontological similitude. The radical inclusivity of the term "Woman" as it is deployed in this text, touched everywhere with homosexual suggestion, sets up a world built upon what might be termed a *homo-ontology*—that is, a fundamental ontological monism in which variance multiplies within a cosmos of likenesses. Alterity here is to be conceived as moments rather than principles, transitory rather than axiomatic; it is produced but also passes away into sameness. We find here an actualization of Lady Buck-and-Balk's wish, couched in terms "a little Callous to Nuance": "I [...] would that we could do away with Man altogether!" (*Ladies Almanack*, 24). This presents one of Barnes's strategies in her art of comic reconciliation: if the subject is melancholically divided from the world it is thrown into via its very constitution, in *Ladies Almanack* however, the bounded ego itself is left behind in a world where alterity is refused at root, replete with desiderators and desiderata beneath and beyond the level of the "human" as integrated subject. It is in this hall of "Woman"'s universal self-encounter that what could be termed the "lesbian sensorium" of *Ladies Almanack* is brought into being.

A specific conjunction of dispersal and utopia is set up here. Such a poetics of decreation has perhaps been developed most significantly in the modern world in the writings of Deleuze and Guattari. Their polemics against the body-as-Gestalt are in fact situated within a specific ontology that rewrites the soteriological narrative of Christianity by beginning, primordially, in flux, and returning, ultimately, to flux. The crux here is a displacement of the anthropological icon—*imago Dei*—as the axis on which the cosmos pivots, from Creation to the Incarnation and Resurrection. From Adam to Christ, *genesis* through *kenosis* to *theosis*, these "permutations of God-Man and Man-God" distribute grace on the basis of this anthropomorphic avatar (Schults 2014, 103). "Oedipus" is merely one of its names, enshrined in the psychoanalytic writings of Freud and Lacan; "Christ," in fact, is another (Schults 2014, 6–9, 25–35). Instead of returning God-Man to Himself in a "U-shaped divine comedy," the Deleuzian project may be characterized rather as a recovery of primordial creativity after its *fall* into the created forms of the material and socio-historical world. The arc of salvation is rewritten: the fall *from* the aboriginal cosmos—or "chaosmos" (Deleuze 2013, 201)—of interacting singularities *into* form will be redeemed via rupturing the world of forms in reactivating these forces and intensities. As will be seen, this names the return not of the *Logos* (anthropomorphically captured) to itself, but of the *virtual* to itself. We begin with the "schizophrenic God," lapse into the world of created forms, and disperse—via a reactivation of these pre-created flows, affects, and intensities—into new assemblages, and finally back into these imperceptible singularities (Deleuze and Guattari 1983, 77). The Deleuzian "glorious body," unlike Saint Paul's, is one "which is divided into disjunctions" (Deleuze 2013, 322).[3] The encapsulated body features here as the vessel of clay in which life is vitiated and contained. Its salvific horizon lies in the release of the life in it that has languished into its borders, hierarchically tamed, organologically fixed. As Peter Hallward observes, a crucial underlying theme in Deleuze's philosophy is "the redemptive re-orientation of any particular creature towards its own dissolution": "[r]ather than a philosopher of nature, history or the world, rather than any sort of 'fleshly materialist,' Deleuze is most appropriately read as a spiritual, redemptive or subtractive thinker, a thinker preoccupied with the mechanics of *dis*-embodiment and *de*-materialisation" (2006, 3).

This movement of decreation is not unique to the DeleuzoGuattarian project and bears affinities with the mysticism of Meister Eckhart—as Kristien Justaert has suggested (2012, 59–70)—as well as that of Marguerite Porete before him, and Simone Weil after them, both of whom Barnes read at different times in her life. Before turning to Porete, it is worth indicating the *autotelic* orientation of *Ladies Almanack* and its difference from the DeleuzoGuattarian scheme. For the latter, all decreation—or molecular-becomings—makes passage via "becoming-animal" and "becoming-woman" before ultimately leading into a horizon of "imperceptibility," returning cosmic singularities to themselves. For Barnes in

---

[3] "To anyone who asks: 'Do you believe in God?' we should reply in strictly Kantian or Schreberian terms: 'Of course, but only as the master of the disjunctive syllogism, or as its a priori principle (God defined as the *Omnitudo realitatis*, from which all secondary realities are derived by a process of division)'" (Deleuze and Guattari 1983, 13).

this *Almanack*, however, the telos of this disassembly is the lesbian sensorium itself, in which the recombinant lesbian constituents of the world meet and flow, returning, thereby, the primordial Sapphic body to itself in renewed guise via the detour of the material and sociohistorical coordinates of the historical present of 1928. The City of the Goddess will rise from the molecularization of the created world. The pre-created and post-created worlds—populated in the DeleuzoGuattarian chaosmos by a tohu-bohu of forces, flows, intensities, singularities, atoms, molecules, imperceptibles, and "non-existing entities" (Deleuze 2013, 322)—are all marked in Barnes's *Almanack* with a Sapphic trace. A seemingly paradoxical formulation emerges here of difference in sameness: in the eternal return of the (same) Goddess, the aleatory shapes of herself resurface, reassembled. In the following, I move on to address the two co-implicated factors involved in this conjunction of shattering, hybridization, and *happiness* witnessed in *Ladies Almanack*: (i) its reformulation of the eschatological Kingdom into that "Single Beatitude" or "Garden of Ecstasy," otherwise "known as Girls! Girls!" (*Ladies Almanack*, 12); and (ii) the foundation of this lesbian sensorium on an ontology of the *virtual* rather than an ontology of *history*.

"Girls! Girls!"—or Utopia

If the utopian dimension of *Ladies Almanack* is often acknowledged, it is just as often elegiacally qualified, as buried past or foiled present.[4] After all, utopia, it is often said, is the glimpsed "good place" (*eu-topos*) only insofar as it is simultaneously the "not place" (*ou-topia*). The sources on which Barnes draws for her *Almanack*, considered alongside her own writings leading up to it, suggest her text's placement in the genre of utopian literature. In the sketches of her expatriate life in "Farewell Paris," Barnes makes a reference to Allan Ross MacDougall's *The Gourmets Almanac*, in which she is listed among the dedicatees at the start of the book, and acknowledged again at its end together with "Millia Davenport and Ossip Zadkin for the valuable books they loaned me" (*Collected Poems*, 255; MacDougall 1931, vi, 358). In addition to the many seventeenth- and eighteenth-century almanacs that MacDougall refers to in his book, the

---

[4] Louis Kannenstine considers it a "lost Eden" (1977, 53). Tyrus Miller reads the *Almanack* in the context of the "utopian celebration of the poetic transfiguration of the body" in the aesthetic practices of Dada and Surrealism. Referring to the 1927 suicide of Barnes's Greenwich Village friend, Baroness Elsa von Freytag-Loringhoven, Miller writes: "[t]he very freedom of her poetic sense in reinventing her appearance revealed an underlying eclipse of the self, a will to self-extirpation that would be definitively consummated by her suicide" (1999, 143).

three publications of the French *L'almanach de cocagne* for the years 1920, 1921, and 1922 are identified as key source texts (Guégan et al., 1919; 1920; 1921). Although it may not be possible to ascertain whether any of these were indeed one of the "valuable books" that Barnes had passed on to MacDougall, it is likely that she had encountered them while writing her own almanac. As Herman Pleij explains, the land of Cockaigne is a kind of medieval earthly paradise, part of "the tradition of the *locus amoenus*, or 'lovely place,' that was a fixed topos of antique literature, usually used to glorify rural life or to portray the nostalgia of a lost Arcadia" (2001, 216).

Ladies Almanack, which Barnes proclaims to hail "from the shores of Mytilène"—a synecdochal reference to the isle of Lesbos—invokes this Arcadian dimension with a particular Sapphic inflection (*Ladies Almanack*, 87). The result of these intersecting topographies—ranging from Mytilène to Cockaigne, Arcadia to Eden—is a relocation of the medieval *locus amoenus* to the textual incarnation of Natalie Barney's own garden on 20 rue Jacob, Paris, presided by its own Doric *Temple à l'Amitié*, which, in 1927, became the seat for her *Académie des Femmes*, where works from Anglo- and Francophone women writers such as Barnes, Loy, Gertrude Stein, Rachilde, and Colette were read and presented (Benstock 1986, 249). In setting up this enclosed world of intellectual, and at times, erotic exchange, Barney's salon might be taken as the localization of a certain imaginative conjunction of Paris and paradise, preserved most notably in Jules Renard's quip: "Ajouter deux lettres à Paris: c'est le paradis" (Renard 1965, 297).

Such a topographical configuration is found in Barnes's own satirical account in "Vagaries Malicieux" (1922). Her opening portrait reveals this dream logic and its moral dodges:

> For years one has dreamed of Paris, just why, no man can tell saving that no pear from an orchard stolen has been atoned for without the mental calculation: "A Frenchman would have understood; in Paris all would be so simple, so charming!"
> (*Vagaries Malicieux*, 5)

Theft, here, is excused in the execution, since this American fabulation of a "Frenchman" seems to know only of desire and its exigencies, not so much of its consequences or its discipline. Debt, material or spiritual, has no place in such a world, where redemption comes on the heels of sin, and the apple of Paradise— metonymically shifted here to the pear of Paris[5]—may be "atoned for" with a

---

[5] Or indeed Augustine's stolen pears (1912, II).

magic calculus that weighs off stolen thing with insincere thought. In Barnes's sketch of her first encounter with Paris, the first two subjects introduced are characterized in terms of a careless profligacy where pleasure and consequence are uncoupled:

> One of these gentlemen is very fond of cats and does a great deal of stroking in the season, the other is a playwright who is utterly reckless about the number of objects in Europe on which he casts what is known as his libido.
>
> (*Vagaries Malicieux*, 5)

The circumlocutory delicacy here is part of the result of a strategic deployment of Freudian terms, achieving the effect of a coy understatement of the hedonism associated with Paris. Further on, an allusion to the land of Cockaigne is inserted as the narrator remarks: "each has eaten ducks in the only place where ducks die for the pleasure of it (I never found out where the place is)" (*Vagaries Malicieux*, 6). So the narrator protests. Yet self-roasting animals make up a prominent motif of the Cockaigne myth, where the entire cosmos serves itself up to human appetite: "wine flows in the creeks," "white and brown bread compete for the honor of being the first to enter one's mouth," fish force their way into homes and grill themselves, and roast geese fly into one's mouth, as Pleij records (2001, 283–5). Like the women invoked by High-Head in *Ladies Almanack*, these cosseted beings are the "spinning Centre of a spinning World" (*Ladies Almanack*, 51). To these queen bees ensconced in their cosmic hive are dedicated the loves, labors, and losses of their subjects: "Do not the Bees belly and blow, hone their Beaks and hoard their Honey to make her Negus and Nectar? The Worm, from Head to Heel, one long contriving inch that she may be wrapped in Silks and Satins, the Seal well suppled for her Coat, and the Seed in the Dirt, fattening and bursting for her Delight?" (*Ladies Almanack*, 51).

Although "Vagaries Malicieux" ultimately segues into the satirical, the utopian dimension it raises becomes the manifest principle in *Ladies Almanack*, which channels a diverse range of myths—pastoral, pagan, and religious—into the concretization of an ontological space of ubiquitous satisfaction. Dame Musset's snide remarks to Patience Scalpel in the August chapter relate Sapphic practice to Christian salvation: "'What,' said that good Dame, 'can you know about it, who have gentlemaned only? Recall, and remember, my Love, that the Camel is forever facing a Needle, but cannot go through it, and a Woman is much nearer the needle's proportion in her probabilities than a Man'" (*Ladies Almanack*, 50). Barnes's occasional habit of using nouns as verbs functions here as an instrumentalization of the male body ("gentlemaned"), measured rather unfavorably against the bodies of women, more likely to facilitate a lover's way to spiritual and erotic bliss. "[I]t is easier for a camel to go through the eye of a needle than for a rich man to enter the kingdom of God," Matthew reports (Matthew 19:23–26); but it is with the body of a woman that one is more likely to pass through this needle's eye, so Musset contends. Along similar lines, a pastoral scene is staged pictorially as an introduction to the May chapter (Figure 2.1).

Here, a cherub rides the sun's rays, a flower in her fist, to bless a sleeping pair of women lovers. Around them, the beasts of the field appear to coexist in harmony, including a capering goat and horse, a bovine couple, and a lion with a serene rather than threatening aspect. Beams of glory radiate from the mattress of the sleeping pair—the bower of bliss in this pastoral—according to a tradition of religious iconography seen also in the collection of folk art from fifteenth-century France up to the Second Empire published in Pierre-Louis

Figure 2.1 Djuna Barnes, "Sweet May," *Ladies Almanack*. © The Authors League Fund and St. Bride's Church, as joint literary executors of the Estate of Djuna Barnes.

Duchartre and René Saulnier's *L'imagerie populaire* (1925), which Barnes names an influence. The figure on the left, ribboned at the waist, similarly emanates an aura of divinity with one hand raised in benediction. It is with this graphic display of beatitude that Patience Scalpel's comically intrusive comments are prefaced: "What [...] can you women see in each other? Where is the Parting of Ways and the Horseman that hunts?" (*Ladies Almanack*, 31). Heterosexual routine—burlesqued here as a kind of division of labor that also involves physical division—is juxtaposed with the contiguity of women's bodies. As a later formula has it: "A man may rage for the little Difference which shall be alien always, but a Woman tears her Shift for a Likeness in a Shift, and a Mystery that is lost to the proportion of Mystery" (*Ladies Almanack*, 57). Patience Scalpel's reproach is, of course, a rather comic commentary on the scene that is taking place, which is succinctly narrated in the following terms: "amid the Rugs Dame Musset brought Doll Furious to a certainty" (*Ladies Almanack*, 31). This "certainty," however, does not turn out to be the *Endlust* that Dame Musset initially thinks it is ("that's all there is, and there is no more!"). Doll's cry—"But oh!"—invites her continued ministrations: "Down Woman [...] there may be a mustard seed!" (*Ladies Almanack*, 31). Not quite the most obscure reference in this almanac, this "mustard seed" seems to indicate some sort of G-spot or another particulate region of pleasure not yet reached by Musset. The parable of the mustard seed recounted in Matthew (13:31-2), Mark (4:30-2), and Luke (13:18-19) comes to mind here, where the Kingdom of Heaven is allegorized as an expansion from particle to cosmos. The third book of Origen's *Commentary on the Song of Songs*, dealing with "the analogical structure of nature," offers a succinct account of the medieval *convenentia* exploited also in Barnes's posthumously published *Creatures in an Alphabet* (1982):[6]

> And perhaps just as God made man in his own image and likeness, so also did he make the remaining creatures after certain heavenly images as a likeness. And perhaps every single thing on earth has something of an image and likeness in heavenly things, to such a degree that even the grain of mustard which is the smallest of all seeds may have something of an image and likeness in heaven.
> (Cited in Curley 1979, viii)

This mustard seed, charged with its biblical associations, presents a particulate manifestation of heaven on earth, an atom of God's omnipresence ensconced

---

[6] See my reading of Barnes's poem in relation to several medieval and modernist bestiaries (Ng 2021).

somewhere in Doll Furious and now hunted down by Dame Musset. What do we make of this mustard seed transmuted into a comic and cosmic orgasm, if not the reterritorialization of medieval correspondence theory as a kind of lesbian sensorium, in which every pleasure, every particle of the universe, announces this queer God's presence in her body of Creation? What Hallward observes of Deleuze's philosophy is pertinent here. There is, in the latter's work, what he calls "a *theophanic* conception of things, whereby every individual process or thing is conceived as a manifestation or expression of God or a conceptual equivalent of God (pure creative potential, force, energy, life …)" (2006, 4).

At this stage it is possible to inflect a French proverb that appears in the popular *Almanach Hachette* of 1899, alluded to in Alfred Jarry's own 1899 *Almanach de Père Ubu* in his account of "les revendications féministes," which Barnes may have come across during her time spent in the Parisian literary salons of Stein and Barney (Béhar, Dubbelboer, and Morel 2009, 49). These feminist vindications are announced and detailed in the *Almanach Hachette* on a single page, at the bottom of which is printed in bold: "**PROVERBE: Ce que femme veut, Dieu le veut**" (Béhar, Dubbelboer, and Morel 2009, 50). Conveniently enough, woman and God are conjoined in a common *volonté*. The operative trope here derived from scholastic philosophy is *synderesis*, which posits the continuity of the divine will or spark of conscience with postlapsarian humanity. Because of this continuity, a reserve of unmediated identity with God is maintained: being "in direct communication with the supersensory," as Agamben notes, this "area of the soul" designated by the "technical term used in the Neoplatonic mysticism of the Middles Ages and the Renaissance […] has never been corrupted by original sin" (1993, 34).

This recuperation of synderesis is also likely prompted by the texts Barnes probably encountered around this time—not just *Ulysses* with its "word known to all men" (Joyce 1986, 9.429–30),[7] but also Thomas Browne's *The Garden of Cyrus* (1658), as well as the 1927 edition of a rediscovered fifteenth-century English translation of Marguerite Porete's *The Mirror of Simple Souls*.[8] Porete's apparent heterodoxy would result in her burning at the stake and earn her the epithet "*pseudo-mulier* [pseudo-woman]" (Hollywood 2016, 135). But if

---

[7] Of this "word," Richard Ellmann writes: "Most readers have supposed that the word known to all men must be love, though one critic maintains that it is death, and another that it is synteresis; the latter sounds like the one word unknown to all men" (Joyce 1986, xii).

[8] The *Mirouer* remained popular even after Porete's execution in 1310, and continued to circulate anonymously or under male pseudonyms for 650 years before its author was identified by Romana Gaunieri in 1946 (Robinson 2001, xii). Authorship is not attributed in Barnes's 1927 copy in the Archive, edited by Clare Kirchberger.

to locate a region of the self aboriginally with God—or whichever conceptual analogue She might take—external to the unfolding of history, is to traverse one's creaturely inheritance and one's socio-political placement to where the incorrigible will resides, then this accusation of being inauthentically woman quite rightly positions Porete orthogonally to natural and historical time. Like Barnes's queer women, who remain in a time of plenitude with a queer God, "*pseudo-mulier*" names an excess beyond any historical or institutional configuration of womanhood. The anti-representational commitment of Porete's mysticism—and Meister Eckhart after her—implicated as it is in a critique of a certain anthropomorphic constriction of God, thus unfolds many of the elements observable in the Deleuze's "iconoclastic theology" (Schults 2014). Decreation, or "creative subtraction," names a common undertaking (Hallward 2006, 79). As Amy Hollywood notes, for Porete, the "final transformation of the Soul demands the annihilation of all creatureliness," such that it is the divine will that remains operative in—and ultimately—beyond it (2016, 142). In repudiating "the mediation of any images," Porete "refuses the path to the divine which lies through humanity, and demands instead the renunciation of all createdness in order to become divine herself" (Hollywood 2001, 96). Salvation is freed from its anthropomorphic end: the soul united in love is "one with its precreated ground and with the divine," returned thence, disencumbered, to "the pre-Adamic state of freedom" (Hollywood 2001, 96, 99). If, for Deleuze, decreation ruptures the organism to rehabilitate the schizophrenic God in him/her—*qua* prelapsarian flows and forces—Porete's pre-created ground of all things is similarly a de-anthropomorphized God, immanently resident in the created world—an "*esse indistinctum*" (Hollywood 2001, 105).

Transcendence and immanence are no longer strictly divided here: "Porete wanted to surpass *all* embodied creation *while remaining within it* in order to realize the true goal of human life: annihilation of the will and transformation into God" (Robinson 2001, 31). An allegorical opposition is set up here, with "Reason," encumbered by an edifice of abstract representations and ethical prescriptions (conventionally, church, clergy, and scripture) placed against "Love," who, aligned as She is with God, remains invulnerable to error: "I am God, says Love, for Love is God and God is Love" (Guarnieri and Verdeyen 1986, 21.44–7).[9] This is "Holy Church the Little" against "Holy Church the Great." As a passage marked out in Barnes's copy of the text has it: "This soul

---

[9] Following Robinson, references are to this critical edition. English translations, unless otherwise stated, are by Ellen Babinsky (Porete 1993).

hath neither thought, word, nor work, except for the exercise of the divine grace of the Trinity" (Kirchberger 1927, 52). With the creaturely will annihilated, the Trinity is enabled free action in the soul, who "has from God what God has; *and is what God is through the transformation of love*" (1986, 135.17–19). The interface between self and world in melancholy is thus reconfigured: the intermittent withdrawal of the Divine Lover, leaving the soul bereaved, stranded in a "dialectic between presence and absence [...] joy and suffering," is overcome via a transformation of the very "*relation* of the soul to the world," enabling "a new relation with God" (Hollywood 2001, 96, 88, 109). Union with the pre-created ground of Being—"the virtual existence of all things within the Godhead"—dissolves the divided world of the melancholic (Hollywood 2001, 104). No longer in existential exile, the soul "swims in the sea of joy, that is in the sea of delights, flowing and running out of the Divinity. [...] She is Joy itself by the virtue of Joy which transforms her into Joy itself" (Guarnieri and Verdeyen 1986, 28.1–5). An ironic reprisal of this finds its way into Barnes's *Almanack*. With a kind of mock-melancholy characteristic of this text, the "Condition of Woman" is likened to a "Fish of Earth": "She was not fashioned to swim in Heaven [..] she swims in Terra-firma" (*Ladies Almanack* 56–7). As with Porete's—and indeed Deleuze's—relocation of transcendence at the level of immanence itself, this "sea of joy" within which the decreated soul swims may as well be "Terra-firma."

It is precisely in this region where the soul is conjoined with God, adjacent to history, subjectivity, and the realm of representation, where an *achieved eschatology* is to be found, making its appearance alongside the production of a world in which one is always already reconciled, always already in joy. Robinson notes that in naming God "Farnear"—or "Loingprès"—Porete resolves the "dialectic of presence and absence, of immanence and transcendence": "God the Trinity is within the soul. Farnear shows the noble soul that her true being dwells within her, *virtualiter*" (Robinson 2001, 54). Synderesis enables the activation of this portion of the soul that remains, as it were, "virtual"—perennially *there*, across the unfolding of history. As Michael Screech points out, synderesis is also at work in the *L'abbaye de Thélème* sequence in Rabelais's *Gargantua*, a common source-text for both Jarry's and Barnes's respective almanacs, said also to be the first of French utopian literature (Rabelais 2006, 372). The motto of the Thelemites, "Fay ce que vouldras," recalling Saint Augustine's "*dilige et quod vis fac* (Augustine 2008, 7.8)" and *Le Mirouer* ("love and do what you will"— Guarnieri and Verdeyen 1986, 13.50), also finds its way onto one of Sophia's five chamber pots in Barnes's *Ryder* (1928) in the inscription "Do what you will"

(*Ryder*, 11). The Greek term *thelema*, meaning "will," from which Thélème is derived, is itself featured in the Lord's Prayer: "Thy kingdom come. Thy will [Θελημα] be done, On earth as it is in heaven" (Matthew 6:10). If it is a *projective* eschatology that is intimated here, however, what *Ladies Almanack* brings into presence may be more aptly characterized in terms of a *realized* Kingdom.[10] In Barnes's *Almanack*, a strategic retrieval of a monist unity between the soul and God as the ground of all being enables the attainment of the eschaton in the here and now of the text—*virtualiter*. The Kingdom of God here, however, is queered into that "Single Beatitude" or "Garden of Ecstasy"—otherwise "known as Girls! Girls!" An infinite variety of girl-forms, girl-parts, and girl-bits—or girl-haecceities, to take on Deleuze's appropriation of Duns Scotus—is contained here in this monist homo-ontology. If the neuter God of the Deleuzian cosmos of flows, forces, and affects is in some ways functionally analogous to Porete's God, a sexed trajectory nonetheless accompanies "*Loingprès*" in the *Mirouer*, who, as Hollywood notes, eventually departs from the "masculine" and "becomes feminized in his union with the soul" (2001, 98). It is this coincidence of the trajectories of becoming-one, becoming-happy, and becoming-lesbian, that is picked up by Barnes's *Almanack*: by virtue of our union with God, we are all lesbian *virtualiter*.

In tilting the axis of history into the axis of the virtual, happiness is reassessed: no longer deferred to future time, it is resituated at the place of the virtual *now*, both immanent and *imminent*. The move is made from an Adornian "*promesse de Bonheur*" to an ontological *prémiss de bonheur* (Adorno 2013, 15). My reading of Barnes's *Almanack* is thus consonant with Julie Taylor's claim that it is "unequivocally committed to the textual inscription and production of happiness" (2012, 151). Although Taylor's use of affect theory does not involve an account of decreation, her reading is to a degree consonant with the utopian dimension of the DeleuzoGuattarian project in its insistence on the

---

[10] As Judith Wolfe has shown, much of the eschatological imagination of the nineteenth and early twentieth centuries may be characterized as projective, or futural, in its orientation. This is witnessed in two opposing tendencies. On the one hand, the move toward "immanentizing the eschaton," initiated most notably by Joachim de Fiore's *Expositio in Apocalipsim* in the twelfth century, culminates in German Romanticism and Hegel's "neo-Joachimite chiliasm," which locates God within history as history's own dialectical self-realization ("World History *is* the Last Judgement"—Hegel 2012, 306). On the other hand, disenchantment with meliorist visions of "sublation of this-worldly effort into eschatological plenitude" would sharpen with later crises including the First World War, accelerating into notions of "eschatological rupture" most notably in the "dialectical theology" of Karl Barth and his circle, whose imputed "neo-orthodoxy" consists in a return to the Reformation's emphatic caesura ("infinite qualitative distinction"—Barth 1968, 10) between the human and the divine (Wolfe 2017, 676–96).

present-ness of happiness: "happiness is a condition of the text's present tense: it is not elsewhere, but here" (Taylor 2012, 177). In the following, I move on to consider the flight from history in the conjugated paths toward happiness, decreation, and Sapphic conversion. I take my cue here from Louis Marin's reading of "the text of 'Rabelais'" as "utopia itself"—that is, "an immense body of joy [*corps-de-jouissance*]" (1976, 36), a body, not of containment, but of transgressive flow, as allegorized by the sculptural centerpiece of Thélème: "a magnificent fountain of pure alabaster, topped by the Three Graces with horns-of-plenty pouring water from their breasts, mouths, ears, eyes, and other bodily apertures" (Rabelais 2006, 368). It is at such a site of ontological seepage, where the body-as-Gestalt is undone, that the lesbian sensorium of *Ladies Almanack* is brought into being.

Becoming-Lesbian

In *Ladies Almanack* the conventional assignation of woman to nature is as often cited as it is inverted, celebrated, as well as parodied, inveighed against, and reconstructed. The book's very subtitle makes such an association its apparent basis, promising a "showing" and "full Record" of the seasonal variations of womanhood according to various earthly and astral influences:

LADIES ALMANACK
showing their Signs and their tides;
their Moons and their Changes;
the Seasons as it is with them;
their Eclipses and Equinoxes; as
well as a full Record of diurnal
and nocturnal Distempers

(*Ladies Almanack*, 3)

When the woman–nature conjunction is taken up again in the October chapter, it is grafted onto a Christian paradigm of the Fall:

There was a time when still rhymed to the wild Rib that had made her, Woman was atune to every Adder, every Lion, every Tiger, every Wood thing, every Water-wight, every Sky-wanderer; every Apple was to her a whole Superstition, and to quiet and to tame that Bone, she whispered "Lord! Lord!"

(*Ladies Almanack*, 61)

A general eroticization of the cosmos is suggested here which threads together ancient and medieval paradigms of the harmony of the spheres with sexual titillation. Musical figures ("rhymed"; "atune [attune]") relate difference to similitude as divisions across sex and species are named and overcome. This prelapsarian conceit is in Barnes's rendering altered by a lust suspended between temptation and discharge, indicated by something like a sustained clitoral erection ("that Bone") rechanneled towards worship: "Lord! Lord!" is this woman's murmurous response and contribution to the *musica universalis*. Between transgression and suppression, the forbidden fruit and the "tame[d]" body, desire expands into ubiquity: "every Apple" holds a mythic promise and every organism an intimation of kinship. If cosmic harmony is parodically inflected here, in the March chapter it is sexologically characterized and sent up: "A Man's love is built to fit Nature. Woman's is a Kiss in the Mirror. It is a Farewell to the Creator, without disturbing him" (*Ladies Almanack*, 23). Having aligned "Nature" and "the Creator," Barnes places "Woman" in opposition to both, with an implication of one-upmanship involving neither strain nor fuss ("without disturbing him"), the effort too negligible and the triumph not worth gloating over. This valedictory move is repeated again in the September chapter, where the love of men is reduced to the "Camp of Nature," and judged insipid against the "Garden of Venus": "Yet do this Fire rage as hotly here in the Garden of Venus, yea, with an even more licorous and tempestuous flame, than in the very Camp of Nature" (*Ladies Almanack*, 57). In this scheme, women's love goes against and beyond nature, involving a certain notion of denaturalization. Staged as "a Farewell to the Creator," the love of women may be understood as a deviation from Creation, a creative detraction from one's creaturely form and purpose.

In placing "Venus" against "Nature," Sapphic love is suggestively characterized beyond the terms of animal copulation. It is in fact this aporetic link between body and spirit at the heart of love in the psychosomatic human subject that has taxed the resources of many a psychoanalyst since Freud. Lacan's consideration of human sexuality in "The Signification of the Phallus (1958)" in particular attempts to bridge this divide between the camps of "Nature" and "Venus." Given the linguistic-being of the subject [*parlêtre*], a certain denaturalizing effect intervenes in intercourse, mutating the nature of this "relation" from "*copulation*" into "the (logical) copula," and along with it, the penis into the phallus: "The phallus is the privileged signifier of this mark in which the role [*part*] of Logos is wedded to the advent of desire" (Lacan 2007a, 581). When, in *Ryder*, this "(logical) copula" is instantiated as "a transitive verb," the conjugation of which ("I lie—he lies—they lie—") results in Sophia's return from her Latin class "a mother," this migration of sexuality from the corporeal to the syntactical is comically staged as the illicit love that founds Wendell's birth (*Ryder*, 35). The phallus, then, is precisely the event of the negation of the penis. Yet Lacan preserves a certain ambiguity when he introduces Hegel's "*Aufhebung*" to articulate this negative relation, effectively confounding "sublation"—in which the negated term (the penis) is retained in the emergent concept (the phallus)— and simple "disappearance": "The phallus is the signifier of this very *Aufhebung*, which it inaugurates (initiates) by its disappearance" (2007a, 581). The result is a hybrid object: the phallus is a mutant penis, partially deterritorialized, a foiled process of becoming-word, not quite in the "Camp of Nature" or the "Garden of Venus." Judith Butler, in her analysis of this text, thus points to the ontological conundrum that it generates: "The phallus *symbolizes* the penis; and insofar as it symbolizes the penis, retains the penis as that which it symbolizes; it *is* not the penis" (1993, 50–1).

The Lacanian account of the passage from the "Camp of Nature" to the "Garden of Venus," from "copulation" to the function of the "copula," may thus be read otherwise—that is, without the recuperative gesture of retaining that inch of masculine morphology in the phallus. Because the varieties of amorous traffic between, across, and among lovers are based on an initial deterritorialization of the "natural" relation of penile copulation, both Butler and Deleuze recognize the creative multiplications that may emerge from this becoming-other of the penis. As Miss Tuck of the sisters Nip and Tuck in the May chapter pines, the "Contortion of Traffic" figuring the entanglements of desire is irreducible, sending whatever path-guiding "Sign-Posts" there are into disarray: "How am I to help it if I go astray [...] when every Law of Love and Desire was long ago as mixed as a Contortion of Traffic?" (*Ladies Almanack*, 38). The love-relation cannot be pinned down. To the potential for a "proliferative catachresis" contained in Lacan's botched phallus, Butler responds with her own conceptual butchery by introducing the term "the lesbian phallus." Since "the anatomical part is never commensurable with the phallus itself," the latter could be said to be a "transferable phantasm, and its naturalized link to masculine morphology can be called into question through an aggressive reterritorialization" (1993, 52–3).

The passage from *physis* to *logos* is given a sexual focus here, recorded as a movement from penises (in the "Camp of Nature") to lesbian phalli (in the "Garden of Venus"). In *Ladies Almanack*, this movement is further specified as an epochal transition, from the "Medieval" to the "modern." In the March chapter, Masie Tuck-and-Frill, "erstwhile *Sage-femme* but now, because of the

Trend of the Times, lamentably out of a Job," thus suggests alternative procreative procedures involving alternative means of impregnation:

> Creation has ever been too Marvellous for us to doubt of it now, and though the Medieval way is still thought good enough, what is to prevent some modern Girl from rising from the Couch of a Girl as modern, with something new in her Mind? To stick to the old Tradition is Credulity, and Credulity has been worn to a Thread. A Feather [...] might accomplish it, or a Song rightly sung, or an Exclamation said in the right Place, or a Trifle done in the right Spirit, and then you would have need of me indeed!
>
> (*Ladies Almanack*, 22)

The penis, as conventional—or "Medieval"—instrument of love, withers away in the proliferation of such modern phalli as feather, song, exclamation, and trifle. Tilly Tweed-in-Blood might despair ("we need them [men] for carrying of Coals, lifting of Beams, and things of one kind or another"), but it seems that in matters of procreation, men are not strictly necessary (*Ladies Almanack*, 24). Dame Evangeline Musset herself is in fact presented as a kind of swashbuckling guru of the lesbian phallus. The almanac's mock-protagonist is introduced in the following terms:

> Evangeline Musset [...] had been developed in the Womb of her most gentle Mother to be a Boy, when therefore, she came forth an Inch or so less than this, she paid no Heed to the Error, but donning a Vest of superb Blister and Tooling, a Belcher for tippet and a pair of hip-boots with a scarlet channel (for it was a most wet wading) she took her Whip in hand, calling her Pups about her, and so set out upon the Road of Destiny
>
> (*Ladies Almanack*, 7)

If reference is made to "that Greek mystery [...] which is known as the Dashing out of the Testicles, and all that goes with it"—some case of self-resolved cryptorchidism it seems—it is made a joke of and said to have occasioned more "Surprise" than "Pleasure" to her seemingly hermaphroditic predecessor (*Ladies Almanack*, 7). Dame Musset is of course "do[ing] it without the Tools for the Trade," and yet "complain[s]" of "nothing" (*Ladies Almanack*, 8). Love suffers nothing, that is, without its conventional instrument. Extending the colloquial reference to the penis as a "tool" into "the Tools for the Trade" brings into relief the inherent denaturalization at work already within heterosexual amorous practice—a prostheticization of the body that attempts to make up for the absence of the sex-relation through renewed practice and signification.

These "tools" and their various modes of deployment, which attempt to fulfil the function of the connective "copula" between lovers, multiply the ways in which their encounters may be inscribed, configured, and realized. Stowed away in Musset's amorous arsenal are hence a compound of words and things, speech acts and bodily practices, which, as uncanny phalli, are often ontological hybrids of one another, *physis-logos* mutants, including "her Slips of the Tongue"—whether Freudian or fornicatory—and "her Genius at bringing up by Hand"—raising great expectations of a different nature from those of Dickens's novel. At the almanac's close we find another catachrestic migration of this "Tongue" at Musset's funeral:

> in the end they put her upon a great Pyre, and burned her to the Heart. [...] And when they came to the ash that was left of her, all had burned but the Tongue, and this flamed, and would not suffer Ash, and it played about upon the handful that had been she indeed.
>
> (*Ladies Almanack*, 84)

This tongue of flame—again a compound of organic flesh, inorganic matter, and language—continues to give pleasure to her women, with Señorita Fly-About the first of the bevy, who straddles the funeral urn and is brought to bliss as "beatitude played and flickered upon her Face" (*Ladies Almanack*, 84).

It is, however, *at the level of art itself*—that is, *at the level of the real*, as Deleuze and Guattari understand it—that this ontological levelling of body and text into forces capable of encountering and interacting with each other immediately takes place. Taking into consideration Deleuze and Guattari's understanding of art as an "event" rather than secondary representation enables a reading of *Ladies Almanack* that is not reducible to the terms of fantasy and even falsity that have plagued its critical history. At this juncture it may be useful to revisit the configurations of art, history, and the utopian impulse in modernist literary practice that have often been raised since Lukács's placement of modernism in antithetical relation to realism, in order to situate the aesthetic practice of Barnes's *Almanack*—as the production of the "real" of sensation itself—against a conception of modernism's retreat from history into fantasy.

The thrust of Lukács's charges against "'modernist' anti-realism" may be summarized as the elimination of objectivity from dialectics—in other words, the eclipse of the historical, socioeconomic, and material conditions of the world, alongside a metaphysical commitment to "the ontological solitariness of the individual" (Lukács 1963, 20). For Lukács, modernism marks the suppression of the "social and historical environment" of humanity for a non-dialectical reconception of "Man" as "an ahistorical being" (1963, 19-21). Crucially, the two terms of *actuality* and *potentiality*, made distinguishable through a dialectical understanding of history, are collapsed under a universal subjectivism. The Hegelian ontology of history that grounds Lukács's analysis denies full ontological status to the "potential" and "virtual": that which is not actualized in time as the "real" of historical progression and the "real" of "reason" is marked as purely "abstract" (1963, 23-4). With the evacuation of the "rational" from history in modernism's extreme subjectivism, however, the infinite phantasmagoria of the mind—"the 'bad infinity' of purely abstract potentialities"—no longer has to pass through the sieve of actuality, and is as a result accorded equal ontological weight as the latter. In dropping the "selective principle," modernism contributes to an unwarranted elevation of subjective fantasy, with "the attenuation of actuality" as its corollary (1963, 22, 33, 25). The following diagnostic is offered: (i) "melancholy," in which "contempt" for the world, which "declines to realize these [abstract] possibilities," is nurtured; and, (ii) "schizophrenic dichotomy," in which, *contra* Hegel, "thought and being are 'quite separate entities,'" where an excess of unactualized life persists alongside attenuated reality (1963, 22, 27). Modernism, in other words, is characterized by the pathos and nostalgia attendant on the awareness of *lost worlds*, and subjectivity's turn inward is as much symptom and cause of the dissipation of these counterfactual potentialities, figured in turns as melancholic failure to let go and schizophrenic cleavage.

I am proposing, however, that a DeleuzoGuattarian turn away from the Hegelian hierarchy of the actual and rational over merely abstract or *virtual* potentiality would enable a reading of *Ladies Almanack* as an instance of a concretized utopia, in which "the possible as aesthetic category" is given "a body, a life, a universe" (Deleuze and Guattari 1994, 177). The related terms "possible," "potential," and "virtual," are here all made *real*. As Daniel Smith notes, the theodistical inheritance of Deleuzian thought inheres in the fact that "[d]ivergences, bifurcations, and incompossibles [...] belong to *one and the same universe*"; the Deleuzian "God," unlike the Hegelian one, "passes through all [...] virtual possibilities" (Deleuze 1997, xxvi). This is where utopia, in its DeleuzoGuattarian form, takes place within an ontology not of "history," but of the "virtual."

Instead of being a realist text, then, where "realism" is understood to imply a subordinate relation of text to world—an instance of linguistic mimesis of reality—*Ladies Almanack* is, rather, a *text of the real*. Its operational mode is *creation*, not correspondence—which is to say that in it language does not enact a self-cancelling gesture to prioritize the extra-textual flesh, history, and mental life of the reader, but *is* the event itself of the lesbian sensorium. It does not represent the world; it *makes* it. Barnes's *Almanack* may thus be read as a specific utopian response to the situation of the melancholic subject, concretizing a world that history is said to foreclose. Instead of a nostalgic throwback to a lost Eden, it produces Eden itself as an affective sensorium—*presenting*, rather than *representing* utopia. Where Lukács considers abstract potentiality to be merely sub- or non-ontological, Deleuze and Guattari confer full ontological dignity to the status of art, refusing the conception of the latter as mere "fantasy," and emphasizing its production of nothing less than "cosmogenetic sensations" (Deleuze and Guattari 1994, 183). As will be seen, this entails a depersonalizing passage from the contingent historical body to what Deleuze repeatedly names a "bloc of sensation" (1994, 164, 179). This abandonment of the "creatural qua creatural" that Hallward refers to includes the abandonment of the "flesh," "subjectivity," "opinions," "perceptions," and "affections" that make up the human-being (Hallward 2006, 30). The overcoming of these anthropocentric affiliations in art is given in *What Is Philosophy?* by the terms "percept," "affect," and "sensation": "Percepts are no longer perceptions; they are independent of a state of those who experience them. Affects are no longer feelings or affections; they go beyond the strength of those who undergo them" (1994, 164). "Sensation," compounded of affects and percepts, is accorded full ontological dignity, and is hence often referred to with such predicates as "being of sensation," "sensation as being," or "pure being of sensation" (1994, 164–7). It is in this ontological region engendered by art that the subject–object dichotomies established by the melancholically divided being are overcome.

For Deleuze, a key component to this process is "style," which, in literary art, is manifested through "the writer's syntax" (1994, 170). "Style" names the means by which "sensation as being" is produced; it is that through which the lesbian sensorium is born, the linguistic medium that dispatches with the "creaturely"— that is, all the historical, local, and corporeal determinants of the human organism—and raises from it a new cosmos of sensation. This function of style is at work everywhere in *Ladies Almanack*. In the May chapter, for example, an account of Dame Musset submitting "one dear old Countess" to her amorous attentions is given as such:

> I, fervid with Truth, had finally so floored her in every capacious Room of that dear ancestral Home, that I knew to a Button, how every Tickling was made! And what a lack of Art there is in the Upholstery Trade, for that they do not finish off the under Parts of Sofas and Chairs with anything like the Elegance

showered upon that Portion which comes to the Eyes! There should [...] be Trade for Contacts, guarding that on which the Lesbian Eye must, in its March through Life, rest itself.

(*Ladies Almanack*, 34–5)

An elaborate system of puns and metalepses here results in the collapse of different categories of being into new percepts. Lexical registers collide and converge as flesh, fabric, furniture, and language pass over into one another. The "Truth" that impels Musset to storm her lover's body and home is a mixture of some kind of sexual authenticity, pseudo-religion, and plain passion, whilst her knowledge of the "Tickling" of every "Button" refers not only to the sartorial item, but also to the nipples, navel, and clitoris. The "under Parts of Sofas and Chairs" also conjure up those of a woman, an effect reinforced by the *chair* which is the word for "flesh" in French; and the "March through Life" functions as a rather grandiloquent military phrase for the process of growing up and growing old, as well as for sexual conquest and its infelicitous visual encounters. Musset's tale is offered as a cocktail of bravado and complaint, stylized with such ingenuity that the resultant affect, in spite of its representational content, is one of pleasure.

The same machinery of affective conversion is deployed elsewhere. In the July chapter, a stylistic stand-off is staged between a sentimentalizing rhetoric of courtship on the one hand ("what a woman says to a Woman"—*Ladies Almanack*, 42), and a critical, censorious one on the other (effectively, what another woman says to such a woman). Yet their differences are not all that easy to measure. The critical voice directed against the sentimental verbosity it chastises is presented with a similarly indiscriminate verbosity. The former's brandishing of its critical wit against the "Blandishments" of the other ends up committing the very vice it rails against. Its target is not just "corrected" with a kind of supercilious glee, but also joyously cited. To juxtapose the criticized passage with the critique itself is hence to reveal their not so covert complicity in the joy of verbal outpour. I set them side by side here:

> You know my quick Step, my real Run, my true Bite. My intake and withdraw are at your behest, I am but a Shade of myself an I am not by your Side, and what I am is because you are, and should you turn and not find me, it is because I have taken that not worthy of you to another, who may blow me bright again to shine toward your Lightning, a Sun to my Beam!

> Nay——I cannot write it! It is worse than this! More dripping, more lush, more lavender, more mid-mauve, more honeyed, more Flower-casting, more

Cherub-bound, more downpouring, more saccharine, more lamentable, more gruesomely unmindful of Reason or Sense, to say nothing of Humor [...] they be not happy unless writhing in Treacle, and like a trapped Fly, crawl through cardinal Morasses, all Legs tethered and dragging in the Gum of Love!

(*Ladies Almanack*, 45–6)

The first is a passage from the inamorata, whose maudlin rhapsody is a string of clichés ("a Shade of myself"; "what I am is because you are") peppered with idiosyncratic detail ("quick Step," "real Run," "true Bite"), and even a dash of ingenious self-exculpation furtively stowed away within the flummery: the conventional formula—"I am not worthy of you"—is deployed here to blot out the lover's faithlessness ("I have taken that not worthy of you to another"), and dilates further on via some verbal cunning into another homage to the original ("toward your Lightning, a Sun to my Beam!"). There is as much glee involved in the reading of this rhetorically suspect passage as in the charge brought against it by the plaintiff, who is, for her part, no more practiced in rhetorical sobriety. "I cannot write it!" she claims, but this turns out to be an instance of what in medieval rhetoric is often termed *occupatio*: a negative is professed, but undermined by what follows. Adjectives compound ("more lavender ... more honeyed"), grow into compound-adjectives that further compound ("mid-mauve," "Flower-casting," "Cherub-bound," "downpouring"), peaking with a bloated modifier ("more gruesomely unmindful of Reason or Sense, to say nothing of Humor"), before a debouchment into "Treacle," "Morasses [Molasses?]," and "the Gum of Love"—that is, a stew of saccharine and smut in which the lover as drowning insect "writhe[s]," "drag[s]," and "crawl[s]," all "tethered" and "trapped." If, at the level of the *content* of these passages, it is possible to attach a negative coefficient to the first and a positive—or at least corrective one—to the second, at the level of the writing itself—its form or style—the affective status is universally positive. Both are, as it were, "twittering so loud upon the Wire that one cannot hear the Message," tending toward the suppression of the referent beneath the sensorial vibration itself (*Ladies Almanack*, 46).

A heightened instance of this reversal may be found in the extensive list of expletives in the August chapter dished out by a man to the women who dare to be more than "just good Distaff Stuff." In a similar logic, negatives are converted into positives as "belabouring" turns into "admir[ation]," and the same content affectively transposed from the perspective of the man into a lesbian bloc of sensation (*Ladies Almanack*, 53). Heterosexual male insults become homosexual female tributes:

> unwieldy, gander-gated, sprung at Hip, unlovely, disenchanting, bearded, hoop-chested, game of Leg, out at Elbow, double-jointed, hook-toothed, splay-footed, wattled, hamstrung, mated with nothing, high-bridged and loose-lipped, no-woman's Meat the length of her Bones, fit for no diddling, dallying Tom, white-eyed and no Wind in her Nostrils but such as blows down her Bellows to make her a neither, and so forth and so on. In no wise worth their pains.
>
> (*Ladies Almanack*, 53)

In imitation of its Burtonian and Rabelaisian sources,[11] each lexical unit in this pell-mell pillory is dispatched from its original evaluative context—under the heterosexual gaze—into depersonalized percepts and affects. Instead of a coherent body, united into a specular whole as a phenomenologically intended "perception," each segment here breaks off into a sensorial nugget that takes flight from the immediate sense of the disparaging terms. The lesbian body, *perceived* by the male gaze as "fit for no diddling, dallying Tom," lifts off into so many lesbian *percepts* ("gander-gated [gaited?]," "sprung at Hip," "out at Elbow," etc.) that the reader partakes of in a sensorium of joyous affects. The reversal managed by the stylistic acceleration here inverts the negative contained in the woman with "no-woman's Meat the length of her Bones" into a universal positive, turning this entire passage "all-woman"—pieces and percepts of women, as it were. So it is said in the preceding chapter:

> were she haggard, gray, toothless, torn, deformed, damned, evil, putrid and no one's Pleasure; or if on the other Hand she were lovely, straight, marble browed, red in her bloom, bright in the Eye, headed with Hair, and Venused to book—'tis all one to a Girl in Love!
>
> (*Ladies Almanack*, 44)

Each term in the series is caught up in a rhythm that propels it on to the next, generating a surge of affects that neutralizes not just the perceptual but also axiological context out of which each arises, mobilizing a syntactical force that sweeps up these cluster-bomb insults and pufferies into a pure bloc of sensation. In this passage from the body caught in the eye of the male subject to the

---

[11] See in particular the extended passage from *The Anatomy* that begins with: "Every Lover admires his mistris, though she bee very deformed of her selfe, ill favored, wrinkled, pimpled, pale, red, yellow, tan'd, tallow-faced, have a swolne Juglers platter face, or a thin, leane, chitty face, have clouds in her face, be crooked, dry, bald, goggle-eied, blear-eyed, or with staring eyes, she lookes like a squis'd Cat," and so on and so forth (Burton 1989–94, III.164). See also the passage from Rabelais's *L'abbaye de Thélème* beginning "in those days no women were put into convents unless they were one-eyed, lame, hunched-backed, ugly, askew, mad, backward, deformed or defective" (Rabelais 2006, 361).

lesbian sensorium, truly, "'tis all one." Style here functions as a kind of linguistic transformer, through which history along with the literary, aesthetic, and moral values that overcode women's bodies, pass and re-emerge as positive affect. Maligned on one occasion for being mere "modernist *bijouterie* (Rascoe 1923, 130)," and backhandedly complimented on another as "sprightly and spinsterish (Glassco 2007, 34)," the lapidary machine of Barnes's writing may now be seen to demonstrate that it is in the very "Jangle" that style *ontologizes* sense (*Ladies Almanack*, 46). Writing itself, in its contact with the reader, concretizes sense as sensation—that is, it produces and gives body to a region of affects and percepts. The heterosexual socium in which these expletives operate breaks open, loses its integrity and the capacity to provide the evaluative frame for the elements it contains, and passes over into the lesbian sensorium. Through this reversal, lesbian "lack" is positivized (in both senses) as affect: "though that Prick is nowhere in the Flesh of Sister for Sister, they cry as loud, yea, lament still more copiously, turning and twisting as if the very Lack were an extraordinary Pain!" (*Ladies Almanack*, 57). Once again, if the sense is "pain," the sensation is joy; though the text writes "Lack," the product is plenitude: the absent "Prick" becomes a ubiquitous "lesbian phallus."

Such rapture founds the world of Barnes's *Almanack*, which in fact prepares its elixir of happiness for the reader in the form of "LOVE PHILTERS," whose magic recipe is given in the October chapter. Here, the alchemizing process itself is its intoxicating product. This aphrodisiac is concocted in the trail of the Goddess, whose passage across the cosmos discharges its virtual constituents as so many Sapphic bits in protean combination:

> So take the first Hair from your Head, and boil it with Mare's Milk and wrap in a Napkin and bring the Goat inside out, then till the old Mother of six pans of her Earth, and next to the fur-side, lay the Nap to the Horns' end, and thereover cast a peep of No-Doubting-Sappho, blinked from the Stews of Secret Greek Broth, and some Rennet of Lesbos to force a get-up in the near Resurrection, and put on a Horseshoe to ride Luck's Mare at a Gallop a trot, and when the Mass bubbles and at the River's lip quivers, call it dear Cyprian, and take her under your Wing on the warm side, and but her no buts!
>
> (*Ladies Almanack*, 71–2)

Maternity suffuses the cosmos here from birthing goats to lactating mares, just as various lesbian molecules of various degrees of palpability from a Sapphic "peep" to a "Rennet of Lesbos" are discharged from Creation. Sexual, spiritual, and eschatological resonances mingle: the "Resurrection" of the body draws in a kind of clitoral erection ("get-up"), while the Holy Communion of the *corpus Christi* turns into a lesbian "Mass" whose Host is compounded of the parts of woman. The sense of an achieved eschatology comes through here not just in the imminence of the Resurrection, which promises beatitude *virtualiter*, but also in the unraveled path of joy: shod with a "Horseshoe" of "Luck," all paths through existence at all paces ("a Gallop a trot") yield happiness. As in the phrase from Alexander Pope's "The Second Pastoral," famously set to song by Handel and referenced by Barnes in *The Antiphon*: "Where'er you walk, cool gales shall fan the glade" (*Selected Works*, 201).

The women of *Ladies Almanack* everywhere undergo processes of molecularization, dehumanized from subjects to sensations, becoming-ceramic, becoming-fabric, becoming-flame, and also becoming-insect and becoming-animal. In the "LISTS AND LIKELIHOODS" segment, which concludes the September chapter, a catalogue is given which includes:

THE Vixen in the Coat of red,
The Hussy with the Honey Head,
[...]
The Doxy in the Vest of Kid
Rustling like the Katie-did,
With Panther's Eyen dark and wan,
And dovës Feet to walk upon.
The Jockey with the Pelvis plump,
The high-hipped Wrestler with the Rump
Or yearling Mare, firm, sleek and creased,

(*Ladies Almanack*, 60)

And so on and so forth. Barnes's strategy of ontological collapse is once again visible here: the categories of being are compressed in "Kid"—causing goat and child to pass into one another—and in its rhymed double "Katie-did," where woman (Katie) and insect (katydid) cross over. The universal reach of this molecularizing process of becoming-woman culminates at the end of the list, where, effectively, time and the cosmos end up traversed by a lesbian vector that queers the created world into a lesbian pleasure-dome:

For all the Planets, Stars and Zones
Run girlish to their Marrow-bones!
And all the Tides prognosticate
Not so much of any other State!

(*Ladies Almanack*, 60)

By congesting the cosmos with lesbian presence—where lesbian molecules overrun the skies, permeate astral bodies, infuse the oceans, and hybridize all creaturely existence—*Ladies Almanack* presents a lesbian Cockaigne, a radical state of reconciled existence in a world in which lesbian desiderators and desiderata everywhere meet and meet again. This spatial takeover is accompanied by a temporal one, as prehistory comes to be overrun by myths of female parthenogenesis—whether through egg-laying, as in the March chapter, or urination, as depicted in April—as well as evolutionary just-so stories involving the "naked backrunning of Nature": "from Fish to Man there has been much Back-mating and Front to Front" (*Ladies Almanack*, 43).

It is this eternal self-encounter of she-desiderators and she-desiderata that provides the *Almanack* with its cartography of love. Right from the outset, the ostensible introduction of the *Almanack*'s protagonist quickly dissolves into a spume of body parts. The tale of a molar entity named "Evangeline Musset" does not quite take off, but is waylaid by an extended account of the various assemblages of organic and non-organic machines of desire. Here, "Hinder Parts," "Fore Parts," "whatsoever Parts," "Itch of Palm" and "Quarters most horribly burning" seek solace "upon warm and cozy Material, such as Fur, or thick and Oriental Rugs," and even "upon warm Stoves," before it eventually pans out that "from the day that we were indifferent Matter, to this wherein we are Imperial Personages of the divine human Race," it is "inflamed" lesbian-parts which best serve the interests of other "inflamed" lesbian-parts: "no thing so solaces it as other Parts as inflamed, or with the Consolation every Woman has at her Finger Tips, or at the very Hang of her Tongue" (*Ladies Almanack*, 6). Such a map of desire, where bodies organic and inorganic are laid out in recombinant reticulations, could be termed "rhizomatic," an alternative vegetable metaphor that displaces the conventional arboreal organization of life, as given in Patience Scalpel's outburst: "Where, and in what dark Chamber was the Tree so cut of Life, that the Branch turned to the Branch, and made of the Cuttings a Garden of Ecstasy?" (*Ladies Almanack*, 12).

"Woman," in *Ladies Almanack*, taken on these dispersive vectors, evades the stasis of molar-being with its negative logic ("I am this, not that"), in favor of an additive one that co-opts all apparent negatives into positives. All exclusions turn out to be inclusions: but's turn into and's and or's, resulting in a vast ontological complex. Where the inscription above the main gate of Rabelais's Thélème accumulates a list of exclusions built on the refrain "Cy n'entrez pas," the "Lists and Likelihoods" of Barnes's *Almanac* reverses this logic of enclosure to include the cosmos within the changing body of "Woman" herself (Rabelais 2006, 364–5).

In the September chapter, it is said: "THE very Condition of Woman is so subject to Hazard, so complex, and so grievous, that to place her at one Moment is but to displace her at the next" (*Ladies Almanack*, 55). In the month before, we encounter another itemization of woman-parts and their expansion into a textual panoply of philosophies, styles and genres: "WHAT they have in their Heads, Hearts, Stomachs, Pockets, Flaps, Tabs and Plackets, have one and all been some and severally commented on, by way of hint or harsh Harangue, praised, blamed, epicked, poemed and pastoraled, pamphleted, prodded and pushed, made a Spring-board for every sort of Conjecture whatsoever, good, bad and indifferent" (*Ladies Almanack*, 47–8). The result, it seems, is that "Woman" includes—and in fact *is*—everything—*even men*, as Dame Musset once suggests ("I never a Woman before nor since!"—*Ladies Almanack*, 24), along with Low-Heel ("she must have had a Testes of sorts, however wried and awander [...] she was called forth a Man"—*Ladies Almanack*, 53); *and even heterosexuals*, like Patience Scalpel, having gone "a Nose-length into the Matter" (*Ladies Almanack*, 50):

> Some have it that they cannot do, have, be, think, act, get, give, go, come, right in anyway. Others that they cannot do, have, be, think, act, get, give, go, wrong in any way, others set them between two Stools saying that they can, yet cannot, that they have and have not, that they think yet think nothing, that they give and yet take, that they are both right and much wrong, that in fact, they swing between two Conditions like a Bell's Clapper, that can never be said to be anywhere, neither in the Centre, nor to the Side, for that which is always moving, is in no settled State long enough to be either damned or transfigured.
>
> (*Ladies Almanack*, 48)

Here, the exclusionary logic of bounded identity is bypassed in order to ramify across all ontological modalities, positive, negative, or the contested zone between. Aristotle's principle of the excluded middle turns out to be a symbolic fiction cut through by the women who "swing between two Conditions like a Bell's Clapper." "[A]lways moving," "in no settled State," Barnes's women not only dodge all kinds of essentialism, but also predestination in another world: neither "damned or transfigured," consigned to Hell or Heaven, they thrive in the Kingdom on the "Terra-firma" of the *Almanack*'s sensorium, all always already in bliss.

In presenting *Ladies Almanack* as the concretization of a positive utopia in which desires, far from being countermanded by the very presence of the objective world, are productive of the real *qua* affects and percepts, I am offering an instance of modernist comedy that steers away from the negative utopias of Adorno and Bloch, as well as the various projective eschatologies of some varieties of Christian thought. Barnes's distance from the negative poetics of a Surrealist writer such as Antonin Artaud, from whom Deleuze adopts the term "body without organs," may thus be measured here. As Adrian Morfee explains, "The *corps sans organes*, by which man will be 'delivered of all his automatisms and brought to his true freedom,' is a way, then, of being finally free from God's influence, the means 'en finir avec dieu'—it could have been called the *corps sans dieu*" (2005, 189). In *Ladies Almanack*, however, this agon of God and poet is now unraveled, as both are brought into a covert alignment. Immanent to the cosmos itself, its author may be said to make a mock cameo-appearance in the October chapter, offering a comic display of God's own becoming-lesbian. After a mythic account of woman's fall from nature, grace, "God and man," the figure of Daisy Downpour is introduced, who, "return[ing] homeward" one day, "Godless and fearless," ends up making "Fear and a God of the yellow Hair of Dame Musset, wandering about the grassless Sods of her Garden" (*Ladies Almanack*, 63). In a moment of theophany, a lesbian part-object—Musset's "yellow hair"—is recognized as God, who turns out to be as cold, cruel, and withdrawn as He or She ever was to Job. Daisy's erotic disappointment unspools in a series of epithets, offering, in one outburst, a depiction of the many faces of God: "by so much Indifference, packed down on Scorn, became she first God, then God Almighty, then God Dumbfounding, and still later God help us, and finally God Damn to Daisy Downpour" (*Ladies Almanack*, 66) In *Ladies Almanack*, Creation and the Creator have become women—"with a Difference" (*Ladies Almanack*, 26)

3

Comedy II: *Ryder*, Rape, and Recurrence

What ho! Spring again! Rape again, and the Cock not yet at his Crowing!
(*Ryder*, 21)

Thus run the opening lines to "Rape and Repining!"—the fifth chapter of Barnes's 1928 novel, *Ryder*. Built on a series of repetitions, the catachrestic unfolding of the chapter—essentially, an extended rape joke—identifies a specific comic mechanism embedded within its alliterative title: first as tragedy, then as farce. Having considered the comic world set up in *Ladies Almanack* as a maximally affirmative response to melancholic existence, this third chapter unfolds how a critique of comedy's affirmative tendency can be included within the comic text itself, and develops instead a minimally reconciliatory stance to life and its associated historical traumas. In focusing on the function of repetition in the production of humor, alongside its ethical implications, the critique of comedy developed here also unfolds a functional disambiguation between the uses of humor and irony in Barnes's novel. The critical tradition that founds humor on a certain principle of "unincremental repetition" will be reconsidered beside an alternate formulation of humor in terms of ironic revision—otherwise put, non-identical repetition, or repetition with difference (Frye 1990, 168). If Barnes's comic novel acknowledges Frye's claim that "[r]epetition [...] not going anywhere belongs to comedy," it stages simultaneously the undoing of this mechanism of humor in favor of a form of ironic reprisal that establishes critical distance from that which it repeats (1990, 168). Irony, as it is deployed in *Ryder*, involves a discriminative disposition that dynamically reconsiders the values that prompt the kinds of jokes they do—and in fact form their very condition of possibility—shifting, in the process, our ethical and libidinal lines of allegiance. It is this dynamism involved in the cultivation of an ironic disposition—one that privileges process over closure—which resists the various forms of premature reconciliation humor is capable of producing, reorientating us thereby away from the present, toward the future.

In *Ryder*, the association of humor and repetition is staged both thematically and formally. The recurrence of rape in particular is attributed to the cyclical time of nature, as seasonal law and genealogical fate:

> A Girl is gone! A Girl is lost! A simple Rustic Maiden but Yesterday swung upon the Pasture Gate, with Knowledge nowhere, yet is now, to-day, no better than her Mother, and her Mother's Mother before her!
>
> (*Ryder*, 21)

Grounded on an anatomical principle of pregnability, the joke here operates by recalling the civilized world to the grim necessities of mere life: generation demands penetration, and every mother, *qua* mother, is a "Girl gone" and a "Girl lost," forming a fateful chain of ruptured hymens. The doubling in the genitive ("Mother's Mother") becomes the formula for an infinite concatenation into prehistory. All mothers, inheriting and bequeathing rape, are leveled by the scythe of Hades, which functions metaleptically as the biological ground-zero encoded in the *memento mori* ("Man is born to die"—*Ryder*, 27), in essence, also a *memento rapi*. Death, to repeat one of Barnes's puns, is the "Grim Raper" (Barnes 1958b). To recall, Persephone, ravished from the flourishing earth to be the caged bride of the underworld, inaugurates winter, becoming the mythic event that divides a perennially green world into the seasons. Yet, if on one level, the humor of the chapter functions via a dogged *reduction*, collapsing civilization into libidinal license and bodily rudiments, historical time into cyclical myth, the linguistic exuberance demonstrated throughout gestures toward humor's other strategy of *elevation*, which, with a kind of manic overwriting, raises suffering into joy. Repetition both de-sublimates and sublimates, rewriting rape as objective fate—in conformity with a physical law—while reclaiming it with subjective agency via an aesthetic reenactment. Repeated textually, the event turns comic, retrieved from the outside world where it was involuntarily undergone to be reprocessed as a redacted narrative, whose wild embellishments and rhetorical relish signal the addition—and, as we will see—the *strain* of the subject's will. Passively suffered, it is now actively relived; the victim triumphs thereby via a diegetic maneuver, recovering from damage a post hoc desideratum, reproduced as the pleasure of the text:

> Ravished, and the Cream not risen in the Pantry! Ravished, and the Weather Fork not turned twice upon its Vane! Ravished, and no Star pricked upon its point!
>
> (*Ryder*, 21)

As the protest augments it is also trivialized, unfolding in an anaphoric sequence that pairs rape with the mundane goings-on of the household, the climate, and the skies. Here already, the lavish redaction of the ravishing points to an ethically dubious relish, its literary arabesques crafted from a body leveled into—and undifferentiated from—so much *materia poetica*.

These two facets of humor (elevation and reduction) will be examined further in this chapter, and set beside the related term, irony, which will be shown to navigate a precarious passage between pleasurable involvement and self-conscious detachment—in other words, between collusion and critique. The tendency for comedy to produce reconciliatory frames of mind via the contrary modes of reduction and elevation does in fact find occasional elaboration within the novel itself. The narrator, at one point, remarks on its mechanism of affective reversal: "By 'humorous' is meant ability to round out the inevitable ever-recurring meanness of life, to push the ridiculous into the very arms of the sublime" (*Ryder*, 9). The examples of malignity and banality strewn across life's passage may, it seems, be recuperated and reversed by a will-to-laughter. The crippling of such a will, however, presents the other face of humor, which runs humanity aground against the bare facts of the hapless body. As Kate protests to Wendell, and his mother, Sophia: if the inevitability of birth chains her to pain, the inevitability of death, turning as it does life into one bathetic peak and trough, is a reminder that both are actually quite "humorous." Infanticide, apparently, is quite funny:

> I've become infatuated with the flavour of motherhood; you poked it under my nose, and I've learned to like it. It makes me ill, and there's no pleasure at either end, but I'm addict, and it's your fault, keeper of the shop, and madame of the keeper! [...] I'll kill it the minute it's born, but I'll bear it! There's humor for you, and you can't prevent me!
>
> (*Ryder*, 170)

Repeatedly subjected to the pains that come with pregnancy and labor, Kate launches the contradictory claims of "ill[ness]" and the absence of "pleasure," despite having "learned to like it": she is, in her words, an "addict." If the comic action pushes her in one instance toward a joyous reconciliation with "motherhood," its contrary tendency is an upsurge into a revolt with limited prospects, returning her to her anatomical destiny, and life, in general, to an eternal recurrence of birth and death, truncated here into the microcosm of the womb.

The two forms of humor that feature prominently in *Ryder* are thus founded on a principle of repetition—one which reduces humanity to its corporeal dimensions, and reverses history into myth, and another which elevates humanity to godhood, raising history into art. Both, however, in repeating life in writing, tend toward a typological closure on the side of comic resolution. The following pages aim to read the two forms of *eternal recurrence* whose logic permeates the linguistic apparatus of Barnes's novel, both of them presenting a false reconciliation to be critically undone, one in the direction of desublimation, and, the other, of sublimation. The names that have been attached to them are those of Mircea Eliade, who reads the return of profane history to its sacred origins as a redemption of violated time, and Friedrich Nietzsche, whose proposal of a will-to-laughter with the power to reverse the fragmentation, suffering, and contingency of life into a redeemed whole has been described as an "atheistic theodicy" and an "aesthetic theodicy" (Young 1992, 109; Williams 2012, 323–48). Kate's "infatuation with the flavour of motherhood" appears in this light as a parodic foil to a disrupted *amor fati*, indicted by Adorno as the "crime of theology that Nietzsche arraigned without ever reaching final court" (Adorno 2005, 98). This "crime of theology," as will be seen, consists in its push toward a problematic theodicy that Adorno considers morally defunct, a collusive misattribution of joyous closure to unreconciled life, prompting the philosopher to develop his own thoughts along the lines of a "negative theodicy" (Geuss 1999, 100). Against these two tendencies toward comic resolution, however, a third form of humor emerges in *Ryder* that may be given the name *irony*. Its defining trait is discernment, and presents the means of negotiating the reader's way—alongside Julie Ryder's own developing subjectivity—between the engulfment of the subject by the primordial community (*à la* Eliade) and the self-arrogation of the subject to a private redemption (*à la* Nietzsche)— between the Scylla of impotence and Charybdis of omnipotence, the crippled and the elevated will. Presenting *Ryder* as an *ironic* comedy thus attributes to it a qualified reconciliation with life that negates joyous closure in the present— alongside the tenuous redemptive formulations that enable it—and reopens the subject instead toward the possibility of renewal in the future. Reconciliation is projected against the horizon.

Having considered the nature of an achieved eschatology in *Ladies Almanack* in the previous chapter, I move on here to a reading of the *projective* orientation toward happiness in *Ryder*, one that involves an investment in the open horizon of the future. If an assent to life and the created world is coded in the comic text of *Ryder*, it is also one that is simultaneous with a refusal of various forms of premature and/or false reconciliation. The premise of futurity on which the text's comic principle is based is thus, on one level at least, secured with an *anti-reconciliatory* gesture: in repudiating a joyous location of the self in the present world, a commitment to the future may be affirmed. *Ryder*, in this light, remains minimally a response in the positive to the question of theodicy, even in its wanton parody of the various false theodicies it relays. The reconciliatory and anti-reconciliatory facets of humor yield a number of antagonisms that will be considered in the first half of this chapter. In the second half, I move on to a consideration of the libidinal implications of irony in relation to the corporeal drives, and hence, its formative role in the production and constitution of the subject. Irony's mode of crafting openings out of a falsely totalized present, it will be shown, is implicated in the open body.

Humor, Satire, Irony

Although a certain degree of automatism is often attributed to its physical mechanism, laughter nonetheless can—and not infrequently *does*—occasion reflection. For many modernist critics, the questions surrounding when and how to laugh are compounded by the fragmentation or even dissolution of ethical norms. Jonathan Greenberg speaks of the "codes of sophistication" that direct emotional responses to suffering, which are themselves complicated by a general attitude of "modernist antisentimentality" (2011, xiii, 12–13), while Matthew Stratton points to the individual and social "dispositions" that prompt or pre-empt laughter, often a marker and dynamic producer of "affiliation and disaffiliation" across subjects and communities (2014, 15–17). In setting aside the taxonomical polarities that have often accompanied critical considerations of irony, whether considered in formal terms ("stable" and "unstable"; "finite" and "infinite"— Booth 1974; De Man 1996), historically indexed ("modern" and "postmodern" irony—Wilde 1981; McHale 1987), or psycho-developmentally tagged ("genital" and "pre-genital"—Sacerdoti 1992; Reik 1929), Greenberg and Stratton direct their attention to the mixed constitution of ironic praxis, which often incorporates elements on both sides of these categorical divisions, in order to consider it as a means of discrimination and discernment. While laughter's spontaneous moment presumes certain affective and ethical investments and dispositions, deriving from a shared situational and/or linguistic context, reflection can nonetheless come in its wake. Irony and satire are capable of recalibrating these investments and reconfiguring dispositions, displacing the lines of allegiance across individuals and communities. Laughter, while "partly a reflex," as Frye claims, may thus also occasion a degree of reconsideration (Frye

1990, 168). They dynamically "affiliate" and "disaffiliate," in Stratton's terms, and constitute, for Greenberg, a "*double movement*": "on the one hand, the satirist speaks for a community [...] on the other, he is a renegade who enjoys the subversion of traditional values"—or, for that matter, non-traditional ones (Greenberg 2011, 7).

Irony, in *Ryder*, affiliates in treacherous ways that in turn prompt critical disaffiliation. As the novel progresses, it becomes increasingly apparent that the reader's collusion and revolt, produced by the linguistic strategies of the narrator, are kin to Julie's own struggle between attachment to her family and community and detachment therefrom—a laborious, intermittent, and unfinished process involving her libidinal and spiritual weaning. This shift from the position of the community to that of the individual is undertaken in the "Rape and Repining!" chapter, which first aligns the reader with its humorous victimization before the overexertion of its comic machinery dismantles it. The subject position of the reader begins with an allegiance with the enunciatory position that centers the chapter—revealed only belatedly as that of a "Council of Women" from Tittencote, comprising "Gossips" and "good Wives"—but ends up with a tentative retreat from the histrionic ventriloquy (*Ryder*, 26, 24). The chapter's prefatory couplet is in fact a concise, if covert, marker of the perspectival frame in which its humor is made possible:

Lock windows, bolt doors!
Fie! Whores!

(*Ryder*, 21)

The enunciatory position set up by the narrator, into which the reader slips by virtue of entering the text, is established against the enemy other: the raped girl—that is, the source of social contamination. "Rape and Repining!" presents the vengeance of the Tittencote population against the individual. The event of rape is understood as a rupture of the archaic order of the community, founded as it is on a mythic synchronization of the seasons and the rhythms of society. Its results are temporal distortion ("You have stolen Time"), genealogical inversion ("Is this not turning the Just Proportion of Generations backward?"), economic ruination ("You mint with your false Metal [...] that from now on, we must watch our Change, lest there be Lead in it"), epistemological confusion ("the Community [...] honoured you as True Coin, only to discover you Counterfeit"), and a general collapse of logic and sense ("Who plants the Staff, Crook down? Who suckles the Wind for a Mother? Who combs the Wind for a Parent?") (*Ryder*, 26–38). Victim-blaming is rife in the vitriol: "There is a 'No' with a 'Yes' wrapped up in it, and there is a 'No' with 'No' enough in the Weave, and we have been sorry amiss that our Girls have not learned of it" (*Ryder,* 26). This girl must have, of course, with classic wile, stowed away a "Yes" within her "No," feigning resistance only to pique his interest. She has, therefore, seized a man out of turn: "Have you not taken that which Better Women have refused [...] Is it well to grab Sweets that an Hundred Guests, at the Same Gathering, have left untouched, and thus greedily to limn their Savour?" (*Ryder,* 26). Her overreaching antics make her traitor to the community and the sacred time it runs by:

> You have stolen Time, such Time as lies thick about Tittencote. Time made stout by Good Wives stitching and washing, baking, and praying. Firm with Household Duties well done, within the narrow excellence of Wedlock, paced to Monogamy, fortified with Temperance, made Durable with Patience. You have bent Time with the Tooth of Lust, torn the Hem of Righteousness, and the Wind may enter and the Cyclone follow!
>
> (*Ryder,* 27)

The "Time" that encloses Tittencote in its seasonal regularity is measured against the cycles of domestic activity, patterned according to "stitching, and washing, baking, and praying," alongside the ritualized stages of life, which make passage—with deterministic force—from "Wedlock" to "Monogamy," sanctified by the values of "Temperance" and "Patience." The community is preserved—or "made Durable"—through a repetition across the generations that safeguards the nuclear family with a recursive production of "Good Wives." The "Girl" who gets herself raped, however, is none such.

The insights drawn from the philosophical anthropology of Eliade and René Girard that inform Michael Seidel's study on "satiric inheritance" enable a closer examination of the relationship between historical and mythic time that satirical literature interrogates. Girard's view that the ethical norms and institutions of a community—given legal elaboration and ritualistic enactment—are codified displacements of primordial violence (be this patricide or fratricide) is taken up by Seidel in his account of historical and "satiric dispensation." The "dispensations of history," Seidel writes, "are the beginnings of necessary cover-ups or sanctifications of violence through disguise," enabling the substitution of founding acts of "sacrifice and scapegoatism" with "communal rituals" (1979, 18). The linear time of history takes hold where the recurrence of violence is minimally displaced. Mythic time, on the other hand, names a repetition without difference. While history begins with an exemption—or "dispensation"—from violence, satire, conversely, *dispenses with* history, exposed now as a long series of compensatory fictions: it "blows history's cover" (1979, 19). In effect, "there is in the satiric act a kind of perverse neutralization of historical progression [...] the satirist maintains that what is represented as legal is really unthinkable" (1979, 21). The legal edifice of the socio-symbolic order, raised and steadily fortified over the course of history—into which primal violence has been displaced—is now desublimated and exposed as ethically and/or epistemologically untenable, a conspiratorial "disguise" of *homo qua lupus homini* in the sheepskin of civilization. In Eliade's view, historical dispensation is a transgression of sacred time (myth) into profane linearity (history), redeemable only via a reconstitution at the origin itself, with a "renewed dispensation": it is only with a *backward repetition* of an "archetype" that such restoration is possible (Seidel 1979, 32). The "structure of this archaic ontology" thus constitutes in this regard, for Eliade, a "platonic structure," which returns "historical man" to his archetypal form, "*ab origine*" (Eliade 1969, 12–16, 34, 49). The cyclical reenactment of a "rite" enables "the abolition of time through the imitation of archetypes and the repetition of paradigmatic gestures," constituting, in essence, the "transfiguration of history into myth" (1969, 49, 52). Within such an "archaic ontology," only that which "participates" in or "repeats" the archetypes of a society's foundational myths retains any degree of "reality" at all. All else remains the illusory dross accumulated with the unfolding of profane time, eliminated anew each time history itself is canceled out in the recurrence of the only *real*, consolidated in the originary myths of the community (1969, 48). The seasonal rite, in short, de-realizes profane history and re-authenticates the sacred archetype. It is this restorative function of archaic repetition, however, that satire interrupts even as it reduces the contemporary world to its primitive coordinates, thereby de-legitimizing both the profane and the sacred. As Seidel points out, satire's dismantling of history into prehistory occurs alongside the perversion of the founding circumstances surrounding the latter, and thus paves the way for a "revisionary inheritance" that enables a forward repetition that includes within it a disinheriting mechanism (1979, 60). Satire, then, as in Mary Douglas's reading of the "joke," may be classed as an "anti-rite" (1975, 102): instead of a ritualistic imbrication of history with the mythic foundations of a community, it hollows out the former with archaeological incision to lay bare the violence that now vitiates rather than legitimates the edifices of society. Satire is capable of dispensing with both history and myth.

Ryder presents rape as a mythic archetype. The suggestion that the daughter is "no better than her Mother, and her Mother's Mother before her" points to an originary ravishing—reinforced here with an allusion to Persephone—

that founds the community, since it reproduces itself only on condition of the production of more such mothers. In this staggering diversion from the immediate victim to her maternal forebears, rape as an isolated case of non-consensual intercourse is first redoubled into a second instance of non-consent ("her Mother"), before its recessive extension *ad originem* pares it down to its skeletal coordinates. It becomes (i) a formal definition of all penetrated (possibly also penetrable) bodies; and (ii) an insinuation that the conditions of heterosexual intercourse itself—physically incursive, socially coercive, with economic stakes and anatomical consequences (*daughters*, for one) so much beyond the remit of the will as to render all "consent" impossible, or, at any rate, moot. Historical dispensation may displace this violence *ab origine* into the sanctioned institutions of "Wedlock" and "Monogamy," as hailed by the council of self-proclaimed "Good Wives," but the satirical action of the chapter goes some way in uncovering the traces of the "Grim Raper" here. In reversing the social institution into its archaic coordinates, the satirist, instead of issuing judgment, ramps up the malicious joy by adopting the voice of the community. Despite the intimation, then, that the marriage institution of Tittencote might be an elaborate and systemic recoding of rape as matrimony, its ethos is not palpably delegitimized, since it is not rape per se that is lamentable, but, rather, the wrong kind. Logical contortions can only emerge here: in opposition to the "timely" rape of wedlock is the "untimely" springtime rape. So it seems, rutting time in the civilized world is post-marriage, not post-winter. Yet the seasonal law inscribed in "Spring again! Rape again" suggests rather the fatalistic timeliness of the event. A phonetic perversion from "rape" to "ripe" marks the convolutions of Tittencotian logic: "'Tis Ripe Time for it, when Unripe Woman falls to Ripening!" (*Ryder*, 23). Each spring, it seems, what is "Unripe" finds the "Ripe Time" for its premature—or, *unripe*—"Ripening."

This satiric touch, which reverses history to primitive time, leaves the victim impotent against the forces of nature and a community enclosed within its myths. But if the mechanism of humor operates here by sealing off the victim as passive object, an alternate function is demonstrated in *Ryder* which is founded rather on a narrative will, retrieving damaged life to be reprocessed in aesthetic form. It is worth approaching the relationship between life and art with some care here. Julie Taylor's cautions against the temptation to critically decode the events of the novel in relation to Barnes's own life are pertinent given the reductive tendency evidenced by past critics. Nevertheless, the numerous allusions in Barnes's fictional and non-fictional writings to some form of sexual infringement in her early years—the exact nature of which remains unclear—

may be registered here rather than suppressed.[1] As Taylor notes, "traumatic testimony" is *produced* rather than uncovered, exhibited in the present via language, symbols, and circulating cultural idioms, and hence offers up an image of history only in *refiguring*—rather than passively recording—a broken past: trauma, in short, is built on a structure of repetition (2012, 36). If the satiric aspect in *Ryder* buries the subjectivity of the victim, trampled beneath the collective mob, another brand of humor sublimates the event into comedy via the will-to-laughter that informs its textual repetition. Narrative overkill "push[es] the ridiculous into the very arms of the sublime." This "Girl" is not just "Ravished," but "Soiled! Despoiled! Handled! Mauled! Rumpled! Rummaged! Ransacked!" (*Ryder*, 21). The trochaic force may be constant here, but it does not quite hammer the point home, with the severity of the offence swerving from "maul[ing]" to "rumpl[ing]" and "rummag[ing]." The catachrestic excess of the accusations accumulates with each retake ("Or put it thus: [...] Or thus: [...] Or so: [...] Or better: [...] Or thus: [...]), multiplying the perspectives from which the victim might be judged and rejudged (*Ryder*, 26-9). Distending from the human community to the animal world, this censuring voice exposes the victim to cosmic pillory, reiterating the sentence against her from one species to the next. Her abjection is refracted thus from eye to eye:

> To the Oblong Eye of the Deer, is not your Condition lengthened? By the Owl, is there not purchased a dreadful Rotundity? To the Shallow Eye of the Fish, you are but a little staled, but to the Bossy Eye of the Ox, you may ride as High and Damned as Jezebel. And what of the Multitudinous Insects, and the Infinitesimal Conclusions of the Ether? To the Myriad Pupil of the Fly, what can it but manifold your Grievance?
>
> (*Ryder*, 25)

Exposed before "the World's Eye," her rape—or "crime," as it were—is reviewed in new dimensions according to whichever "thing it walks before" (*Ryder*, 25). Violated once, she is violated once more and ever more; first raped, she is now rent through a host of disparate lenses ("Oblong," "Rotund," "Shallow," "Myriad" etc.) to different effect ("lengthened," "staled," "Damned"), wrenched apart by a kaleidoscope of shame into a series of mutilated shapes. Raising ridicule to sublime proportions, the hyperbolic linguistic machine turns the eternal

---

[1] Whether or not Barnes's father did rape her, or facilitated it via a neighbor, and to what extent the bawdy letters from *the mother* of this father are evidence of some form of grandmother-daughter incest is not an issue I am able to follow up here. See Taylor for a sober overview of these claims (2012, 7).

recurrence of rape into a thing of laughter. This capacity for textual repetition to reverse tragedy into comedy is in fact suggested by the narrative pleasures of Molly Dance in the novel itself:

> She consumed one after another some hundreds of shilling shockers, laughing with hearty delight when a knave got his mouth clean slitten, or a damsel suffered rape: "For at least," she said, "it never hurts in the reading."
>
> (*Ryder*, 193)

The accumulation of "shilling shockers" to the "hundreds" drains the "hurt" from the "reading," turning murder and rape into occasions for "hearty delight." The more *written* the text, the more the contribution of the narrative will, which, in reappropriating the contingency and suffering of life into the ambit of subjective agency, raises these into joyous affirmation. That this repetition of tragedy as humor involves shifting one's allegiance from the side of the victim to that of the victimizers is encapsulated pithily in the caption of an earlier drawing by Barnes for the *Brooklyn Daily Eagle*: "The Joke in the Tragedy of the Other Man's Life." (Figure 3.1).

In situating tragedy on the side of the "other," suffering and misfortune may be consumed as comedy. A certain degree of sadism is intimated in this libidinal affiliation with fate rather than fate's victims, indicated by the slightly sinister aspect created by Barnes's contorted faces. The rising curve of the grimace is, in both figures, broken by smaller undulations that suggest the spasmodic motions of laughter, which, in turn, visibly traverse the entire body to rupture physical composure into interrupted lineaments, concentrated at the abdomen and torso where the jagged strokes aggregate. In dispatching with sympathy, laughter here seems momentarily to snatch the human from himself. This libidinal redistribution from sentiment to *Schadenfreude* is produced via a shift in our allegiance from the victim to the victimizers, and is at work throughout "Rape and Repining!" When, for instance, the offended community points the finger at the source of contamination, its manic rhetoric betrays a sadistic hue: "'Tis such who Poison Wells, and make the Hackle rise on every Pubic Inch, and do split the very Bells by which we tell Time!" (*Ryder*, 25). The affective complexity coded in the accusation is revealing: rising hackles, a conventional marker of anger, move south to turn into a pubic disturbance that modulates disdain into desire.

Such a libidinal redistribution is not far from Nietzsche's characterization of the laughter of the gods. The philosopher's declaration—"our *laughter* itself may have a future!"—marked out in Barnes's copy of *Beyond Good and Evil*, follows a pronouncement of universal comedy on the same page:

Figure 3.1 Djuna Barnes, "The Joke in the Tragedy," 1913. © The Authors League Fund and St. Bride's Church, as joint literary executors of the Estate of Djuna Barnes.

we are prepared as no other age has ever been for a carnival in the grand style, for the most spiritual festival-laughter and -arrogance, for the transcendental height of supreme folly and Aristophanic ridicule of the world.

(Nietzsche 1914, 166)[2]

Such "*golden* laughter," related later in the text to "*The Olympian Vice*," is produced from the vantage of "transcendental height," the sublime peak beneath which the mundane world shrinks into "ridicule," presenting to the distant eye a miniature of human civilization, not as canny enterprise, but as "carnival." The "Gods," Nietzsche claims, "also know how to laugh [...] in an overman-like and new fashion—and at the expense of all serious things!" (1914, 260). In *Thus Spoke Zarathustra*, the titular prophet—"*the teacher of the eternal recurrence of the same*"—is in fact not so much a soothsayer as a "soothlaugher [*Wahrlacher*]," figured as a harbinger of redemption and conqueror of death, in a revisionary take on the Biblical resurrection (2006, 177, 158, 108). In the following section headed "*On Redemption*," the repetition of the past ("it was") into a willed act in the present ("thus I willed it!") names the process by which the shards of life are shorn up against ruin to re-create a whole:

> And all my creating and striving amounts to this, that I create and piece together into one, what is now fragment and riddle and grisly accident. [...] To redeem those who are the past and to recreate all "it was" into "thus I willed it!'—only that would I call redemption!
>
> (2006, 110)

These passages, leading up to the formulation of the "eternal return of the same" in Part III of *Zarathustra*, point to the creative will involved in redeeming linear time and the debris accumulated with its flow, with a retrospective gaze that gathers it up and reproduces it "piece[d] together into one." If deficient in organization, significance, and reason, the past nevertheless comes into completion refigured by an aesthetic will. Such a form of "redemption" is achieved via a willed repetition of life as art. Eternal recurrence here serves as the litmus test for the vigor of this will. Given this, the cumulating excesses of "Rape and Repining!" may be read alongside the logic embedded within Nietzsche's account of eternal recurrence, which several critics have associated with the trope of hyperbole:

> the idea of eternal recurrence is not about proportion; its whole emphasis is on disproportionate acceptance, acceptance with a vengeance so extreme that the

---

[2] I cite from Barnes's edition in the Archive.

terrifying power of what is is subverted in a hyperbolic leap from resignation to desire[.]

(Magnus, Mileur, and Stewart 1993, 145)

Mere "resignation" remains on the level of Stoicism. Nothing less than "positive desire" answers to the "challenge of wanting unconditionally what is the case"—that is, *amor fati*, or the love of fate (1993, 145). The greatest pains incurred in the trajectory of history are thus reversed into a joy to be repeated unto infinity: reality as it is—"what is" and "it was"—is redoubled into sublime form and redeemed. As with Nietzsche's emphasis on song and rhyme in relation to metaphysical gaiety, in *Ryder*, versification is often a concise means of rewriting life as art, a comic affirmation of that which, in the first instance, elapses beyond the remit of the subjective will, only latterly reappropriated by it.

If "the Horrid Outcome of Wendell's First Infidelity" is the death of a woman in childbed ("Impaled upon a death that crawls within"), it is retold with verve in a sequence of iambic pentameters that begin and end "to the point":

> And died so—in pitched child bed, ere the North
> Gave up its snowy custom, and came down
> To waters in the heavy watered sea,
> [...]
> And so this girl, untimely to the point,
> Pricked herself upon her son and passed
> Like any Roman bleeding on the blade—
>
> (*Ryder*, 77)

Pathos, here, is prematurely terminated in the chapter's bathetic opening, cutting short grief in life with comic precision, just as the life of this woman—referred to only as "Wendell's First Infidelity"—is cut short to be served up as so many *bons mots*: "For men die otherwise, of man unsheathed/ But women on a sword they scabbard to" (*Ryder*, 77). Similarly, after the reader is told of another death occasioned by Wendell's procreative animus—this time that of one of his daughters, "born feet first"—the following chapter, "And Amelia Sings a Lullaby," retells the death of a young boy and his mother's response to it:

> She with true philosophy
> Made no cry how it must be.
> Since he was all three-quarters lost
> She would make whole at any cost!
> Fol di ril de re do!
>
> (*Ryder*, 103–4)

This "true philosophy," it seems, takes the step beyond Stoic resignation ("Made no cry how it must be") to joyous affirmation, rounded off in two rhyming couplets and ending in the gay refrain of the lullaby. *Amor fati*, operative here on several levels, overlaying the losses of the mother here with—perhaps—Amelia's own, is, however, also burlesqued. The willed recurrence of misfortune put forward by Nietzsche morphs into collusive action, with the mother joyously finishing off what was "all-three quarters lost" to "make whole at any cost," effectively turning herself into lover *and* accomplice of fate, crafting a redeemed "whole" of sorts from the "grisly accidents" of life. More than Chaucer's Knight, who thinks it "wysdom [...] To maken vertu of necessitee," she makes of necessity complicity (Chaucer 2008, l.3041–2). Narrative will, here, domesticates death into versified epigrams:

> For when a boy's more in than out
> Of this world's gate, what can one do
> But push the rest of him out too?
>
> (*Ryder*, 103)

In the form an inverted pregnancy, this boy is given death to by a mother who "push[es] the rest of him out" *from* rather *into* life—quite likely, in the comically retold drowning: "He, in other words was—phut!/ Head-first in the water-butt. [...] Fol di ril de re do!" (*Ryder*, 103).

While Nietzsche's own references to "redemption" justify readings of his notion of eternal recurrence as an "atheistic" and/or "aesthetic theodicy," *Ryder*'s satirical edge tends rather toward its dismissal as another instance of false reconciliation. If, on the one hand, allegiance with the comic apparatus of the text is achieved, its humor quite often redounds on itself, disassembling the very machinery by which it operates whether by overworking it, or by prompting a renewed sentimental response, thereby disaffiliating us from its sadistic tendency, and in turn affiliating us with an alternate axiological position. Although Barnes's own references to Nietzsche suggest that the influence of the philosopher on the artistic circles of New York's Greenwich Village in the 1910s did leave its mark on her,[3] the most pointed intertextual revision in *Ryder* that subverts the redemptive omnipotence of the will is based rather on a parody of the proto-Nietzschean figure, Kirillov, from Dostoevsky's novel, *Devils* (1872). A letter from Barnes's mother, dated January 5, 1927, suggests Barnes's encounter with the novel prior to *Ryder*'s publication the following year (*Nightwood: The*

---

[3] For an account of "New York, Nietzsche, and the 1910s," see Stratton 2014, 23–52.

Original Version, 231). The pages detailing Kirillov's meditations on the nature of the "will" and the "former God," alongside his eventual suicide, are in fact all marked out in one of Barnes's two copies of the novel, and serve as the model for the satirical undoing of the redemptive will of the belated creator in *Ryder*.[4]

Kirillov's search for a "salvation for everyone," entailing nothing less than the "physical[] transform[ation]" of humanity, registers a number of the distinctive features of the spiritual project of the Nietzschean overman (Dostoevsky 2008, 693–4). An agon is staged here between the "divinity" of the individual and that of God—otherwise put, "Self-Will" against "His will":

> If God exists, then everything is His will, and I can do nothing of my own apart from His will. If there's no God, then everything is my will, and I'm bound to express my self-will.
>
> (2008, 691)

The grounding evidence for the revised soteriology Kirillov envisions takes shape as an act made possible only with the primacy of "self-will" over that of the "former God": suicide, he claims, shifts "sovereign[ty]" over to the subject ("To realize there's no God, but at the same time not to realize that one's become God oneself is absurd"—2008, 693). While not a requisite for future generations, an originary act of violence is nonetheless necessary to secure the ground for the new order: "I must certainly kill myself to make a start and prove it" (2008, 694). This basic opposition between "Self-Will" and "His will," however, finds itself in a logical imbroglio: "I'm still only God against my will and I'm unhappy since I'm *obligated* to express my self-will" (2008, 694). "Self-Will," here, loses foundational status in the acknowledgment that it fails to be self-grounding, since its very existence and expression are based on a prior "obligat[ion]": suicide no longer stands sufficient as an unconditional act, or the cynosure of the will's freedom. In fact, where this putative "self-will" takes Kirillov is nowhere other than the paradox of willing "against [his] will" in an attempt to supersede God.

This metaphysical morass that Kirillov runs himself into, first paralyzing him with inaction, then pressing him into an ignominious suicide when cornered, is raised in *Ryder* in an exchange between O'Connor and Wendell, with the pathos of its precedent, however, drained into a truncated summary. In the chapter, "Dr. Matthew O'Connor Talks to Wendell on Holy Inspiration," a gendered spin is given to Kirillov's predicament: "'It's God in them [women],' said Matthew

---

[4] These are pages 578–87 of Barnes's 1916 copy. In the following, I cite, however, from the *Oxford World's Classics* edition.

O'Connor. 'It accounts, I think, for the peculiar difference in the suicides of man and woman'" (*Ryder*, 203). The logical conundrums involved in a self-grounding will are compressed into a bathetic *non sequitur* in O'Connor's account. The "young man" is "[t]roubled—why?"

> Because he cannot kill himself without including his will in that action. He knows that if he kills himself, he is the slave of that action, so with the soul of the slave he bargains, and makes great argument about a thing that has not only no base for argument but no way but the way including its will. He says to himself, "I must abandon you. How shall I abandon you?" Thus, he makes for himself a pact. If I kill me, my corpse shall be, in my terms absolute, and by myself, myself made myself—voilà!
>
> (*Ryder*, 203)

If the point of the suicide is "to place himself on an equal footing with God" and bring about the "death of God *and* the father" in an act of self-siring, he balks before the circular inclusion of his subjectivity in the negating process ("he cannot kill himself without including his will in that action"), relegating his self-will from sovereignty to the place of the "slave" (*Ryder*, 203). "[A]rgument" is made where "argument" is out of place and a "way" out contrived where there is "no way but the way including its will." Finally, however, with a preposterous syntactical legerdemain, he reasserts himself, tripping over his "absolute" will into his "absolute" corpse by smuggling both terms—subject and object—into the reflexive pronoun "myself." In an act of sovereign self-grounding—or, rather, self-ungrounding—he is, as it were, "by myself, myself made [*not*] myself." In addition to terminating the trammeled sophistry with a curt intervention, "voilà," here, also indexes not so much the self-positing subject or even his empirical body, but the fast dissipating hocus-pocus of his logic. With this, the redemptive will of the overman is dispatched. The woman, conversely, bypasses these metaphysical snares since, unlike the Oedipal man who attempts to father himself, her will is ceded to God in the act:

> take what woman you like, the virgin in her nightshift, the mother in her maternity gown, the actress in her beaded buskins and ruff, the queen in her leg-o'-mutton sleeves, the peasant girl among her wheat, the shop girl among her percales, the market harridan in her filth and degradation, the whore in the stews; one and all commit, in that act, their body to death's custom, neither making bargain nor asking for precepts and points of departure, nor platforms for philosophy, because women know that there is God only, but man knows that there is God and the father.
>
> (*Ryder*, 203–4)

Against the omnipotent will, now gendered male and scattered into aporias, there is the impotent passivity of the "woman," who, in another variant of *amor fati*, consigns herself to "death's custom" and the way of God. Humor, once again, operates in both directions, abetting, then betraying the insurrectional will on one side, and on the other, reducing the "woman" to an anatomical ground-zero. Death the leveler cuts his scythe across the ranks of "virgin," "mother," "actress," "queen," "peasant," "shop girl," "market harridan," and "whore."

As previously discussed, the narrator herself is complicit to some degree in this essentialist take on "woman." Her humor, as with O'Connor's here, operates via reduction. The third form of humor that is available to *Ryder*'s readers, however, prompts a process of disaffiliation that withdraws from the libidinal complicity of comic engagement: *irony* cuts its way through both the reductive repetition that abolishes the subject (*à la* Eliade) and the sublimating repetition that enthrones it upon its own will (*à la* Nietzsche). Where humor tends toward closure—whether by an aesthetic repetition of life into the product of the subjective will, or a reductive repetition of life into an archetype—irony reopens these forms of premature reconciliation to resituate the subject in history, with a gesture toward an unwritten future. These openings, as will be discussed below, are both psychic and corporeal.

Just months before Barnes's death on June 19, 1982, her last poem is published with a reference to another infamous spring sacrifice—namely, Stravinsky's 1913 *The Rite of Spring*. Barnes's own "Rite of Spring," like Stravinsky's ballet, exhibits the defeated body, collapsed into anatomical stasis:

> Man cannot purge his body of its theme
> As can the silkworm on a running thread
> Spin a shroud to re-consider in.
>
> (*Collected Poems*, 145)

The "theme" of the mortal body, subjected as it is to contingency, pain, and decay, persists throughout "Man"'s existence. This opening declaration disables history's capacity to relieve—much less to redeem—the stigma of fate on the flesh, insisting instead on the eternal recurrence of its needs and symptoms. If symbolic existence is often cited as a marker of species difference—if not species *distinction*—it is here crippled in the contraposition of man's "cannot" with the silkworm's "can": Man repeats his body's "theme" without difference while the silkworm is given the chance to "re-consider." The intimation here of a certain degree of thought displaces consciousness from the human, anatomically immured, onto an insect capable of metamorphosis, and hence, of a "purg[ing]" of the inherited body for the "re-considered" form of a silkmoth. While the familiar resurrection motif commonly attributed to the butterfly may encourage such a reading, Barnes's choice of the silkworm produces a degree of semantic dissonance that is further intensified by the reference to a "shroud," affiliating the chrysalis hence with the winding sheet more than the womb—an association reinforced by her citation of Joseph Addison in a marginal note to another of her late poems: "The silkworm after having spun her task, lays her eggs and dies" (*Collected Poems*, 145). The silkworm, in "re-consider[ing]" life, deems it not worth living, and departs. Negating the prospect of the transfigured body, it reverses resurrection into suicide, issuing its counter-judgment against Creation and the Creator. Never to unfurl from itself, it consciously chooses that which "Man" is coerced into, sealing off its body in an integument of its own making. Unlike its other insect cousin, the Keatsian spider—who may "spin from his own inwards his own airy Citadel"—Barnes's silkworm has for its home no dwelling in the symbolic spaces of the imagination, but only in death (Keats 1935, 102). Spring, once again, functions as a reverse archetype, advancing only the "anti-rite" of a rebirth perverted into suicide, one that fails its task of a ritualistic reanimation of the world.

With these oppositions between the open and closed body, historical and mythic time, critical irony and collusive humor, set in place, it is not hard to understand how Adorno's condemnation of the false redemption associated with *amor fati* (Nietzsche's "crime of theology") is closely linked to his analysis of irony, as well as his negative assessment of Stravinsky's *Rite*. Irony, for Adorno, is indissociable from the existence of various openings, gaps, or rifts, between the world-as-it-is and the world spiritually and libidinally re-envisioned—otherwise put, between its immanent guise ("That's-how-it-is") and its "transcendental" commitment (Adorno 2005, 212). His dismal assessment of the prospect of irony in the modern world is founded precisely on a perceived collapse of the differential zone between immanent reality and its transcendental reconsideration: "Irony's medium, the difference between ideology and reality, has disappeared. The former resigns itself to confirmation of reality by its mere duplication. [...] There is not a crevice in the cliff of the established order into which the ironist might hook a fingernail." As with *amor fati*, humor has now been realigned with fateful necessity: "Irony used to say: such it claims to be, but such it is"; "today, however, the world [...] falls back on the argument that things are like this," which now "coincides," quite simply, with the good (2005, 209–10). Laughter, hence, switches sides, dispatching with the subject to affiliate itself with the community or the cosmos at large: "our situation [...] makes a mockery of mockery" (2005, 209-10). This "sadistic gesture," which transfers allegiance from the victim to the mob, is attributed equally to Stravinsky, whose works are repeatedly characterized in terms of an "anti-subjectivism," a "distrust of subjectivity," and a "taboo on subjectivity" (Adorno 2002, 155, 162–8). Stravinsky's "restoration," as Adorno sees it, is closely related to his "archaism," which proposes a "magic regression" from history into myth, abolishing, in the process, the subject, now "sacrifice[d]" to "collective power": "the music does not identify with the victim, but rather with the destructive element" (Adorno 2016, 100, 108–9).

As in *Ryder*'s "Rape and Repining!" the *Rite*'s sacrifice of the victim is aesthetically refigured and affirmed. Here, too, elements of Nietzschean and Eliadean eternal recurrence result in a false theodicy that repeats destruction as desire, and constitutes "the innermost deception of objectivism: the destruction of the subject [...] is transformed into the victory of the subject in the aesthetic complexion of the work" (2016, 108). Allegiance, here, is once again shifted from the subject to the "objective" elements of fate and the community. As with the vitiation of irony in the modern world, the "ontological illusion" of Stravinsky's art confirms its affiliation with a redoubled immanence: "This is how it is" (2002, 149–50). If, for Adorno, "music" has always been "a protest against myth, against a fate which was always the same," Stravinsky's contrived objectivism turns music, with its temporal dimension, against itself:

> Instead of overcoming the fate of Sisyphus by virtue of its intrinsic historical structure, it comes to grief on a concept of time as the unconnected sequence of ephemeral events and on the illusion that salvation lies in using art to conjure it away. Ernst Bloch's comment that Nietzsche's Eternal Recurrence was simply a poor imitation of eternity consisting of endless repetitions applies literally to the inner core of Stravinsky's music. [...] [H]is works create the impression [...] that they have abrogated time and achieved a state of pure being.
>
> (2002, 151–2)

Time and "historical structure" are once again "abrogated" here. The secular, profane world "comes to grief" against the fundamental ontology of the sacred in its undivided "state of pure being." A dubious soteriology is attached to this achievement of unity, as "salvation" here—like "Nietzsche's Eternal Recurrence"—reveals itself "a poor imitation of eternity," lost to a cyclical fate. Both rites of spring, Barnes's and Stravinsky's, exhibit a form of stasis that retreats from the wounds of time, folding "becoming" over into "being" as a mechanism of preservation that is at best contrived, if not destructive in its enclosure of life in myth. Both artists raise the closed body before us, and in each case, this closure counts as a *redoubled closure*: first as fate, then as the love of fate. Aesthetic complicity, by sublimating the cruelty and contingency of life, affiliates desire with the agents of destruction. Instead of seeking for some transcendence beyond the stasis of the present, it spiritualizes the immanent world: immanence is thus redoubled as its own transcendent horizon.

Ryder, in fact, begins with such a theology of immanence with the chapter "Jesus Mundane," which has been read—with unsettling consistency in the history of Barnes scholarship—*without irony*. The second half of this chapter, in proposing an ironic reading of "Jesus Mundane," seeks to challenge this critical complicity in the destruction of subjectivity and to reconsider irony's role in forging openings. These openings, as mentioned above, have a corporeal basis. By relating ironic voicing to the polyphonic texture of Barnes's novel, the rest of this chapter considers how the psychic structure of the embodied subject may be recalibrated via strategies of affiliation and disaffiliation.

To Spit or Swallow?

If *Ryder*'s patriarch, Wendell, has quite rightly been the target of much feminist criticism in Barnes scholarship, its matriarch has eluded the attention of many of these readings (Broe 1991; Dalton 1993). Yet Wendell is very much his mother's son, his identification with Sophia signaled not only by his last name (Sophia "gave him no father's name"), but also his first, changed from John— after his father John Peel—when "he spoke up for an unfatherly given name," by way of "Rufus" and "Wolfgang" (*Ryder*, 17). In *Ryder*, the Law of the Father is supplemented by that of the presiding Mother, whose representative is not so much Julie's mother, but her mother's mother, Sophia: "She was the law" (*Ryder*, 16). Kate's protest against their brand of nature philosophy and free love, which redoubles anatomy as destiny, is directed at both Wendell ("keeper of the shop") and Sophia ("madame of the keeper"): "you and your son came forward with his notions about women loving one another when they were not meant to love one another, or to get their children from the same spigot" (*Ryder*, 170–1). Readings directed unilaterally against Wendell's patriarchal role are thus wanting on two counts: they fail not only to account for the maternal supplement to the oppressive familial law, arguably more insidious for its invisibility, but also fail to note the complicit structure of the narrative itself, which, framed within the formal coordinates of a picaresque novel, establishes allegiance from the outset between the reader and the position of the roguish mock-hero (more "ranchman" than "father"—*Ryder*, 170), who is himself situated in opposition to the orthodox state values of monogamy, public schooling, and species difference. The Law of the Ryder family, already divided between the matriarch of the house and its filial delegate, is pitted against what is more conventionally associated with the Law of the Father—that which expropriates the subject from the mythic family to relocate it within the symbolic order of society at large. Susan Edmunds quite rightly points to Wendell's position in the novel as both "emancipatory hero of nonconformity," and "domestic and sexual predator whose practices merit suppression" (1997, 218–19). Given the conflicting enunciatory positions staged by the formal apparatus of Barnes's novel, the reader is often affiliated with the embedded value systems of each of these voices and brought into their circle of laughter, and is disaffiliated from them only by means of a critical process of judgment and discernment.

I have suggested that another form of humor, irony, contributes to this mode of disaffiliation via corporeal and psychic means. Since Freud's synthesis of his accounts of identification and melancholic incorporation, critics have often pointed to the heterogeneous constitution of the subject. Freud's claim in *The Ego and the Id* (1923) that "[t]he character of the ego is a precipitate of abandoned object-cathexes" implicates the subject within a structure of derivation, emerging belatedly as the site of its losses (*SE* XIX, 29). The self is constituted by its incorporated others, making it, in essence, an "elegiac formation" (cited in Bahun 2013, 28). Bahun hence speaks of a "porous ego [...] constantly formed and re-formed by abandoned/lost loved objects" (2013, 28), while Sanchez-Párdo, in her close engagement with Kleinian thought, writes of the processes of "introjection" and "projection" in negotiating the boundaries between the self and other as a "continual activity of interiorization and exteriorization" (2003, 11). Both critics, in relating the heterogeneous composition of the subject to the formal heterogeneity of much modernist art, point to the instability mobilized in the reading experience itself, demanding "responsive understanding" more than mere "receptivity" (Bahun 2013, 168). Affiliation and disaffiliation are continually and dynamically processed. If the subject is produced via the melancholic incorporation of its predecessors, and hence affiliated from its inception with certain figures of authority, then the project of disaffiliation may be said to involve the reverse process of a "'disincorporation' [...] of the Master" (cited in Bahun 2013, 39). In *Ryder*, this manner of satiric disinheritance tethers ironic praxis to the body in the form of a buccal revolt. If laughter is, on a primitive level, identified with the convulsive mouth, exhalant or expectorant, irony—one of its forms—is in *Ryder* engaged in analogous acts of buccal and oral resistance. Disrupted from its normative action, textually displaced and mediated as comedy, laughter here is registered in the form of an ironic vocalization that continues to bear its corporeal trace—of *spitting*.

Melancholic incorporation and buccal revolt are in fact staged quite literally early in the novel. Deploying the model of the Eucharist—associated already with tribal practices of incorporative affiliation in the preceding decades by James Frazer's *The Golden Bough* (1890) and Freud's *Totem and Taboo* (1913), both of which Barnes encountered—the unity of the Ryder family is said to be preserved via the incorporation of the body of the matriarch. Julie's move to "think[] something outside the family," in essence, a disaffiliative gesture, thus involves the disinheritance of the familial name via ironic citation, judgment, and revolt (*Ryder*, 169). "[S]he is none of mine," Wendell protests midway through the novel, with the explanatory addendum: "Did I not hear her *deriding* me greatly?" (*Ryder*, 110; my italics). In refusing to incorporate the body of the matriarch, Julie opts out of the communion of the family. Sophia, the narrator relates, exacts "obeisance": "she loved, but she would be obeyed."

> She was the law. She gave herself to be devoured, but in the devouring they must acclaim her, saying, "This is the body of Sophia, and she is greater than we!" Devour her they did, and said, "This is the body of Sophia, and she is greater than we"; all but Julie, who loved her most. It was Julie who gave this queen her mortal hurt, for that she loved her best. Sophia offering her heart for food, Julie spewed it out on a time, and said, "I taste a lie!" And Sophia hearing, cried in agony, but Julie went apart.
>
> (*Ryder*, 16)

The "affective amalgams" that compose the subject, as Bahun puts it, are recalibrated via a negotiation of its borders (2013, 167): the love between grandmother and daughter may be mutual, yet the latter achieves individuation with an act of disaffiliation archaically associated with the refusal to be fed. The maternal forcemeat is, as it were, expelled to reopen the subject to a life outside the family. If the Ryders establish communion by partaking of "the body of Sophia," forming a consubstantial unity bound by "the law," Julie finds her way "apart" only with a form of archaic judgment that reveals discernment to be a function of "taste": the refusal to be *taken into* the tribe with its enshrined "lie" is a refusal to *take in* its nutritive substance. This understanding of a corporeal archaeology supporting mental activity does in fact find a focal point in Freud's account, at the oral cavity. Having staked the claim that the Eucharistic host, like the totem meal, forms the *"sacred cement"* and the "sacred bond" that unites the community in "the same substance" in *Totem and Taboo* (*SE* XIII, 154), Freud goes on in his 1925 essay, "Negation," to locate the faculty of judgment at the site of the archaic mouth. "Judging," he writes, "is a continuation [...] of the original process by which the ego took things into itself or expelled them from itself" (*SE* XIX, 239). In other words:

> Expressed in the language of the oldest—the oral—instinctual impulses, the judgement is: "I should like to eat this," or "I should like to spit it out"; and, put more generally: "I should like to take this into myself and to keep that out." That is to say: "It shall be inside me" or "it shall be outside me."
>
> (*SE* XIX, 237)

Julie's act of "spew[ing]" out the totemic "body of Sophia" thus functions as a "disincorporation of the Master"—or Mistress—that involves a form of discernment compounding bodily and psychic factors.

Eating, in *Ryder*, is often a sign of compliance. The sanctification of the primitive family and community operates alongside a redoubling of nature as law. Such a framework constitutes a spiritualization of immanence through which anatomy is sublimated into destiny. Sophia's efforts to preserve the sacred bonds of the family are thus echoed by Wendell's own philosophy of immanence, which finds itself actualized in the bodies of women. "All women," so Wendell claims, "are equal, until one dies in child-bed, then she becomes as near to saints as my mind can conceive. Why is that? you ask; because they died at the apex of their ability" (*Ryder*, 202). Once again, a reductive gesture levels all women to an anatomical ground-zero via an abrogation of the socio-historical world, in a radical transvaluation of all values onto a single axis of reproductive capability. The life he envisions for his daughter, Julie, according to his philosophy of immanence, locks her within the sacred time of myth, prescribing for her the "simple" path of conformism, with no wayward deviations "outside the family," or indeed, outside nature:

> She [...] will follow her mother, she will become both buxom and coarse. It will have saved her from the pale existence of those women who, from cradle to the grave, have but two odours—celibacy and monogamy. My daughter will be frank, neither promiscuous nor childless: those two things are appropriated by flat-chested women whose hearts beat sideways for want of room. She will eat, function and die, looking neither backward nor forward.
>
> (*Ryder*, 202)

Julie, in repeating the life of her mother, will be another derivative exemplar of the family. Evading the external law of the state ("celibacy and monogamy")—characterized here in terms of the libidinal restrictions that psychoanalysis designates "castration" (as the "pale existence" of "flat-chested women whose hearts beat sideways for want of room")—she would cleave instead to the law of the Ryders in a return to the archetype of the animal-woman. Withdrawn from history back into myth, "[s]he will eat, function and die, looking neither backward nor forward," reduced to an operative vessel without memory or aspiration. Eating, here as elsewhere, signals her enclosure within "nature." Those who partake of the same flesh, becoming consubstantial in the process, are brought into the extended circle of the holy family. In the chapter "Ryder—His Race," Wendell hence "explains his mission in life" beginning with "a treatise on canivora": "Of all canivora man holds woman most dear":

> To see some sweet creature, couched in splendour, putting away sides of ox, fills him with pure ravishment. [...] In like manner, consuming whole lamb, trawls of fish, an hundred guinea fowl, woodcock and grouse per annum, does she not eat, that through her office slaughter may be transfigured? [...] Has not wild venison rhymed her coquetries of throbbing bosom, spaced the heaving stomach to a strophe, as she lies dreaming in all capacities, mundane yet meticulous?
>
> (*Ryder*, 205)

The ritualistic elements of the feast are raised here with a reference to the "transfigur[ation]" that turns "slaughter" presumably into sacrifice, spiritualizing the act of incorporation. In Wendell's philosophy of immanence, nature is redoubled as spirit: poetic devices here point to the repetition of life as art, sublimating anatomy into a rudimentary blazon as the "throbbing bosom" finds "rhyme" and the "heaving stomach" its scansion, "spaced [...] to a strophe." That Wendell's "pure ravishment" recalls the "ravishing" of "Rape and Repining!" is hardly accidental given how both chapters stage the closure of women within the mythic archetype. Wendell's profane soteriology, which seeks to found a form of universal love that operates by conflating the sexual and spiritual, *eros* and *agape*—to the point of traversing the species boundary[5]—may in fact be described with another iterated term here: it is, in brief, a sanctification of the "mundane."

---

[5] "By bedding in all beds," he plans "to be Father of All Things," redeeming all of Creation into a single "Race": "Now this is the Race that shall be Ryder—those who can sing like the lark, coo like the dove, moo like the cow, buzz like the bee, cheep like the cricket, bark like the dog, mew like the cat, neigh like the stallion," and so on and so forth (*Ryder*, 210–11).

I choose to conclude this chapter with a reading of "Jesus Mundane" that relates irony to *Ryder*'s polyphonic practice partly as a corrective to the unsettling tendency demonstrated in previous scholarship in using the novel's opening lines as a stable hermeneutic frame within which further instances of ambivalence and indeterminacy may be sorted and embedded. Of the many injunctions issued in this prefatory chapter, the imperative—"Reach not beyond the image" (*Ryder*, 3)—has in particular often been isolated as evidence for the novel's own putative investment in a project of immanence. Brian Glavey pronounces *Ryder*'s first chapter "a lesson in iconology" that cautions against libidinal and epistemological "overreach" (2016, 63), while Tyrus Miller reads it as a foil to "modernism's desire" to raise "the wordless 'depths' of meaning' into 'speech'" (1999, 167)—a claim that is thereafter cited by Taylor in her argument for Barnes's investment—"against hermeneutics [...] grand narratives [...] cosmic certainties and universal truths"—in "the bodily, the affective, the immediate and the uncertain" (2012, 85). Such a facile binary between a modest or "mundane" modernism against its repudiated others—variously characterized as too deep, too grand, and too certain—winds up stabilizing the very uncertainties that have been worked into Barnes's text itself right from its opening pages, and becomes the critical accomplice to Wendell's own religion of the mundane—otherwise put, his *grand narrative* of philosophical immanence. Taylor goes so far as to cite the "choreographed laughter" of the community as "a powerful alternative to depth psychology," arguing finally that in *Ryder* "Barnes suggests that individual subjectivity should not be privileged over collective forms of expression" (2012, 87). Once again, evidence is marshalled with non-ironic citation: the injunction—"Let thy lips choose no prayer that is not on the lips of thy congregation" (*Ryder*, 4)—is taken to be Barnes's.

As I have suggested, the polyphonic apparatus of the novel produces treacherous affiliations that are further reinforced by its pervasive humor, from which distance is established, conversely, via the disaffiliating effects of irony. Critical collusion on the side of the victimizers is, on one level, solicited by the novel, but, on another, internally challenged through various libidinal realignments. The heterogeneity of Barnes's text, arguably, dynamically engages the heterogeneous constitution of the melancholic subject, variously prompting, shifting, privileging, and suppressing its disparate allegiances through a variety of enunciatory positions. As Bahun argues, "heterogeneity obscures the signifying system within which one is expected to interpret the utterance [...] and, by extension, challenges our presuppositions about particular adequacy of certain types of utterance to certain kinds of content" (2013, 168).

Ryder is presented as a formal and vocal conglomerate. Its Menippean mix of prose and verse is complicated by the epistolary, its picaresque trajectory framed by a series of biblical injunctions. The satirical and the sentimental cohabit as much as the religious and the profane. Bungled Chaucerian verse meets the bungled lullaby and the bungled bedtime story, and, as letters make their way across the Atlantic, tall tales and fairy tales, a confession, treatise, sermon, and a will enter the fray. This "pastiche of genres and styles," Sanchez-Párdo notes, produces a "chasm between referentiality and figurality," an "incommensurability of the effects of narration with narrated events" (2003, 306, 318). If the formal mosaic of the novel ends up disarticulating language from the content it inscribes, it redirects attention to the provenance of each instance of vocalization—that is, from *what* is said to the *how* and the *who* of the saying. These are occasionally signaled by the chapter titles, or derivable from context, but are not always immediately clear. For example, "Amelia Sings a Lullaby," "Midwives' Lament," "Amelia Hears from Her Sister," and "Sophia Tells of Wendell" may give the reader enough indication regarding the various enunciatory positions that center these chapters, but it takes some time before the victim-blaming of "Rape and Repining!" is attributed to a "Council of Women," while the circumlocutory slut-shaming of Kate-Careless—who could be anything from "Kate-Why-Not" to "Kate-the-Doll," "Kate-the-Whirlwind" or "Kate-the-Swoon" but *not* "Kate-Careful," a pruner of "wanton brambles"—is never pinned to any subject position in "What Kate Was Not" (*Ryder*, 88–92). A discriminating reader might think it is Amelia's jealousy doing the talking here, but given its waffling prolixity, note its incongruence with the tussles wife and mistress more often get themselves into, which favor physical assault and invective—and the occasional foray into the epigram—over yarn-spinning.[6] In *Ryder*, quite often, these enunciatory positions are mixed or unidentifiable.

A certain conjunction, then, between a mosaic formal apparatus and the mosaic topography of the subject is witnessed in *Ryder*. While a vocal polyphony is in evidence on one level, distributing distinct parts across the novel's disparate participants, each characterized by recognizable variances in tone, diction, and content, on another level, the narrative solvent of the writer's own voice—held at a steady pitch of urbanity, mischief, and affected pity—returns these

---

[6] "'One was owner', said Amelia, 'and one was poacher'.
'One was gift fruit, and one was gotten' quoth Kate.
Therewith, a doughty clout Amelia fetched her alongside of her head [...] and as good as was sent she gave in return, till blood flowed, and hair fell, and there were tears amid the equal anger.
'Filthy slut!' cried Kate." (*Ryder*, 173–5).

individuated accents to a common flow commingling satire and sentiment. The lines that divide subjects from one another are as frequently displaced as the lexical accents that distribute formal ground. *Ryder*, in this sense, inherits a feature common to much satirical and ironic literature—that of a degree of complicity or even collapse between those who laugh and those who are laughed at—otherwise put, a treacherous affiliation. Critics have thus spoken of satire's "purloined territory": like the subject founded on melancholic incorporation, it begins as a derivative formulation (Seidel 1979, 14). Kenneth Burke's term for the lost boundary between satirical agent and object emphatically returns the two to a single body: they are, he notes, "consubstantial" (1945, 514).

Given this, *Ryder*'s ironic praxis may be understood as a means of working a way out of this consubstantiality of the belated subject and its predecessors. Ironic voicing *colludes* with a prior enunciatory position in order to *critically* disengage from it. The mechanism most often deployed in Barnes's novel for this purpose is that of hyperbole, no longer simply to "push the ridiculous into the very arms of the sublime," but to push the ridiculous into the *sublimely ridiculous*. Hyper-bole, in *Ryder*, goes beyond Nietzschean sublimation by, quite literally, *throwing up* the contents that have been subjectively incorporated. Ironic (over-)voicing—a kind of *ventri-loquy*, or belly-speech—constitutes a disincorporative method. Rejecting the words and the values coded in the nutritive contract between parent and child is thus figured as the refusal of communion: the body of Julie's forebears, as much as their language, is "spewed out." If ironic speech may be characterized on a basic level as *saying what one does not mean*, such an act of dissociation, framed otherwise, may be understood as the expulsion of the words that have been seeded in the nascent self, whose boundaries are thus renegotiated in the process. Paul West's keen observation that in *Ryder* Barnes seems to be after "ventriloquial recoveries of the beloved voice gone" thus captures half the picture. These melancholic traces of the lost voices of one's forebears are retrieved only to be reworked into grotesque semblances that are thereby disincorporated (*Ryder*, 246). Irony tracks this process of iteration and differentiation.

Redacted as a series of anaphoric biblical injunctions, "Jesus Mundane" solicits the reader's compliance by adopting the enunciatory position of the patriarchs. If its first lines, cautioning against "fanatics" and protesting care for "thy physical body and thy temporal agony," are rather palatable, they nonetheless arrive at an intensity that becomes harder to stomach, moving us from affiliation to disaffiliation. Taylor's characterization of its tone as "authoritative but benevolent" is about as misleading as the chapter itself seems designed to be (2012, 85). Its philosophy of immanence is formulated via appropriations in both form and content of the King James Bible, which, in redoubling nature as spirit, prove to be, as the novel progresses, recognizably Wendell's. The voice of this prophet of the mundane enjoins its listener to withdraw into the cyclical time of myth:

> Art thou not part and parcel of thy pastures? Thank thy melons for what thou art, and blame thy figs for thy failures, and gather in thy differences, and go to thy mourning as one a little gathered from the earth, and as one going a little toward the earth, and of the earth judged.
>
> (*Ryder*, 5)[7]

As with the prescribed existence Wendell has in mind for Julie—to "eat, function and die"—the voice of the master here returns its subject to "the earth," foreclosing any departure from a purely immanent existence by collapsing life and law into "the way" of the world (*Ryder*, 4). What is, *is*. Divinity and mundanity are synchronized here. Wendell, it seems, has managed the double infringement underlined in Barnes's copy of Pascal's *Pensées*: "Two errors: 1. To take everything literally. 2. To take everything spiritually" (cited in Caselli 2019, 148). If the chapter opens somewhat "benevolent[ly]," it graduates into shades of petulance as the imperatives compound and the oppression turns personal with the introduction, towards the chapter's end, of the pronoun "I":

> Go now, and lift up thy cries from about me, for I have done with thee awhile and thy ways, and thy way's ways, and the things that thou hangest about the places of the soul. And speak not of Me, for thou knowest not of what thou speakest, nor knowest thou of thy need, nor knowest what thou hast given or taken [...] Knowest thou if thou hast troubled me, or how thou hast inconvenienced me for thy sake? Or if thou hast pleased me in any way, or hast not? [...] These things are as the back of thy head to thee. Thou hast not seen them.
>
> (*Ryder*, 5)

The novel's opening lines may be voiced seemingly out of nowhere, sourcing authority from the impersonal accents of the law, but by the time its final paragraphs are arrived at its floating enunciation touches ground with an all-too-human "I." Citing Saint Paul's claim in Romans 10:17 that "from hearing comes belief [*ex auditu fides*]," Steven Connor relates the "experience of a voice without an obvious origin, whether in divine annunciation, oracular utterance," or other instances of displaced vocalization to an "experience of the overload

---

[7] Barnes's reference here is presumably to Job 12:7-9.

of sound": "The long association between the dissociated or ventriloquially dissimulated voice and the exercise of various kinds of divination, in particular in the traditions attaching to the oracle at Delphi, seems to testify to this close link between the autonomized voice and the control and signification of time" (2000, 23-4). More than just the authority over time, what is shown in both psychoanalytic thinking as well as Barnes's novel is the command over the formative processes of the self and its relation to the world that the voice without apparent origin wields. This voice of the master, melancholically incorporated as the "superego" in the Freudian topography of the subject, regulates the self, its actions, and ethical commitments, in this case curtailing all epistemological and spiritual ambition within a theologically framed account of immanence. While seemingly autonomous, it is genealogically attributable to the self's predecessors. In *Ryder*, the archaeology of the self turned up by the text ends up returning the disembodied voice of the law to its human sources, exposing in the process its foibles and pretentions: the Wizard of Oz, it seems, is Wendell. Mapping out the various wheretos and wherefroms of the diverse voices that constitute Barnes's novel thus simultaneously maps out the mosaic constitution of the subject, with its affective and axiological distributions laid out for critical stocktaking. In "Jesus Mundane" in particular, ventriloquy enables the daughter to inhabit the enunciatory position of the father by activating that part of her that is consubstantial with him from melancholic incorporation. In a further step, this vocalization from "purloined territory" effectively divides the speaking from itself, alienating its overworked formal mechanism to open up a residual space of discontent from which the subject might come into its own. Ironic engagement and disengagement thus form the process by which the belated subject, in spewing out its incorporated predecessors, comes to be.

The extent to which the voices of literary and genealogical patriarchs and predecessors co-entwine in Barnes is perhaps made most explicit in a letter to Coleman, dated August 7, 1938, in which she reports on her recent reading of Tolstoy during a trip to Petersfield with Peggy Guggenheim and her children:

> I have read three of Tolstoi's books in Petersfield, his later religious and polemic ones, why of life, of art? etc, and now his biography, what a very great, prolific, and at times deluded man. Still I think him less of an idiot, than I did (that is for his later repudiation of himself along with Beethoven, Dostoevsky, Turgenieff, Gogol etc) than I did before I read his books. I can imagine what a great lumbering, dispotic fiery [sic] genius he must have been, hell to live with, particularly to himself, with better intentions than temper, better conceptions

that [sic] ability to follow them up, and a power of concentration and ability to work that I envy like poison. He had the good and the evil of a fanatic (which you cant [sic] thole) I think I understand him better for the fact that I knew Peter Neagoe, all those hairy, open shirt prophets have something of the same footing, like my (upsidedown) father, Thoreau, Whitman, you know the kind, full of theories and whiskers, but underneath a really passionate feeling for truth and right and "how to live?" as its theme.

Admiration and dismissal are threaded together here. By means of some caricaturizing accents, Barnes's depiction of the Russian "prophet" and "fanatic" departs from its immediate referent to include other preeminent father figures, both literary and familial, all subsumed—with a conspiratorial nudge—into indexical tautology: "you know the kind." Sororal solidarity is established here against the grandiloquence of their predecessors, as esteem is wrecked against charges of misconduct. The universalist tendencies that characterize the thought of Tolstoy, Thoreau, and Whitman—founded on visionary pronouncements on "human nature" or "nature" *tout court*—are also attributed to the renegade spirituality of Barnes's own "(upsidedown) father," as well as her sometime lover, Peter Neagoe. Their philosophical bulk, however, is linked somewhat deterministically to a similar profusion on a physical level ("full of theories and whiskers"), with a reductive touch that pits their predilection for hyperopic sapience against the subtlety—and, ultimately, the greater ethical validity—of the women. While "great" and "prolific," Tolstoy is also "at times deluded," even "an idiot"; as a "great lumbering dispotic fiery genius," he must have been "hell to live with," and, like "all those hairy, open shirt prophets," rhapsodized across the standard repertoire of the sages ("why of life, of art? [...] 'how to live?' "), churning up in the process, "the good and the evil of a fanatic." The oppressive paternity of a Tolstoy or Thoreau, a Walt Whitman, Wald Barnes, or indeed a Wendell Ryder, it is suggested, is the common result of male visionaries who miss the trees for the forest—or, rather, the women for the world ("To man is the vision, to his wife the droppings!") (*Ryder*, 114).

In *Ryder*, Sophia's mother, Cynthia, dispenses some cautionary advice to her daughter when she finds that "madness had crept upon her" after her fourteenth pregnancy: "Your father is a hairy atheist [...] all nature lovers are, especially these. Remember" (*Ryder*, 7). Two generations later, the warning is repeated between Sophia's daughters. To her sister Amelia, about to depart for America in marriage to Wendell, Ann protests that he is "free-thinker" (*Ryder*, 47). As far as Ann is concerned, Wendell's counterfeit religion is not just blasphemous, but also epigonic:

> Did you ever know a dog [...] who was free to choose him a home, who would not nose out a dung-heap? For free-thinking dog or free-thinking man [...] never seem to come by anything with their thinking but the refuse of other people's!
>
> (*Ryder*, 47)

Like Barnes's own "(upsidedown) father," Wendell's profane soteriology, which doggedly conflates sexual and spiritual love across all of civilization's taboos against incest, polygamy, and bestiality into a vision of universal kinship, is derided by Ann as the excreta of the luminaries of the past. Wendell, we might say, is "Jesus Mundane" in several senses of the term: instead of the Good News of Christ he offers nothing very *new*—and nothing very *good*; promising naught by way of transcendence, he veers into territory claimed already by Luther's *princeps mundi*—that is, Satan, prince of *this world*.

If the suggestion comes through Barnes's novel that it is sometimes better to "spew" than to swallow, to throw rather than lap up the "refuse of other people's," this focalization of the subject's will over the oral cavity can only be reinforced by certain events from her own life. As retold in her 1914 article, "How It Feels to Be Forcibly Fed," an "experiment" undergone in solidarity with the British suffragettes who had been force-fed since 1909 while on hunger strike, the subject's "passive revolt" can sometimes be "reduced to one simple act—to swallow or to choke" (*New York*, 174–6). The stunt-journalist theatrics of the piece notwithstanding, Barnes's recapitulation of the event firmly underscores the collapse of the subject into her body, her "spirit" reduced to a "physical mechanism": "I had lapsed into a physical mechanism without power to oppose or resent the outrage to my will" (*New York*, 175, 178). Hardly any less literal is the link between buccal revolt and the opening into subjectivity made in another surviving anecdote from the Barnes household, retold this time by Janet Flanner of the young Djuna:

> My favourite story of hers dealt with a period when her father, who entertained odd ideas of nourishment, decided that since chickens ate pebbles to aid their digestion, a few pebbles in the diet of his children might be equally salubrious.
>
> (Cited in Broe 1991, 155)

Herring's suggestion that Wald Barnes has, here, taken a leaf out of *Walden* adds just one more layer to the derivative stack that weighs upon the belated subject (1995, 34). This comic literalization of the necessity of disincorporation is nonetheless an opportune reminder of the place reserved for irony in *Ryder*—

that is, to open up a space in which the subject might come to be, away from the premature reconciliation of, on the one hand, absorption into the community, and on the other, the humorous reappropriation of its forces—the one eliminating the will *in toto*, the other raising it to godhood. After all, even in Nietzsche is the tendency for this metaphysical gaiety to trip over into *indigestion* acknowledged: instead of the sublimation of the past ("it was") into an act of the will ("thus I willed it"), one sometimes finds the "will's gnashing of teeth" against "the stone 'it was'" (2006, 111– 12).

4

Tragedy I: *Nightwood* and the Eschatological Body

In the penultimate chapter of *Nightwood* (1936), "Go Down, Matthew," the manic Doctor of the novel makes a note of Robin—"a wild thing caught in a woman's skin"—before launching into another one of his *non sequiturs*, comparing her to a "paralysed man in Coney Island":

> who had to lie on his back in a box, but the box was lined with velvet, his fingers jewelled with stones, and suspended over him where he could never take his eyes off, a sky-blue mounted mirror, for he wanted to enjoy his own "difference."
> (*Nightwood*, 131–2)

Immobilized, supine, and sunk within his ornamented coffin, this "paralysed man" appears determined to retrieve for himself the image of his own end with "a sky-blue mounted mirror," on which his gaze is fixed. While this may not constitute any recognizable form of extreme unction, his preparation for his death nonetheless reveals the close association between one's eschatological orientation—or being-toward-the-end—and the frozen image of the body: the corpse, vacated of life, may be secreted from decay and immortalized in and as image. His bejeweled body, anticipatorily embalmed as the imperishable image of himself, is thus "raised in glory," as it were, by technical means (1 Corinthians 15:43). If something of a "literal error" comes through here in the jewels over his flesh and his velvet cocoon, what remains visible in his "enjoy[ment]" of his posthumous form are the lineaments of a certain dialectic between the mortal body, subject to time and contingency, and its transfiguration into the eternal stasis of an image (*Nightwood*, 80). The "difference" emphasized here points to his infirmity, the anatomical shortfall that opens up the margin between the image of the normative human body and his own. That this is prefigured—in *falsetto*—in an earlier passage when the Doctor's "voice cracked on the word 'difference,' soaring up divinely," suggests, however, that this intervening tension between the fallen flesh and its glorious form is one that extends to all of *Nightwood*'s "damned" and "disqualified"—all who fail to approximate, as will be seen, the corporeal idol of a normatively conceived notion of Christological Man— including, as his rogue leap up the octave betrays, his own the transfeminine self (*Nightwood*, 83).

Resurrection history, in its basic coordinates, may be mapped out as the movement of the body beset by time, error, and contingency, toward its pleromatic reconstitution at the end of time as the restored image of Christ.[1] This trajectory, however, is in the first instance stalled in melancholic indecision in *Nightwood*, raising the question of the eschatological body: does the body that is projected against its end direct infirmity toward formlessness and putrescence, or is it refigured, rather, in the light of the Resurrection, "sown in corruption [....] raised in incorruption," "sown a natural body [...] raised a spiritual body"? (1 Corinthians 15:42-4). Is this a body plagued by the "eschatological affliction" of radical finitude that Heidegger names "being-toward-Death" (2001b, §50-3), or is it rather a body in the form of a Christian being-toward-eternity, which, as Ricoeur notes, reads "the meaning of my existence in the light of the Resurrection, that is, as reinstated in the movement which we have called the future of the Resurrection of the Christ"? (1974, 409-10). This chapter, in picking up on Barnes's concern with the eschatological body—evidenced from the early comic *ars moriendi* of "What is Good Form in Dying?" (1923) to her late poems—charts the diverse forms of the body and the meanings embedded in them in the mirror of death.

Throughout *Nightwood*, the Doctor's own apocalyptic imagination summons up a motley fellowship of the dead in a series of apostrophes and invocations, rupturing his many, plangent digressions in spasmodic intervals. The "Widow Lazarus" and "the widower bird at the turnstile of heaven" make an appearance, alongside the Biblical King Saul (accompanied by Handel's "Dead March"), trailed by some variant of the Death and the Maiden motif (imaged here "with a crupper of maiden's hair" and a "grim horse")[2] and the heliophagic *Sköll* of Norse mythology who consummates his quest at *Ragnarök* (*Nightwood*, 124, 85, 127, 114). Surveying himself from the end of time, the Doctor retrieves his body not in elevated form, but pared down to its essential architecture, reduced after accumulated suffering into its skeletal substratum:

---

[1] Such a theological anthropology, founded on the typological interval between Adam and Christ, broaches numerous unresolved issues of embodiment and sexual difference, as discussed in Dunning 2014.

[2] "The grim horse is death," Barnes explains to Wolfgang Hildesheimer in a June 5, 1959, letter.

> But when you inbreed with suffering [...] you are destroyed back to your structure as an old master disappears beneath the knife of the scientist who would know how it was painted. [...] [W]e all carry about with us the house of death, the skeleton [...] Time is a great conference planning our end, and youth is only the past putting a leg forward.
>
> (*Nightwood*, 117)

What follows this is another sketch in apocalyptic tones of the stations of the damned (London, Marseilles, Singapore), with their necromantic host of "Tuppen[ies]," "*grue[s]*," and other "ladies of the *haute* sewer," all altered by the touch of death into the caparisoned fauna of a modern *selva oscura*, pressed into confrontation with the last things—*ta eschata*—of existence. They are brought to their "last stand," "taking their last stroll," "sauntering on their last Rotten Row," frozen by O'Connor into so many terminal images. Some remain "standing still, [letting you do it,]³ silent and indifferent as the dead, as if they were thinking of better days, or waiting for something that they had been promised when they were little girls" (*Nightwood*, 118). Projected against the horizon of the end, these women join the company of the dead and deathward bodies—variously "shock-abbreviated" or "stripped" of "the hide of time"—that are imaged throughout the Barnesian corpus, "vivid and repulsive/As the truth" (*Collected Poems*, 49, 55; *Nightwood*, 121). A paradox emerges here concerning the eschatological body: where mortal life enters the terminal zone of the apocalyptic gaze, the organism, arrested in its insentience, nonetheless ends up succeeding itself in the afterlife of the image. As will be seen, this eidetic stasis has at times been affiliated with the notion of the resurrected body in Christian salvation history.⁴ *Nightwood*'s enclosure of a tragic world is thus implicated in the delivery of not just the body, but the *image of the body* itself, over to death. I begin here with Barnes's formulation of the corporeal *eschaton*.

The Resurrection of the Body

Just a few years after *Nightwood*'s publication in 1936, toward the end of the decade, Barnes somewhat facetiously refers to the post-Resurrection body in

---

³ This clause apparently did not escape T. S. Eliot's censoring eye (*Nightwood: The Original Version*, 110).
⁴ According to Agamben, the conception of the resurrected body in terms of its *eidos* rather than its material constituents was historically put forward by Origen (*contra* Aquinas), and suspected of heresy (2011b, 92–3).

a letter to Coleman with the cryptic remark—"How odd to write 40—a date younger than myself and older than God" (1939–40). The allusion here is to Augustine's claim—which she would also have come across in Émile Mâle's study of medieval art in *The Gothic Image* (1913)—that the body is "born again at the perfect age of thirty years" (Mâle 1961, 374–5).[5] At "the age of the fullness of Christ," the body reaches its pleromatic form (Augustine 2008, 462). That Mâle's remark is made in the context of the religious significance of the "image" in the Middle Ages is of some relevance here: the "mystic" Doctor of *Nightwood* is after all an epigone of not just the biblical prophets, but also— christened Matthew-Mighty-grain-of-salt-*Dante*-O'Connor—of *il Sommo Poeta* (*Nightwood*, 28). Barnes's words to Coleman on two separate occasions suggest that the significance of the Italian poet for her concerns his signature memorialization of the visionary and the worldly at the crossroads of the poetic image. As she formulates it in her letter dated October 30, 1938:

> Dante, for me (perhaps because I cant [*sic*] read him in the Italian) has a marvellous under-tow, a weight and an importance thats [*sic*] near to the <u>weight of dreams</u>, occasionally a line will absolutely rpostrate [*sic*] one with its accuracy and beauty—but its alsays [*sic*] the accuracy and beauty of something that is a phantasmagore [*sic*], the taking of a vision and pinning it through like a butterfly, its [*sic*] one of his powers, and then theres [*sic*] the other no man can explain, something grasped of another reality and set down so stoutly that it must be real, the father and mother of visions, midwife of two worlds.

The poet's access to the nebulae of visionary heights is partnered with a firm grounding in the material realm. If the noumenal intimations of "another reality" are disclosed here, they nonetheless manifest themselves in the coordinates of the phenomenal plane, "set down so stoutly" as to condense into the "real." In this accretion of substance, reality itself is re-envisioned and remade. A certain gravitational field shapes the oneiric expanse of the imagination, magnetizing its flow into regions of density with a "<u>weight</u>" and "under-tow" that gathers the diffuse into the contoured boundaries of the image. The referenced dualism of the "two worlds" (spirit/nature, noumenal/phenomenal, transcendent/ immanent) meet here in the crucible of Dante's mind where—in an archetypal analogy—as "father and mother," they birth the visions overseen by the "midwife" poet. The solecism of "a phantasmagore" here is striking in its anticipation of the figural elaboration that follows: as the wild motility of the "butterfly" is

---

[5] A 1958 edition of Mâle's text is held in the Barnes Archive.

fixed into the image of its death, so the multitude of phantasms contained in a "phantasmagoria" is seized—and singularized—in a coinage that carves out a recess in the flesh borne at the heart of the static *eidos*.[6] The reduced suffix here, from "*agoria*" to "*gore*," encapsulates one of Barnes's idiosyncratic formulations for the body's relation to its idealized form: it is, as it were, "impaled" upon its image (*Nightwood*, 3, 123).[7]

The following year, on June 6, 1939, a similar reference to eidetic unity and contingent plurality is made in relation, once again, to Dante. To Coleman, she writes: "you [...] seem to have just one long dream through which, with Dantesque terror, man after man goes and disappears in that mad limbo." In the same letter, she observes: "I believe you have only had one lover in your whole life—the one <u>in your head</u>." The image that one is "impaled" upon, in short, is a loved image that bears the imprint of the self, toward which one is eschatologically oriented. Nora's attempt to repair her fractured relationship with Robin is thus envisioned against a final horizon of recovery: "In the resurrection, when we come up looking backward at each other, I shall know you only of all that company" (*Nightwood*, 53). A blasphemous intransigence is recorded here: like Catherine Earnshaw of *Wuthering Heights*, after whom she seems to have been initially named, the ultimate desideratum here is not God, but refracted back to her earthly love.[8] As Ramie Targoff points out, Jesus's words in Matthew 22:25-8 ("For in the resurrection, they neither marry, nor are given in marriage, but are as the angels of God in heaven") have been taken from at least the time of the Renaissance to indicate "no real possibility for a shared afterlife between husbands and wives" (2014, 29). Nora's envisaged reunion with Robin, situating eschatological fulfilment within the framework of same-sex desire, draws angelic-being and sexual *indifference* into proximity. As this chapter will show, the pleromatic body as formulated in *Nightwood*, insofar as it is retrieved in "glorious form," is resituated in a prelapsarian region before the Fall into sexual difference—the very place from which the "damned" are exiled.

The dialectical relation of the body and its own repetition in the image is implicated here in a concomitant dialectic between temporality and eternity. The paralyzed man's attempt to reappropriate his infirm anatomy as glorified image

---

[6] In a letter to Coleman on October 13, 1938, Barnes makes the Freudian observation on the psychic traces embedded in parapraxes: "misreadings are often the unconscious revising, like your mirth for myrrh, like my mouthing lark for mounting."

[7] Barnes also recounts her impression of Salvador Dalí to Daniel Mahoney with a similar turn of phrase: "bandolined moustaches, gold topped cane and all/ the sloe-eyes head completely skimmed of human moisture., bead [beard?] sharp, impaled upon his ego" (1958b).

[8] Plumb notes: "Catherine [...] was later combined with Nora" (*Nightwood: The Original Version*, xii).

ends up functioning as a *memento mori*, bringing to the fore the stigma of death that accompanies the raising of the flesh. This eschatological presentation of the body enables us to retrieve the theological coordinates—often suppressed—that frame the Lacanian mirror-stage. As Lacan himself notes:

> There is something in images that transcends the movement and changeability of life, in the sense that images live on after the death of living beings. According to Antiquity's *nous*, this is one of the first steps of art: that which is mortal is immortalized in statuary. This is also the function that is served in a certain way by the subject's image in my theory of the mirror.
>
> (2015, 351)

The *constitution* of the body itself as Gestalt via a mirrored repetition effectively projects it against the image of its end—that is, in the pleromatic form of the Adult that, *qua* phantasm, will however always remain a "subjunctive delineation" (Butler 1993, 44). In this sense then, the body is always constituted via its eschatological orientation, the flesh anticipatorily refigured in perfected form, of thirty years or not. Prior to the Second Coming, the body in its properly human dimensions, is *always already the body post-Resurrection*, predicated on the negation of its infirm flesh and its sublimation into the vessel of a transfigured double. O'Connor, said to be "dead in the beginning," has, along with Dante, made passage beyond his death to retrieve for himself his posthumous form (*Nightwood*, 137).⁹

The structural genesis of the psychoanalytic body before the mirror thus reformulates the coarticulation of death and resurrection already registered in the sacrament of baptism, which, as the initiation rite into Christendom, mortifies the "body of sin" to raise from it a Christic body, ushered into a "newness of life" that is also "eternal life": Christological Man is produced an imago of God, projected "in the likeness of his death" and "in the likeness of his resurrection" (Romans 6:3-23). To be a body, from Saint Paul to Lacan, is in the first instance to be alienated from the immediate flesh ("whilst we are at home in the body, we are absent from the Lord"), and in the second instance, re-oriented toward the "glorious body" of Christ ("we are [...] willing rather to be absent from the body, and to be present with the Lord"—2 Corinthians 6:6-8). The anthropological minimum here, marked by the entry into the Holy Community of Christic bodies, is the swerve in the eschatological horizon of the embodied

---

⁹ On Dante's "necropolitan pilgrimage to God," see Balsamo 2004, 9-42.

subject from the self-coincident animal to the glorious Other: the manner of one's being-unto-the-end is thus refigured here, dividing those who "live unto themselves" and those who live "unto him which died for them, and rose again" (2 Corinthians 6:15). Dying to itself to be raised *imago Dei*, the body is thereby "clothed upon" (2 Corinthians 5:2): it sheds—to use a Barnesian formula—its organic integument to be re-skinned, on one level, in civilized garments, and on another, in the ethical and spiritual codes of the socio-historical world. Humans, in this sense, have second skins.[10] It is this logic that enables Barnes's facetious characterization of "Eskimos" as animal rather than human, since they can be "killed for their fur" ("Why Actors?" 42–3), and of the fate of "little beasts in their mothers" as lamentable, for "having to step down and begin going decent in the one fur that would last them their time" (*Nightwood*, 94). Robin, on the other hand, becomes the insupportable image of a Venus that would not stay *im Pelz*, an animal slipping from the "'picture' forever arranged" to which she remains precariously pinned: as the eland in spiritual raiment, she is "outside the 'human type'—a wild thing caught in a woman's skin" (*Nightwood*, 131–2).

Melancholy's reference to a soteriological indecision may thus be focalized here as a crisis in corporeal assumption, in the arrested zone interrupting the redemptive arc from the ontologically incomplete to the pleromatic body. The place of "damnation," otherwise put, is lived out in a corporeal limbo *between* skins—that is, expropriated from the hide-bound existence of the Animal, without, however, a corresponding reappropriation into the raiment of glory, *denaturalized* without being *divinized*. Insofar as the self-coincident Animal is seen to remain immersed in nature, the motive O'Connor gives for desisting from stealing one of Jenny's calf-bound books—probably *The Satyricon*—appears slightly less eccentric in this light: 'I might steal the mind of Petronius [...] but never the skin of a calf" (*Nightwood*, 93). As for the Doctor himself, however, he remains in the divided state of transfemininity ("I divorced myself"—*Nightwood*, 138), ek-statically cast from his mammalian masculinity yet "clothed upon" by neither the image of Woman nor of Christic Man, equidistant hence from Animal and God. He resides between bodies, *skinless*, homeless in the home of the flesh yet homeless in the home of the Father, with death alone, as his ersatz refuge: "I was doing well enough [...] until you came along and kicked my stone over, and out I came, all moss and eyes; and here I sit, as naked as only those

---

[10] See also Barnes's gloss on her poetic image of Absalom's death: "I always feel that the dead body is second body to the living." Like her melancholic Doctor, she finds herself in posthumous existence: "I should be writing about Absalom, when I myself was hanged long ago" (1938h).

things can be, whose houses have been torn away from them to make a holiday, and it my only skin" (*Nightwood*, 138).[11] The place of the "damned" is, therefore, of ontological exile; its ontic analogue is the "outhouse." As the Doctor descants: "I haunt the *pissoirs* as naturally as Highland Mary her cows down by the Dee" (*Nightwood*, 81–2).

The margin—or "difference"—between the "glorious form" one is "impaled" upon and the infirm organism is thus implicated not just in a general question of "love," but also in *soteriological desire* in particular. The purgatorial interval, between the self and its transfigured image, disrupts the consummation of love, which, in the definition that Nora ventures, is perhaps "Man seeking his own head": "The human head, so rented by misery that even the teeth weigh!" (*Nightwood*, 122). This open region of the body's non-coincidence later comes back to her when her pursuit for Robin—said to be "incest," "like a relative found in another generation"—leads her to a young girl in Naples:

> Looking from her to the Madonna behind the candles, I knew that the image, to her, was what I had been to Robin, not a saint at all, but a fixed dismay, the space between the human and the holy head, the arena of the "indecent" eternal.
> (*Nightwood*, 141–2)

Sexual and soteriological desire are mapped out in parallel in this doubled reflection, with a coordinated fault-line between woman and image: Nora's paralysis—in "fixed dismay"—in the limbo that divides "the human and the holy head," is Robin's vision given back to her through her own eyes witnessing the failure of the Madonna to coincide with herself, and who hence falls asunder into the two parts of her transcendent significance and her material vessel, stalled, therefore, before her own "saint[hood]." The structural homology of two missed encounters discloses the invisible "space between," the "arena" where the agonistic tension toward grace tows in the "eternal" into a warped—even "indecent"—eternity of anticipation: from out of this girl's gaze, Nora retrieves the Madonna *manquée* of herself in Robin's gaze.

This revelation of love through a crossing of the gaze on the plane of the divine discloses the transferential frame that supports these mirror-identifications. *How one loves*, it is suggested, is informed by *how one is loved*, just as *what one loves* is informed by *what is loved in one*. Nora's love for Robin is situated where Robin's

---

[11] See also Daniel Mahoney's own description of his plight to Barnes in his September 8, 1950, letter: "I am always happier in rainy weather—less exposed somehow. When it is fine, I always feel like some poor old crustacean with its shell pulled off" (cited in Herring 1995, 213).

love is: "I said to myself, I will do what she has done, I will love what she has loved, then I will find her again" (*Nightwood*, 141). Locating herself in Robin's field of desire, Nora retrieves it eventually in the disrupted soteriological relation between a girl in Naples and her Madonna. I will go on in this chapter to examine this soteriological relation that binds the subject to her/his Other, but note for now the importance of the function of transferential love in Lacan's conceptualization of the mirror-stage. As he writes: "It is inasmuch as the third party, the Other with a capital O, intervenes in the relationship between the ego and the other with a lowercase o that something can function that gives rise to the fecundity of the narcissistic relationship itself" (2015, 353). The attachment to one's specular reflection is *mediated by* the Big Other. This is to say that the "Other's gaze" is from the outset "internalized" in the bond between the subject and her image, implicating hence the "ideal ego" ("an imaginary projection") within a realm of significance, as the "ego-ideal" ("a symbolic introjection."—Lacan 2015, 356). Deploying Freud's term—*ein einziger Zug*—Lacan conceptualizes this "reference to the Other" already present in the narcissistic relation as the "single trait" that sutures the organism to its reconstituted form (2015, 355). The "sign of the Other's assent" is thus sedimented in the apparition of the glorious body, libidinally legible where the gaze of subject and Other "coincide": *I love myself where S/he loves me*. The *einzige Zug* may thus be reformulated in Barnesian terms as the point where the subject is "impaled" upon her eschatological form.

Robin's love for Nora and the Neapolitan girl therefore find a point of intersection in their common reference to the Madonna, albeit one that falls short of her own saintly image. As I go on to show, it is in this fault in the Other that the interval between the subject and her significant form—or *significant other*, as it were—is aggravated, ushering in a soteriological crisis that leaves the body precariously suspended alongside the image it fails to assume. Citing Karl Barth's observation that Christological Man, as *imago Dei*, "signifies an *analogia relationis* rather than an *analogia entis*," Carl Raschke writes that the human being is, therefore, "ontologically constituted as a relationship" (Raschke 2014, 59). The disruption of this soteriological relation, in a co-implicated crisis of subjectivity and the sovereign Other, thus produces the panoply of bodies of the "damned" in *Nightwood*, misshapen torsions of the glorious image, exceeding or untethered from its lineaments, all on the cusp of a humanity they fail to fully assume. Whether—as with Nikka's black body—inscribed over with salvifically drained words ("hack-work of the devil") and images ("an angel from Chartres"), skinned over with a taut "bodice" to become "unsexed as a doll" (Frau Mann), prostheticized with a "pine board" (as with the legless Mademoiselle Basquette), cross-sexed (Doctor O'Connor), cross-speciesed (from Robin to the Breton cow and "the horse who knew too much"), or, in fact, simply Jewish (Felix, Guido), these denizens of the night incarnate a theologico-political critique of the image of Man itself (*Nightwood*, 14–15, 12, 23–4, 102).

In the following, I direct my critique of soteriological desire toward a comparative disambiguation of the pleromatic body of the Aryan forged by the Fascist imaginary and the volatile body of *Nightwood*'s transfeminine Doctor. That a certain link between conquest—here, Fascism in particular—and art is suggested by Barnes herself on the basis of a common root in the infirm body raises the question of where and how the "power of the deformed"—of "Toulouse[-]Lautrec, Gaugin, Rimbaud, Verlaine, Proust," on the one hand— may be distinguished from that of "Napoleon, Hitler, Mussolini" on the other (1938i). She observes in her October 30, 1938, letter to Coleman:

> note all great conquerors, Mussolini (sexually all right perhaps, but—) Hitler, (hasnt a mouses [*sic*] rations in his trousers I understand) Napoleon, <u>nearly all geniuses something damned in them sexually</u>, so that the instinct, or whatever it is, leads them onto other roads, and better ones, degrade the sex instinct enough and it becomes vulgar crime, or bragging at best, like D'Anunzio [*sic*], George Moore, the Marquis of Senningalt (?) de Sade thinking hes [*sic*] being mighty by using whip and match, or perhaps a Hitler and a Napoleon should be in the most degraded class, not above it where Jack the Ripper takes satisfaction immediately on the body of three or more children,—Hitler, Napoleon need to ravage a world,—all beauty and all ugliness (?) seems to come from the physically "deformed."

In her own throwaway contribution to the discourse of degeneration popularized in the preceding decades by Max Nordau and Cesare Lombroso, Barnes ends up reducing all "<u>genius</u>"—whether aesthetic or military—to the common denominator of "the physically 'deformed.'" Where its etiology is further specified in terms of "the sex instinct," Barnes's critical attention seems to hone in on the libidinal redirection from the mortal flesh to its sublimated substitutes ("other roads, and better ones"), associated with world-making desires, whether manifested in the production of a textual or colonized, "ravage[d] [...] world," in which the redoubled body might live. As formulated in an earlier letter, the "deformed" body attaches all the more vehemently— and *creatively*—to its projected double in glory: "inferiority complex [...] made Napoleon, Mussonini [*sic*], Hitler, etc and gives hunch-backs a feeling that they are Gods [*sic*] miracles, not errors" (1938d). Sexual deficiency from Hitler's measly share to Mussolini's passable one prompts the ersatz production of everything from the Sadean whip, Post-Impressionist painting, French Symbolism and its Decadent precedents, to the military imagination and serial infanticide. Insofar as physical deformities render the ontologically incomplete status of the organism more acute, its typological completion in the repeated form of its glorious double may go down the direction of "beauty" or "ugliness." Some spiritual significance may be attached to the aesthetic discrimination referenced here. Having ventured a tentative distinction between the "ugly" and the "beautiful," Barnes elaborates with another ambivalent formula: these "geniuses" bear "the holy imprint of the Devil hoof." The turn from anatomical mediocrity onto "other roads" is signaled by a metaphysical trace, indeterminately condensed here into that which is both "holy" and "of the Devil." If a common expropriation from the mortal flesh is indicated by the rebus of this "holy Devil hoof," which way one turns—toward "beauty" or "ugliness"—it seems, is still open to be determined. This turn, as suggested, lies in the eschatological orientation toward the glorious body of God, or the Devil. As Catherine Pickstock observes, the fact that the body is constituted via an original repetition through which the Other is internalized leaves it structurally open to alterity: it is always already "possessed"—always already available to be repossessed or dispossessed—by the *divine* or the *diabolic*, in the image of Christ or his double, the Antichrist (2013, 124). The crisis in corporeal assumption thus involves several dimensions: it is possible to remain sutured to an image of salvation that is never attained, leaving one "damned" in the interim, or, in a tragic turn, to reorient oneself eschatologically toward an image of Death, in devotion to, as it were, a "god of darkness" (*Nightwood*, 114). A third possibility, as will be seen, lies in the way of another kind of false redemption: the body can also be given over to the ersatz God of the fascist leader.[12]

I move on, in the following, to a critique of the libidinal structure of *narcissism* that undergirds fascism and the production of its corporeal idols, to disambiguate it from the soteriological crisis of *hysteria*, which structures the Doctor's simultaneous attachment to and inquisition of his God. In contrasting the "fascist body" with the "hysterical body," I seek to account for the psychic logic co-implicating narcissism and fascist eschatology in order to dissociate it from the expressive enactment of hysteria in O'Connor, and in so doing, offer

---

[12] As Wolfe points out, Hitler at times frames himself as the redeemer: "Thus I believe myself to be acting on behalf of the almighty Creator: By resisting the Jew, I fight [*kämpfe*] for the work of the Lord" (cited in Wolfe 2013, 312).

a revisionary account of the novel's political unconscious. Placing narcissism beside hysteria—and, as will be seen, their bodily correlates of Nazism's "blond beast" and *Nightwood*'s "damned beasts"—is thus an attempt to disambiguate two psycho-political states of mind, whilst taking into account that their disparate strategies of synthesizing fracture and revolt nevertheless relate to a specific dialectic of woundedness and cure. Both narcissism and hysteria bind the split subject to the figure of the sovereign in a soteriological relation. However, where the narcissist disavows the lack internal to his constitution in the identification with his idol, the hysteric, though placed in the field of the sovereign's desire, ultimately foregrounds the failure of the redemptive promise encoded in this relation.

Of Beasts Blond and Damned

In her peremptory writ to James Scott on April 1, 1972, Barnes launches the following accusation: "I want you to subdue your genital solution for everything—but <u>everything</u>!"[13] While the ostensible targets here are the reductive readings proposed by the literary critic, a strident metaleptic reference nonetheless comes through: the "genital solution" of critical reduction is likened to the "Final Solution" of Nazi eschatology. That a certain psychoanalytic logic informs this comparison is suggested not just in the encryption of a Freudian "genital stage" here, but also in Barnes's earlier accusations targeting Scott for his "superficial drive [...] to drag the author back his or her works to confront him or her at the porch of the mother" (Barnes 1971b). Decades earlier, repeated allusions to "the Hitler complex" or "'little Hitler' complex" (1939i)—applied quite often, though not exclusively, to her mother[14]—suggest a capability on Barnes's part to engage in psychoanalytic diagnostics, often flippant though occasionally also earnest, on issues running the gamut of Freudian motifs from ego-development and mass psychology to infantile sexuality and narcissism.[15]

In her reference to the Final Solution of the Nazis, Barnes locates the Queer alongside the Jew as figures of embodied otherness in opposition to the mythic

---

[13] A variant of this section has been published in *Twentieth-Century Literature* (Ng 2020b).
[14] Stephen of Cloyes, a "shepherd boy" who led the 1212 Children's Crusade, is also "like Hitler etc." Barnes misdates the Crusade to the twelfth century (1942b).
[15] In her December 15, 1938, letter to Coleman, Barnes reports: "I've read the psychoanalysts from time to time, a bit here, a bit there, all of them, but of course I would have to go through them again and properly ... dont [sic] recall much, case history makes me sick, the one on dreams (not the popular one) and cant [sic] recall who wrote it."

Aryan body. As the term "genital" seems to suggest, the Adult that figures at the end of a Freudian teleology of the drives, whereby pre-maturational "polymorphous perversity" is subdued to its hierarchical configuration in later life, is considered a form of violent foreclosure. As narrated in Freud's *Three Essays on the Theory of Sexuality* (1905), the final image of the body that one is to inhabit is genitally centered, with the libidinal disorder of the maturational process brought to order, delivered over to a procreative end, enabling the disavowal of individual finitude in favor of the fetish of reproductive immortality (*SE* VII, 191). Barnes's irate epithet thus imbricates the Freudian Adult with the Nazi Aryan. A preliminary delineation of a corporeal eschatology may already be found here: desire is directed toward its immortal fetish, given in the image of the Adult or the Aryan, ensuring both racial continuity and the millennial reign of the Reich. The Freudian *Endlust,* in gerrymandering the corporeal map of the drives, works in tandem with the *Endlösung* that gerrymanders the map of the world, redistributing—or annexing, rather—*Lebensraum* along purportedly "racial" lines. Both the body and the body politic are organized here in the fabrication of idols promising redemption (*Erlösung*). Judith Wolfe's account of the messianic heritage of modern European thought thus points out that the "identification of eschatological kingdom with earthly *Reich*, and the consequent need for its political and military realization, is a foundation stone of National Socialist ideology" (2013, 311).

Barnes's formula of a "genital solution" postdates *Nightwood*, and quite likely draws on her later reading of ideological critiques of the Third Reich in texts by Kenneth Burke, Simone Weil, Hannah Arendt, and also William Shirer's best-selling *The Rise and Fall of the Third Reich* (1960), which is particularly emphatic on the ideological sequence from Nietzsche and Wagner to Hitler. An account of the narcissistic libidinal structure operative in Nazism, alongside its eschatological promise, is, however, already present in Wyndham Lewis's *Hitler*, published in 1931, the same year in which Barnes's attempt to interview the latter falls through (Herring 1995, 177). In Lewis's reconstruction of the "'Blonde Beast' theory," narcissistic identification serves to actualize the mythic body of the *Volk* in the living tissue of its members (Lewis 1931, 132). Within their metaphysical framework of "*Blutsgefühl*," these "germanic blood-mystics" are said to "desir[e] a *closer and closer* drawing together of the people of one race and culture," into a "true bodily solidarity." The "bodily attraction" involved here is depicted as a mutually implicating dynamic of inclusion and exclusion. Blood, sinew, and neurons are synchronized as the "alien interference" is expelled:

> Identical rhythms in the arteries and muscles, and in the effective neural instrument—that should provide us with a passionate *exclusiveness*, with a homogeneous social framework, within the brotherly bounds of which we could live secure from alien interference[.]
>
> (Lewis 1931, 106–7)

In this "brotherly" hall of mirrors, bodies, in imitation of each other, reproduce the units of individual Aryans who, agglomerated into a "homogeneous" whole, bring into existence the Aryan *Volk*: both the single body and the body politic are here produced as a function of mimesis. Nazism's racial body, the fetish object of a "cult of the Kolossal," could thus "find a place in the anatomical cosmogonies of Hildegard [von Bingen]" (Lewis 1939, 63). Its desire is eschatological in its attempt to recreate a "Golden Age" of the past in the future, if not the present (Lewis 1939, 129). Out of the numerous misfires of Lewis's analyses of the political project of Nazism, an astute account of a corporeal myth invoking narcissistic investment to encode a specific racial eschatology emerges.

With a different critical apparatus, this forms the crux of Andrew Hewitt's argument that a "textbook Lacanian *objet a*" is lodged in Nazism's "mythic objects of desire"—most notably, its *völkisch* body—the attainment of which marks the end of history, the overcoming of the lack incurred upon entrance into the symbolic order, and the passage to redemptive Being. In this case, the split subject of history is phantasmatically overcome in the whole subject as the political body of the Aryan:

> If the fascist projects the condition of subjectivity into a mythic future as the representation of a racially purified *Volk*, he nevertheless performs subjectivity in the very act of that representation. The political collective is both the object of a mythic representation and the subject of that act of representation. The *Volk* is not merely that which will come, but the collective of those who await its coming. In other words, the desiring structure of fascism is specific not in its projection of the condition of subjectivity [...] but in its performative reversal of the condition of lack, in its organization of those who lack Being into the collective subject on the *Zeppelinfeld*. What is specific to fascism is not, then, its mythification of political subjectivity or its inability to constitute a political subject, but quite the reverse—its *enactment* of subjectivity, its withdrawal of political subjectivity from the semiosis of a representation into the immanence of a performance.
>
> (Hewitt 1996, 202)

The "enactment" or "performance" of the Aryan body, as a temporal contradiction that is at once *projective* and immediately *present*—a contradiction that is as such disavowed in the very staging of the acquisition of the mythic body—leaps over the moment of disruption in the Lacanian model of identification to collapse into the fetishized political body. The impossibility of this move in the Lacanian account, which preserves a dialectic of identification and dis-identification, is suppressed in these transfigurative rites on the Nazi assembly grounds in Nuremberg, likened by Lewis to nothing less than the "'Nordic' temples" of Hitler the "Jingo God" (Lewis 1939, ix). Citing Alfred Rosenberg's claim—"Odin is dead, but in another way, as essence of the German soul, Odin is resuscitating before our very eyes"—Hewitt holds that the "characteristic of Nazism [...] is to have proposed its own movement, its own State, as the effective realization of a myth, or as a living myth" (Hewitt 1996, 18). The political body of the "Blonde Beast," together with its constituent units, is thus resurrected.

The foregoing analysis encodes the specifically bodily element to what Saul Friedländer has termed the "redemptive anti-Semitism" of Nazi ideology (2003, 18). Distinct from previous forms of "racial anti-Semitism," it integrates an "apocalyptic dimension" that enables the formulation of a Final Solution (2003, 18). Narcissistic merger, in eliminating the interval between the absent political subject of Nazism and its eschatologically realized form, recovers the pleromatic Aryan body in ritualistic performance. Roberto Esposito hence characterizes "totalitarianism" as "the phantasmatic temptation of abolishing the limit, of filling in the fault, of closing the wound" such that the "community might be definitively healed of its melancholy" (2013, 29–30). The joyous fascist body is thus produced out of a soteriological relation with the sovereign, whose several faces—*qua* Führer or Odin, Aryan or "Blonde Beast"—serve as the fetish objects that enjoin its subjects in the mimesis of its own form, both promising and presenting in the process undivided Being out of the wounds of history. Disabling the production of this restored body of the Reich by turning away from the "phantasmatic temptation of closing the wound" thus names a restructuration of the political unconscious—that is, from narcissism to hysteria.

As I have suggested above, the attribution of a narcissistic libidinal structure to the various characters of *Nightwood* is not entirely unwarranted.[16] In 1935, toward the end of her long and meticulous editing of the novel, Emily Coleman cites a passage from George Barker's "The Bacchant" to Barnes, indicating its similarity to *Nightwood*'s "prince-princess in point lace.' The overcoming of lack that narcissism promises is, in the subject's self-encounter in the mirror, formulated as an overcoming of sexual difference:

---

[16] For readings of *Nightwood* in relation to narcissism, see Carlston 1998; Rupprecht 2006.

> within the confines of that long mirror lives entombed a person wavering between the feminine and masculine, whom I adore. My God, how impossibly secure that person lives, behind a cold wall of impenetrable thinness! I could with a passionate hand this moment burst that wall open to attain to him, to her, and find, dark on the wall, like my despair, my shadow.
>
> (Coleman 1935b)

Coleman's observation is on point. This eschatological trajectory of the body from its divided state *qua* sexed mortal toward the salvific recovery of the whole body is one that has made its way from Plato's *Symposium* and Gregory of Nyssa's theology to Heinrich von Kleist's "On the Marionette Theatre" (1810) and Lacanian psychoanalysis, inflecting also Barnes's thoughts on sexual difference and desire. She writes to Coleman in 1938:

> Why angels were made men that they should grow is a mystery to me, does the long falling down make them better? It shouldn't, but perhaps in heaven (?) angels are to that place what babies are to our world, they must grow up, for tho [sic] children are pretty dreadful (they are not those n[i]ce pink bottomed little angels that people like to make out, they squash flies and tear dragons [sic] wings off, and occasionally drown their brothers and sisters in a frenzy of childish experiment and amusement) but they are not learned, is learning the whole plan?
>
> (1938g)

Characteristic of Barnes here is the synchronization of salvational and ontogenetic histories: divine creation and human procreation form the departure gates from which angels and babies make their passage into sexed, mortal beings via the Fall. The questions remain: is it a *felix culpa*? If innocence in children is not to be found, is perfection to be sought in the formative process of becoming-Adult? Does the "whole plan"—or Divine Economy—lie in the production of neo-angelic bodies through "learning," understood in the larger sense of a spiritual education or *Geistesbildung*? In the conception of the cross-dressing Matthew O'Connor as an "angel on all fours," and again as an "uninhabited angel" (*Nightwood*, 85, 134), *Nightwood*'s response is to disrupt the eschatological trajectory of the body from its mortal, sexed form to its pleromatic fulfilment as a "glorious body." Such a body, having fallen from the path of salvation history, is not just "disqualified," "*détraqu[é]*," and "excommunicat[ed]," but also "damned" (*Nightwood*, 8, 47, 85). It is within this theological frame that *Nightwood*'s "tales of men who became holy and of beasts that became damned" are to be situated (*Nightwood*, 9). O'Connor's failure to become-angel names the failure of the split subject to accede to its whole body—that is, the fetishistically repaired body that has overcome sexual difference. If narcissism disavows this failure, hysteria brings it to the fore as a dialectic involving two antinomian moments: (i) the *false positivization* of the body, come to fulfilment whether as Aryan, Adult, or angel; (ii) its *negative reversal*, emptying out the putatively "completed" or "whole" body. Hysteria, as such, is founded on a crisis in the soteriological narrative that narcissism pushes to fulfilment. As I will go on to show, the manic switchbacks between angel and beast, condensed into the formula of a haloed quadruped, are productive of an alternative *jouissance* from that of narcissism.

Conscripted into O'Connor's angelology are the transfigured anthropomorphs of the "doll" and the "Prince," both of whom present the supersession of sexed difference. The "prince-princess in point lace" that Coleman refers to is "the pretty lad who is a girl [...] neither one and half the other," and is raised in O'Connor's attempt to explain "this love we have for the invert, boy or girl":

> The girl lost, what is she but the Prince found? The Prince on the white horse that we have always been seeking. [...] We love them for that reason. We were impaled in our childhood upon them as they rode through our primers, the sweetest lie of all, now come to be in boy or girl, for in the girl it is the prince, and in the boy it is the girl that makes a prince a prince—and not a man. They go far back in our lost distance where what we never had stands waiting; it was inevitable that we should come upon them, for our miscalculated longing has created them. They are our answer to what our grandmothers were told love was, and what it never came to be; they, the living lie of our centuries.
>
> (*Nightwood*, 123-4)

The prince *qua* "Prince" presents a prelapsarian body that has not suffered the wound of sexual difference. Located "far back in our lost distance," s/he stands in as the primordial desideratum in the prehistory of the split subject, reached for during pre-maturational childhood and again, phantasmatically, in the present. Like the "last doll," who, as "the girl who should have been a boy, and the boy who should have been a girl," s/he is "foreshadowed in that love of the first [doll]," presented during childhood (*Nightwood*, 133-4). The overcoming of sexed finitude exhibited by the "glorious bodies" of these anthropomorphs, however, is also explicitly formulated by O'Connor as "the living lie of our centuries"—a statement that encapsulates, as it were, the hysteric's critique of narcissistic desire. It is partially accounted for via a genealogical explanation (handed down by "our grandmothers"), and adduced additionally to desire's eschatological bent, never satisfied with the objects of this world, and hence its "miscalculated longing."

This exposure of the false positivization of the body accounts for O'Connor's self-ascription of the epithet "uninhabited angel": while directed toward the body's eschatological form, its attainment can lead only to the evacuation of the life of the body itself—its mortal substance. The "third sex," like the "doll" and the "immature," exhibits the body redeemed from sexual difference only to have the life drained from beneath it, in its apocalyptic transcendence of history: "The doll and the immature have something right about them, the doll, because it resembles, but does not contain life, and the third sex, because it contains life but resembles the doll" (*Nightwood*, 133–4). The fetish of the glorious body is thus envisioned, in hysteria, alongside its negative reversal.

While the placement of the hysteric's body "outside sex" has often led to its association with the figure of the "transsexual," Patricia Gherovici's recent contribution to the critical discussion highlights the impossibility of sustaining such a position "*hors sexe*," and hence, the various symptomatic attempts to reconstruct a habitable body (Gherovici 2017, 90–1). The logic of hysteria involves both positive and negative moments, between which the subject moves in the making and unmaking of the body. Affinities between Lacan's conceptualization of hysteria and *Nightwood*'s O'Connor emerge here through their reference to a common literary and religious tradition, culminating in the Surrealist reclamation of hysteria in the 1928 edition of *La Révolution surréaliste*. In an article commemorating "The Fiftieth Anniversary of Hysteria," co-signed by André Breton and Louis Aragon, two key features of this "supreme means of expression" are raised: (i) "the subversion of the links established between the subject and the moral world"; and (ii) its basis in a "reciprocal seduction" (Breton and Aragon 1928, 22).[17] Hysteria, understood as a specific kind of social bond, involving paradoxically attraction and refusal, "seduction" and "subversion," becomes formalized by Lacan as a "signifier link" or a "signifying articulation" between the split subject ($) and the sovereign (S1) (Lacan 2007b, 89, 94–5). This aporetic relationship complicates the libidinal structure of narcissism insofar as the moment of "seduction" between subject and sovereign is at the same time "subverted," in effect, negating the production of the pleromatic body. Hysteria, unlike narcissism, foregrounds a ruptured soteriology.

The Lacanian account of hysteria thus points to the body's traversal by contrary vectors directed toward positivization and negation. Projected, on the one hand, into the form of an uncanny anthropomorph—"*l'être-ange* [being-an-angel]" (Lacan 1998, 8)—the hysteric mobilizes, on the other hand, "the body's

---

[17] The same issue contains an extract from Breton's novel, *Nadja*, whose name is given to *Nightwood*'s Princess Nadja.

refusal," and "goes on a kind of strike" (Lacan 2007b, 94). In the moralizing accents of Lorenzo Chiesa's formulation, *l'être-ange* is "a deceitful mirage of ontotological reconciliation that would eliminate sexual difference through the body as One [...] the hysterical angel intends to occupy the mythical place of the desexualized partner of the noncastrated and hence fully enjoying Father, who would thus be himself asexual" (Chiesa 2016, 11). The hysterical subject is bound to the sovereign in a soteriological relation. In their co-habitation of a fantasy of wholeness wherein sexual difference might be superseded, they produce, as it were, the glorious couple of Father and angel in a bond of mutual repletion. The hysterical angel thus stands in as "the alleged essence of femininity" to be "the fusional partner of the Father/Phallus." Her body is projected against the image of "the being-One of a chimerical body" (Chiesa 2016, 128, 3).

Chiesa's work, however, tends to operate by constructing static models based on Lacan's "logic of sexuation," the drawbacks of which are at least twofold: how these models relate to the complexities of living subjects are often cursorily indicated or even reductively assumed.[18] Furthermore, the antinomies internal to their structure lead more often to complacent judgment than to an examination of how these models push beyond their own boundaries—that is to say, folded within them are their own dialectical reversals. Chiesa's account of the hysteric focuses unilaterally on the push toward eschatological fulfilment, neglecting, however, the opposing vector of the aforementioned "strike on the body." His claim that the hysteric's only partner is the "noncastrated Father" may thus be set beside Lacan's own statement that the hysteric's discourse "is divided into [...] the castration of the idealized father" and "the assumption, by the subject [...] of the *jouissance* of being deprived" (Lacan 2007b, 99). This forms the crux of his adoption of the Surrealist Paul Éluard's line, "*le dur désir de durer*": by lasting (via a sustained margin of "deprivation") rather than culminating, joy here is located *in time*, instead of an eschatological fulfilment at *the end of time* (Lacan 2007b, 57). These antinomies are operative in O'Connor's relation to his sovereign, none less than God himself, who is said to be both set up and unseated by the hysteric. If both the narcissist and the hysteric deliver their bodies over to their masters in the hope of redemption—be this the Führer or the Father—it is the hysteric finally who, in her interrogation of Him who authorizes her being (and as a result her own ontological status) exposes the ruptured relation between the split subject and the sovereign, and lives out her wounded existence in an alternate mode of enjoyment: this, Barnes names a "hilarious sorrow" (1958b).

---

[18] See especially the rather smug note on "transsexuals" and "the transsexual" (2016, 193).

A page after he refers to himself as "[t]he uninhabited angel," O'Connor makes a political-theological invocation of "the holy Habeas Corpus, the manner in which the body is brought before the judge" (*Nightwood*, 135-6). The legal summons, presented in the subjunctive—"have you the body"—is relocated onto spiritual ground, setting up a divine court of judgment to which the subject is interpellated.[19] The bond between the Father and his subject is distilled here into a relation between mortal body and holy judge, exhibited on the stage of O'Connor's spiritual theater. The result, here as elsewhere, is not just the mortifying exposure of the inadequacy of the angel's fallen body, but also the "castration of the idealized father" himself, disrupting thereby the soteriological relation between subject and sovereign: "pray to the good God, she will keep you. Personally I call her 'she' because of the way she made me; it somehow balances the mistake" (*Nightwood*, 135). Remaking the God who "made" him/her in *her own image*, O'Connor irreverently implements a *quid pro quo* justice to even out the botched patches of Creation. The hysteric, we might say, in both setting up her God and removing the pedestal from under his feet, takes ironic and critical distance from her own libidinal structure. O'Connor's body, shuttling between its eschatologically realized form and its subsequent mortification, is alternately positivized and negated, pushed toward repletion yet drawn back and depleted: as "the last woman left in this world," he is continually, yet inconstantly, projected against the images of a fast-volatilizing glory (*Nightwood*, 90). His phantasmatic presentations of the Absolute Woman are thus continually ironized: "it was a high soprano I wanted," he croons, "and deep corn curls to my bum, with a womb as big as the king's kettle, and a bosom as high as the bowsprit of a fishing schooner." On the contrary: "what do I get but a face on me like an old child's bottom" (*Nightwood*, 81). Of opera and its making of the "Diva," he muses: "there's something wrong with any art that makes a woman all bust!" (*Nightwood*, 92). The Father's interpellation of the angelic body produces not its pleromatic form, but an ironic exhibition that burlesques His desire as an interrogative strategy, mounting, as such, hilarity over sorrow. The "holy Habeas Corpus" thus opens up a histrionic space in which the vicissitudes of the relation between the split subject and the sovereign, ruptured yet retained, play out, and is perhaps most strikingly witnessed in O'Connor's missed encounter with God in the St Merri Church, to which I now turn.

Ellie Ragland-Sullivan has characterized the hysteric's predicament as the simultaneous demand for "affective proof of an ontological place" and a

---

[19] See also 2 Corinthians 5:10.

self-sabotaging refusal of any answers that might come by way of the sovereign (Ragland-Sullivan 1988, 77). Her interrogative repertoire thus includes: "Who am I?"; "What do I want?"; "Am I man or woman?" O'Connor, described as a "volatile person," requires incontrovertible proof of his ontological status (*Nightwood*, 16). Affects are the privileged indicators here given the immediacy by which they are received. No such phenomenological guarantee or "revelation," however, comes to him despite his divine solicitation: his blasphemous apostrophe—"O Book of Concealment"—alludes to the occlusion of the sovereign's desire (*Nightwood*, 120).[20] O'Connor's demand relates to the Real itself, that which may be extricated from time as his perdurable essence, the place of God's desire: "So tell me, what is permanent of me, me or him?"—that is, his speaking self, or "Tiny O'Toole," cephalus or phallus (*Nightwood*, 120). His eclectic songbook, ranging from Paisiello to Schubert and emerging in snippets through *Nightwood*, now seems to reverberate as the lyrical accompaniment to the hysterical *idée fixe*: "*Chi vuol la Zingarella* (how women love it!) [...] *Who is Sylvia?* Who is anybody!" (*Nightwood*, 139). The disruption of the antiphonal call and response between subject and sovereign foils the eschatological and erotic union coded in his earlier allusion to the biblical Song of Songs: "Why is it that whenever I hear music I think I'm a bride?" (*Nightwood*, 29). O'Connor is bride here to an absconded Father. Invoking the presence of God, he enters the box pew in St Merri "for the souls in Purgatory," and pulls out his penis, which becomes his one co-actor on this tragicomic stage:

> Kneeling in a dark corner, bending my head over and down, I spoke to Tiny O'Toole, because it was his turn, I had tried everything else. There was nothing for it this time but to make him face the mystery so it could see him clear as it saw me. So then I whispered, "What is this thing, Lord?" And I began to cry; the tears went like rain goes down on the world, without touching the face of Heaven. Suddenly I realized that it was the first time in my life my tears were strange to me, because they just went straight forward out of my eyes; I was crying because I had to embarrass Tiny like that for the good it might do to him. [...] And there I was holding Tiny, bending over and crying, asking the question until I forgot, and went on crying, and I put Tiny away then, like a ruined bird, and went out of the place and walked looking at the stars that were twinkling, and I said, "Have I been simple like an animal, God, or have I been thinking?"
> (*Nightwood*, 119–20)

---

[20] Like John of Patmos in Revelation 10:9, O'Connor, too, has "eaten a book [...] a bitter book" (*Nightwood*, 115).

O'Connor's visit to the church is in fact prompted in the first place by an ecclesiastical demand in the person of Father Lucas: "Be simple, Matthew, life is a simple book, and an open book, read and be simple as the beasts in the field" (*Nightwood*, 118). Being one with Nature, presumably, would resolve the predicament of his divided self, a mind–body opposition common to all but brought to acuity here by its sexed inflection, explaining hence his later outcry, after Dostoevsky's Underground Man: "To think is to be sick" (*Nightwood*, 142). The angel's "being-One of a chimerical body" is envisioned here as the undivided body of the Animal. The Father's final desideratum, "simpl[ifying]," as it were, the cross-dressing human being to its bare coordinates, marks out and encloses the mere life in him. O'Connor, however, parses this demand into its antinomian moments: "[t]his is a terrible thing that Father Lucas has put on me—be simple like the beasts and yet think and harm nobody" (*Nightwood*, 118).

A dialogue between the soul and body in the person of a transfeminine doctor who professes himself "as good a Catholic as they make," but also something of a "mystic" and a "charlatan," takes place in St Merri (*Nightwood*, 139, 28). A complex libidinal map emerges: at one level, O'Connor seems to be humiliating himself as a last resort ("I had tried everything else") by exposing his aberrant penis before the Father's gaze, in a kind of spiritual discipline after Saint Ignatius of Loyola, who finds a devotee in Felix Volkbein; on another, he seems to be vacating himself into a trance-like state, drawing himself close to the condition of the "animal" by crying and "asking the question until I forgot"; on yet another level another kind of joy seems to accrue to his masochistic self-exhibition: "It is I, my Lord, who know there's beauty in any permanent mistakes like me" (*Nightwood*, 119). The ostensible aim here is the conversion of "Tiny O'Toole"— and by synecdochal extension, himself—from desiring men to, possibly, desiring women, but primarily to desiring God. In the morphological reconception of his body, from something of a woman to something of a man, O'Connor delivers himself over to the desire of his sovereign: his genitalia, isolated here as the putative cause of his inversion—and perversion ("*c'est le plaisir qui me bouleverse!*")—emerges from this process a "ruined bird" (*Nightwood*, 120).

In Ellis Hanson's study of *Decadence and Catholicism*, the "hysterical symptom" is raised in relation to "spiritualization": the hysteric, modeled after Christ, "experiences through the symptom an irruption of the Real on the body, a fragmentation of the familiar fantasy of the body to make way for another, more occult fantasy" (Hanson 1997, 122). The "familiar fantasy of the body," *qua* genitally organized, is dismantled to be reconfigured in the light of Christ's body. The devotional practice of *imitatio Christi* thus takes place via the libidinal rearticulation of the subject, often displacing the centers of affective intensity from the genitals to the "stigmatic wounds on the body of Christ" (Hanson 1997, 123). This is where "hysterical conversion" and "religious conversion" meet: in the body's exposure to the "Real," conceived here as the enigmatic signifiers of the Lord's desire, the subject is mortified to be reconfigured in the image of His desire. Hanson's formulation does, however, seem to interrupt a "genital solution" in favor of a Christological one. Insofar as hysteria ultimately ruptures its soteriological relation with the sovereign, the refiguration of the invert's body into that of the convert fails to be sustained as a final solution to wounded existence. The fact that the pleromatic body of Christ is often exhibited with the ostentation of his wounds suggests that the mimetic forms of its subjects might not after all be fully consolidated.[21] The wounded body, rather than the whole body, preempts the false reconciliation that would resolve the predicament of the split subject: without an eschatological resolution, the hysterical conversions the body might undergo continue *in time*.

Sexual difference, for Barnes, implicates bodies in both infinitude and finitude, projecting, on the one hand, the eschatological image of the undivided angel, while, on the other hand, placing the spiritual ceiling *this* side of it, where the subject remains lodged. The body that reconceives itself in the image of the whole is also a self-negating body, living out its changing libidinal zones. As given in Barnes's cryptic formulation to Coleman:

> what the artist craves is the beautiful untruth, that might be made reality, and then, were it so made, would discharge, like the ink-fish, his venom against that, and make another. Man hangs downward, the stalactite wishing to join his stalagmite, sex the double deposit, trying to reach the circle of the whole.
>
> (1938h)

The "circle of the whole," however, does not come to fulfilment so long as "sex," broken into a "double deposit," remains the stigma of ontological division, geologically figured here in the open region between "stalactite" and "stalagmite" where the "artist" writes and unwrites, inks out and inks out his or her "reality." The absence of *the* sexual relation that would produce the pleromatic body thus coincides in the hysteric with the absence of *the* soteriological relation between subject and sovereign. In the same letter, Barnes remarks wryly on her numerous idiosyncratic formulations: "the value of my mind (such as it is) is that

---

[21] Many examples of these from the French Middles Ages are printed and discussed in relation to the Last Judgment in *The Gothic Image* (Mâle 1961, 365–89).

it wanders! (Matthew). [...] What nonsense I am writing—losing my mind no doubt, along with kidneys, liver etc." Likening her own manic thought processes to those of O'Connor suggests that Barnes's understanding of speech and writing in relation to the open wound bears affinities to the unlicensed doctor's avowal that he cannot really heal: "I am no herbalist, I am no Rutebeuf, I have no panacea" (*Nightwood*, 17). Continually solicited for help by the suffering, his attempts "to take the mortal agony out of their guts" leave him "the greatest liar this side of the moon" (*Nightwood*, 122). Words, in Barnes's account, do not heal or redeem, and are more appropriately inscribed in a "Book of Concealment" rather than Revelation:

> You see now why one must be secret? One must not betray that place, or it will heal up [...] Why did I just say "will heal up"? Thats [*sic*] exactly it, it just came out. The wound in the side of Christ?
>
> (Barnes 1937)

As she later claims in a letter to Edwin Muir: "As I told Eliot, I'm not a 'writer'; once in every twenty years or so, the wound bleeds, that's all" (1957). The artist's corpus is produced out of the confluent tributaries of blood, ink, and text.

The implications of relating Christic wounding to writing and the body may in fact be found graphically exhibited in an eighteenth-century engraving by Joseph Ottinger, which survives, with eight other Ottinger engravings, in the Djuna Barnes Archive (Figure 4.1).

While printmaking is often associated with broad dissemination, consequently shifting value from the material of the artwork to its informing concept—that is, from the substantial body to the replicable form—the inlaying of colored paper and gold foil recuperates to some degree the density of matter that circulation vacates. The supposed Protestant tendency of privileging the word over the body, spirit rather than letter, more conformable to the practice of printmaking, encounters here a reverse force that sediments value onto the page itself. One specific form of engraving is in fact referenced in *Nightwood* to magnetize affect within the body itself: "in the heart of the lover will be traced, as an indelible shadow, that which he loves. In Nora's heart lay the fossil of Robin, intaglio of her identity, and about it for its maintenance ran Nora's blood" (*Nightwood*, 51). Robin's eternal form, incised into Nora's heart as the grooves of a printing plate, brims over with circulating blood-ink. This conjunction of serum and print condenses the libidinal map of the body into a region of affective intensity, redistributing its zones of investment and reshaping its contours and, in this case, delineating the icon of Robin within

Figure 4.1 Joseph Ottinger, *Crucifixion*, c. 1750–1800. © The Authors League Fund and St. Bride's Church, as joint literary executors of the Estate of Djuna Barnes.

Nora herself. In Ottinger's engraving, the prominent fuchsia of Christ's side wound focalizes the gaze onto the source of his sorrow and of humanity's succor, setting in relief (via the literal material addition) the place where the ingress of his body simultaneously signs and secretes the redemptive fluids of his blood—conflated here not so much with the milk and vaginal fluids of medieval piety—but with ink and sweat. Framed by the *arma christi* held up by the cherubs, the ostentation of his stigmatic wounds partakes of the glory indicated by the effulgent gold of his aureole, inlaid as it is with the same material. Pain and glory, mutually conversive, coagulate into affectively dense segments over the body. The Christic body, far from being genitally centered, is traversed by intensities that shatter it into passionate zones, refiguring it as a dynamic patchwork imprinted by the chromatic ciphers of the Real.

Ottinger's engraving is in some ways therefore a collage *avant la lettre*.[22] As developed in the 1930s by the Surrealists, collage, Elza Adamowicz points out, enhances "the fetishistic appeal of part-bodies and the elliptical erotic narratives of advertising images and slogans" via a "cutting and pasting practice" (1998, 11). This fractured and reassembled body disrupts "mimetic models of representation" by unveiling the fault-lines in the constitution of the visible world, breaking up "the normally seamless surface of reality by smashing the mirror and importing the other" into its cracks (1998, 12). Such an aesthetic strategy, moreover, functions in tandem with the political commitment of the Surrealists, expressed with increasing urgency in the thirties in opposition to Nazi encroachment: the "watchword" here, as reiterated by Breton, concerns "transform[ing] imperialist war into civil war" (Breton 1972, 238, 249). Considered in the context of the political formations of the body, Breton's insistence on the redirection of exogenous to endogenous hostilities names the conversion of the integrated body into the body in internecine strife. If Nazism attempts to forge the imperial Aryan body via a suppression of lack, the Surrealist resistance envisions a libidinal reconfiguration that would enervate such a body to supply the critical forces that would preserve the turmoil within the organs of the self and State. That the Surrealist resistance is based on an opposing libidinal model may be observed in Aragon's claim in *Le Paysan de Paris* (1926) that "the geography of pleasure" can "constitute an effective weapon against life's tediums":

---

[22] See also Barnes's faux-woodcut drawing of O'Connor for a chapter in *Ryder* held in the Archive, whose body is covered with tattoos, ink hatchings, and segmented into bright—almost lurid—colors ("The Soliloquy of Dr. Matthew O'Connor," *c.* 1928).

No one has assumed the responsibility of assigning its limits to the *frisson*, of drawing the boundaries of the caress, of charting the territory of ecstasy. All that man has succeeded in extracting so far from the individual experience is a series of vulgar localizations.

(1980, 44)

To unfetter the body from these "vulgar localizations" under the rule of genital primacy, Aragon conjures up alternative cartographies of the body's "erogenous zones," their changeable contours, alongside renewed "meanderings of pleasure." Other "atlases" of being are opened up (1980, 44).

The hierarchical consolidation of these "erogenous zones," to recall, forms for Freud the final image of the Adult body at the end of the history of the drives. Nonetheless, Freud's own admission that "any other part of the skin or mucous membrane can take over the functions of an erotogenic zone" indicates that other regions of the body may be raised into affective centers, opening the "whole body" up once more to be scrambled into another shape. This "displacement," Freud writes, is common to the production of "erotogenic" and "hysterogenic zones" (*SE* VII, 183–4). The body, in short, may be converted by pleasure and by pain. Freud's observation that hysteria "behaves as though anatomy did not exist" is elaborated by Lacan: the body of the hysteric, fallen from its angelic apotheosis, is riven along various "lines of 'fragilization,'" suffering an "aggressive disintegration" that simultaneously enables its morphological reconstitution via an "organ-morphic symbolism" (cited in Gherovici 2017, 74). It is, in this sense, put together as an assemblage of interactive organs, affects, and ideas—that is, "confusions," as the Doctor diagnoses:

> I, as a medical man, know in what pocket a man keeps his heart and soul, and in what jostle of the liver, kidneys and genitalia these pockets are pilfered. There is no pure sorrow. Why? It is bedfellow to lungs, lights, bones, guts and gall!
>
> (*Nightwood*, 20)

Here, the "heart and soul," first displaced into the "pocket[s]," are subsequently "pilfered" therefrom by the spasmodic intensities—some kind of "jostle"—of other organs, producing a changing morphology. This scrambled anatomy of the volatile body is most attributable to the "volatile person" of O'Connor himself, unable to drop ontological anchor in relation to his vitiated sovereign. Incapable of situating himself in relation to the Father's desire, he avows: "this lover has committed the unpardonable error of not being able to exist" (*Nightwood*, 84). In the company of his "Sodomites," who, he knows, cannot love him since "it's a woman loving one of them," he "comes down [...] a dummy in their arms"—that is, another fallen anthropomorph, an empty form of life (*Nightwood*, 83-4). The hysteric fails to exist since her only partner is a sovereign who also does not exist: her "ontological status as pure in-existence," Chiesa points out, means that she only "*in-exists* [...] in relation to [mere] *man*" since her postulated partner is none less than the Father (Chiesa 2016, 126-8). O'Connor thus withdraws into his spiritual theater where he remains, in his words, "shadow-boxing" with God (*Nightwood*, 84). Ragland-Sullivan explains this impossible predicament: "Enjoined by unconscious desire to stay true to a denigrated father, to float in the nether land of being neither man or woman, the impotence in her structure shows up as an impossible desire: to exist by not existing" (1988, 79).

In this indeterminate region of "in-existence," however, the hysteric's body is continually negated and reformulated. If, in "hysterogenesis," the body is said to be infected by ideas and hence "converted," O'Connor's self-mortification may be said to occasion its energetic renewal, setting in motion the process by which corporeal zones of intensity are toggled and re-contoured. This is thus the body he delivers over to the gaze of the Other—not, finally, an angelic body—but a disinherited body of jarring constituents, trawled up from the wreck of Creation, articulating, by sheer force of contiguity, a variegated wasteland of fragments from history:

> What an autopsy I'll make, with everything all which ways in my bowels! A kidney and a shoe cast of the Roman races; a liver and a long-spent whisper, a gall and a wrack of scolds from Milano, and my heart that will be weeping still when they find my eyes cold, not to mention a thought of Cellini in my crib of bones, thinking how he must have suffered when he knew he could not tell it for ever— [...] And the lining of my belly, flocked with the locks cut off love in odd places that I've come on, a bird's nest to lay my lost eggs in[.]
>
> (*Nightwood*, 90)

Presented as a historical collage, O'Connor's body becomes both the inscriptive and storage space for a motley gathering of lost tales and relics, holding everything from a "kidney" to a "shoe," a "long-spent whisper" to "a wrack of scolds." It is eschatologically visualized not so much as a resurrected body but an anatomized one, with its tangle of guts, posthumous heart, and a stillborn narrative in his "crib of bones," gestating—not Eve here—but the Florentine sculptor and rogue lover of men, Cellini. The archetypal "wandering womb" of the hysteric seems in fact to have found its way for the moment back into O'Connor, inspiring the "belly" wherein the fruits of his "love" are to be incubated. These "locks cut off love in odd places," Barnes has suggested, have a pubic provenance, their passage from one body to the next made presumably with the Doctor "going down" on his lovers.[23] The "bird's nest" they put together, makes for the flimsy gestation chamber for his "lost eggs"—that is, his lost progeny as much as his lost ovaries. That this hysterical body is produced in "hilarious sorrow" is made more explicit perhaps in Barnes's memoirs of Paris, where she relates the verbal and medical praxis of Daniel Mahoney to lacework:

> When Doctor Dan [...] held the entire Latin Quarter in the grip of laughter, the great unpaid, funny, medical man drunk every night [...] The truths he told and the lies he told made a sort of Venetian rose point of his life.
>
> (*Collected Poems*, 249–50)

Here, Barnes returns "text," "tissue," and "textile" to their etymological kinship in the Latin *texere*. It seems that her reported advice to Antonia White might after all be a bit more than a joke: "Keep on writing"—that is, even though "one may write the most lamentable balls"—since, after all, "[i]t's a woman's only hope, except for lace making" (cited in Herring 1995, 235). Writing and bleeding, alongside collage- and lace-making, figure as the processes by which the fibers of the body are pulled apart to be strung together again. In this weaving and unweaving of the body, hysterical joy, we might say, involves the caterwaul of the damned that, in its very lugubrious but implacable process, makes of hilarity and sorrow its woof and warp to yield a tracery of pleasure and pain—of pleasure *in* pain: "A broken heart have you! I have falling arches, flying dandruff, a floating kidney, shattered nerves *and* a broken heart!" (*Nightwood*, 139). Drawing these catachrestic formulations into his body like so many renewed lacerations, O'Connor continually re-sutures his open flesh into new form. The hysteric's "hilarious sorrow," seen in this light, enables desire to endure in the face of suffering: there may still be "beauty," even joy, in "permanent mistakes" (*Nightwood*, 119).

This, unfortunately, is not where *Nightwood*, finally, ends.[24] As I have suggested, O'Connor ultimately reorients himself toward a horizon of radical finitude, a convert to a regnant "Death in Heaven." Toward the end of the novel,

---

[23] Barnes's awkward formulation to her Italian translator Signor Maffi runs: "among other things will be found in his stomach body hair, implication obvious considering that he is homosexual" (Barnes 1948).

[24] See also Drew Milne's moving account of "*Nightwood*'s journey into wits end," folding the "tragicomic" over into the "tragic" (2019, 118, 122–3).

his accelerated speech breaks forth into the frenzied brushwork of a rudimentary allegory, haunted by a Düreresque scheme:

> Here lies the body of Heaven. The mocking bird howls through the pillars of Paradise, oh, Lord! Death in Heaven lies couched on a mackerel sky, on her breast a helmet and at her feet a foal with a silent marble mane. Nocturnal sleep is heavy on her eyes.
>
> (*Nightwood*, 146–7)

While the prosopopoeia of Death, animal symbolism, and even the detail of the "mackerel sky" are reminiscent of the woodcuts of Dürer's Apocalypse reproduced in Barnes's copy of the Book of Revelation (1926), O'Connor's iconoclastic move here supplants the cloud-ensconced Christ with a female Death (Figure 4.2).

If it is now an image of an Angel of Death that he leaves himself "impaled" upon, some of its significance may be traced in a passage marked out by Barnes in her copy of Jacques Maritain's *Art and Poetry*:

> All sin is a sorry thing, injuring nature. […] I did not make myself, nor save myself; my sin injures the work of another, and disfigures the visage of another. In making of your sin beauty, you send it like an angel among your brothers. It kills them without a sound. However, this is not your first fault. But that of yourself within yourself for having hidden a corpse in the branches of your arteries, as if God did not see.
>
> (1943, 51)

The Catholic paradigm here, which locates "sin" beyond subjective intention as a kind of objective "disfigur[ation]" and "injury" of Creation—the defacing, as it were, of the glorious "visage"—is unfolded with another call to humility: genesis and grace are beyond the remit of the will. If it is the crisis in corporeal assumption in *Nightwood* that spawns its life-forms all in excess of the image of Christological Man—in its narrower delineation at least—in effect, incarnating a "criticism of the Most High," these bodies nevertheless are all through the novel clothed upon in beauty ("Why Actors," 42).[25] Barnes herself, not too impressed with Coleman's reading of her novel as a "Catholic Sermon" (Coleman 1947), and, given to parodies of the association of Creation with order ("the mad strip of the inappropriate that runs through creation"—*Nightwood*, 93), would

---

[25] See also Coleman's remark in her August 27, 1935, letter to Barnes: "You make horror beautiful—it is your greatest gift" (cited in Herring, xvii).

Figure 4.2 Albrecht Dürer, print from *Apocalypse*, 1497–8, woodcut. New York, Metropolitan Museum of Art.

nonetheless have seen the tragic import of a turn away from the Good News of Life. The corporeal *eschaton* here is no longer the resurrected body, but the "corpse," resident in the temporal flesh that is now reoriented toward an idol of Death: *the body is now repeated in the image of its decay*. At the outset of *Nightwood*, the Doctor is still able to pronounce, "putting his fingers on the arteries of the body": "God, whose roadway this is, has given me permission to travel on it also." By the novel's end, however, what he has made of this "permission" is indexed with another deictic gesture: "Here lies the body of Heaven" (*Nightwood*, 28, 146). In this turn to Death, he is now "the god of darkness" incarnate. *Dies irae*, for the Doctor, thus comes as a tragic judgment on the melancholy division of his being. Divested of the Word, the body in tears—*like* the body in laughter[26]—torn and turned from itself, is now decisively stranded in an eternal ek-stasis: "I've not only lived my life for nothing, but I've told it for nothing [...] the end [...] now *nothing, but wrath and weeping!*" (*Nightwood*, 149).

---

[26] Robin—similarly *and* conversely—is stranded in the ek-stasis of laughter in the final chapter, "barking in a fit of laughter, obscene and touching" (*Nightwood*, 153).

5

Tragedy II: *The Antiphon* and the Refusal of History

In a letter to Natalie Barney dated February 29, 1968, Barnes reports of her invitation by the Istituto Acaddemico di Roma to a congress on "Valeurs permanentes dans le devenir historic [sic]," to be convened in October. Her response is characteristic of an attitude increasingly solidified in her later years:

> I [...] had to tell them that I no longer travel, and never, never speak in public. [...] [A]s Sylvia Beach said in her book, I never was one to "sell my wares"... and less and less as time goes on. Perhaps I am becoming as silent as Ezra Pound, or as a better one before him, St. Thomas Aquinas.

Allusions to her withdrawal from life increase: she is an "anchorite," "Tibetan-like," and, in a phrase also applied to Miranda in *The Antiphon* (1958), "trappist-like" (1968d). In place of "reticence"—"absolutely the thing not done these days"—"advertising" is "all the Rage" (1968c); and, "for not being more amenable to the market," she finds herself 'whipped around the world" (1968d).

The invitation by the institute and her subsequent abstention thus occasion some irony. Asked for her contribution for a discussion on "permanent values"—values the Institute seems to find enshrined in *The Antiphon*—Barnes's response turns out to be a refusal grounded on a rejection of the historical trends of the day, namely, the dominance of the market, public advertisement, and the language that has been subordinated to their purposes. Withdrawing from "public" discourse, the economy, and even from the body's displacement in "travel," Barnes stages her recoil into privacy as an aesthetic and spiritual resistance to the fads of the day, authenticated not just by one of literary modernism's luminaries (Pound), but also by an emblem of the medieval mendicant orders (Aquinas), alongside his monastic kin, whether of Tibetan or Trappist leanings. As will be seen, the choice of silence over speech indicated here is, in Barnes's imagination, backed by a broader opposition between a general *retention*—across the levels of discourse, time, market economy, and the body—and, conversely, the *circulation* of the same. Art, for Barnes in her later years, comes increasingly to be situated against history, preserved against the flow of time, and along with it, the flow of capital, the flux of words, and the effluvia of the body. On April 15, 1969, she writes to Christine Koschel, one of the pair of German translators of *The Antiphon*: "I am not a 'modern' after all! Which sound [*sic*] strange for one who is considered <u>avant guard</u> [*sic*]!"

This chapter seeks to account for the tragic judgment on life in *The Antiphon* as a specific refusal of history. Such a refusal consists in a radical disinvestment of the historical world, involving a libidinal withdrawal from the terms of the socio-symbolic order, whether coded at the level of the market, in discourse, or in the passage of time itself. Reality itself is reconceived in this total recoil of the subject from a deconsecrated world: the "real" is now relocated from the order of time and being to a region of non-being outside of time. All of history, along with the entities and events that emerge and elapse within it, is de-authenticated—and in fact, *de-realized*—in this libidinal drainage. Following the terms set out in my introduction, the tragedy enclosed in Barnes's late play consists in its negative response to the question of theodicy: the past time of Creation is summed up here as *false*, evil, and the source of irremediable suffering, in an aesthetic judgment that places it below the threshold of any minimal reconciliation.

This account of tragic negation outlined here may be traced by returning to the double negations found in the quotations from Barnes's letters above. In her letter to Barney, the symptomatic doubling of the word "never" recalls *The Antiphon*'s reprisal of the proliferating negatives in *King Lear*. Not long into the commencement of the play, Dudley, one of the conspiratorial duo of brothers who later indulge in histrionic attacks on their mother and sister, relates death in the family, and death on the scale of nations, into a genealogical and historical *cul-de-sac*:

> We'll never have so good a chance again;
> Never, never such a barren spot,
> Nor never again such anonymity as war.
> All old people die of death, remember?

(*Selected Works*, 101)[1]

In the event, it is Augusta—"Mrs King Lear," as Barnes christens her to Coleman in a September 24, 1942 letter—who brings the curfew-bell down on Miranda,

---

[1] Unless otherwise stated, I follow Julie Taylor in citing from the 1962 edition of *The Antiphon* (2012, 189).

negating nativity itself in the reversal of the mother from life-giver into death-dealer. Barnes's "never, never" to Barney echoes its appearance in this passage, buried in fragments of negating morphemes: two more "never"s, above and below, brace its already redoubled occurrence, amounting to just one less than Lear's notorious five; the voicing of a "nor" returns encased in "anonymity," sounding another "non" while the negating prefix "a-" foregrounds the namelessness the word denotes. Where the end—or "n"—coded in "barren" lexically and aurally tail-ends both natural life and human history, the iterated "d"s in the tautology, "die of death," similarly encode that terminus within "old" itself, aural signs that return, in a dilatory echo, lines on: "Of man's despairs we've had the deal and dole" (*Selected Works*, 108). In Act Two, Augusta's claim—"I've seen my daughter die before, and make it" (*Selected Works*, 180)—phonetically encrypts the finality that its sense denies, fatefully consigning the "daughter" not to generation but to the general "Doom" she sounds (*Selected Works*, 217). If the ear does not catch on immediately, four lines on from the conjunction of daughter and death the plosive beats return: "Be dead, be done, be modest dead."

Such phonetic reprisals are a feature of a certain brand of typology that the title of Barnes's play gestures toward. *The Antiphon* names, on a basic level, a phonetic antitype. Words here are often reiterated in a series of distortions, sounded out only to place their conventional associations under erasure. Enacted as the last movement to a "Key-gone generation," whose "figured base [bass?]" is now let loose into "So many scattered minims on the wind," Barnes's last play sets up a profane acoustic chamber in which the harmony of the spheres might rebound, distorted, to be found again as mutilated motifs (*Selected Works*, 218). As with *Nightwood*, which throws back Creation's founding invocation in Genesis 1:3—"Let there be light"—in inverted form ("Lord, put the light out"—*Nightwood*, 146), the call-response structure encoded in *The Antiphon* sends the cosmogenetic address ricocheting back as so much desecrated echolalia.

In my introduction, I have considered one aspect of the "antiphon" as the artist's production of an antitype to Creation via Pinkerton's notion of a "transgressive typology." Pinkerton's reading of "blasphemy" within the framework of such orthodox thinkers as T. S. Eliot and G. K. Chesterton, however, ultimately neutralizes the tragic import of some of Barnes's writings, insofar as "blasphemy" itself is reassimilated to the continued "*necessity*" of Christian faith (Eliot 1975, 231): "What blasphemy requires is not 'spiritual sickness' but rather a commitment to playful and critical reworkings of orthodoxy, coupled with a respect and even reverence, not for God, or scripture, or the church, but for *religious faith itself* and its enduring cultural sway" (Pinkerton 2017, 5). For

Pinkerton, Barnes's *Nightwood* drives "transgress[ion] farther and deeper" but ultimately "in pursuit of salvation," leading to "sacred regions below and beyond the human," while *The Antiphon*—read as "an irreverent counterdiscourse aimed at male-dominated institutions of oppression"—comes across more as a political challenge to patriarchy than a total recoil from the created world (2017, 130, 120).

"Blasphemy," in Pinkerton's account, never exceeds the framework of a minimal theodicy as set out in my introduction, insofar as it remains oriented toward a redemptive horizon, *revising*—rather than repudiating—the terms of our engagement with the world. Where transgression remains committed on a minimal level to the unfolding of time itself, the *regressive* vision that *The Antiphon* presents—in seeing the "creeping catafalque/ Toiling backward to the cot" and the "Perambulator rolling to the tomb"—preempts any retrieval of an afterlife from the ruins of present time by *reversing* temporal progression itself (*Selected Works*, 219). *The Antiphon*'s refusal of history is fulfilled in a totalizing vision that encloses all of Creation within its tragic theater, to be denounced and returned to the void. It is, after all, a general collapse of Creation that is announced at the play's end: "This is the hour of the uncreate" (*Selected Works*, 223). Straining toward a form of negation *without* a dialectical afterlife, Barnes's method of coining additive prefixes in *The Antiphon*, from the "uncreate" to "disoccur," reverses life into fallow seed, drawing back from the linear trajectory of history into retrograde implosion (*Selected Works*, 213). The antiphonal reversals that take the "catafalque" to the "cot" to "uncreate" Creation and "unbreath" the living "breath," thus, function to further countersign the "daughter" in the image of "death," "wisdom" as "winter," "resurrection" as "bootless roar," and to bring back to "child-bed" that which would otherwise, in the Resurrection, "un-bed [...] in paradise" (*Selected Works*, 217, 202, 222–3).

In these systematic reversals of salvation history, *The Antiphon* may be viewed along the lines of a black sacrament and black Mariology, as the tragic artist's profanation of the Eucharist and the Marian antiphons (*Selected Works*, 212). I will follow up on the ambivalences in the idea of "antiphony" later in this chapter, but note for now the range of its religious, musical, and literary meanings, which Barnes brings up in a terse response to Peggy Guggenheim: "You ask what the word ANTIPHON means. the Oxford Dictionary: Antiphon, n. Versicle, sentence, sung by one choir in response [*sic*] to another; prose or verse composition consisting such passages—"(Barnes 1958a). My claim here is that *The Antiphon*, published in 1958 and set in 1939 during the commencement of the Second World War, articulates a tragic temporality in opposition to *two* forms of redemptive time, each conceptualized according to a certain dialectical principle: (i) the time of history as the dialectical unfolding and self-revelation of God in the immanent world; and (ii) the time of a specific form of intersubjective encounter understood as dialectical "witness" and "testimony" (Taylor 2012, 36–73; Wallenfang 2017, 37–50). The Hegelian structure of the former situates history on a linear trajectory, at the end of which a "real theodicy" is to be revealed (cited in Agamben 2011a, 5), while the latter reads salvific promise in the *apertures* in history from which new beginnings emerge, produced each time subjects meet outside the terms of alienated exchange in the socio-economic world. This alternative model of time is conceptualized in terms of an "I-Thou" relation by Martin Buber, whom Barnes read probably around the time *The Antiphon* was written, and has since been given phenomenological elaboration as a form of "prosopic intercourse"—a "dialectical relationship" structuring the liturgical practices of the Eucharist and Mariology (Wallenfang 2017, 183–214).[2] If an antiphonal relation is suggested in the call and response of the I-Thou encounter, *The Antiphon* itself, however, ultimately drains it of its salvific significance.

The judgment against history staged in *The Antiphon* is tropologically unfolded most prominently in a chain of reversals. This quite often involves a co-conception of salvational and genealogical time, with filicide standing in as a key emblem for retrograde finality. Allegorically sketched, this is "Death with a baby in its mouth" (*Selected Works*, 219). The allusion here to Cronus's devouring of his children—memorably depicted in Francisco Goya and Peter Paul Rubens—may be placed alongside a line from Barnes's *Notebook* which refigures the iconography of the Virgin and Child: "the child decays in the lap of the Madonna." The same two motifs are brought up decades earlier in Barnes's response to a book of drawings from Coleman in a letter dated September 2, 1938: "I prefer the madonna and child with child in those really horrifying woollies with the two buttons at the neck, its [*sic*] worse that way than naked, more horrifyingly child and mother, nursing enigma and rodent, all the horror you feel for the Christ child in early Italian paintings but with the wicked cleverness of putting him back view." The second of the "two best" in the collection is that of "the man holding the squirming boy [...] gets the exact feeling (I remember it as a child) of being held against the will and not being strong enough to break out of it" (1938f). In Coleman's drawings, these intergenerational passions—Oedipal or Saturnine—are reduced to the primitivist lines of her pencil-work (Figures 5.1 and 5.2). A few diacritical marks on the page produce affective masks of moroseness, malice, or motor shock. As for the blank occiput of the infant, its spherical absence, set

---

[2] The "prosopic trait," Wallenfang clarifies, relates "to the person or face" (2017, 183).

in relief by the displaced ocelli of the "woollies," records the *horror vacui* of the measureless hunger of a child at the breast of its mother. Barnes's appreciation of the religious context of Coleman's drawings reveals her awareness of the larger implications of intergenerational relations. *The Antiphon*, it might be suggested, is her later attempt to refigure the various Madonnas of art history, in particular those of the Italian Renaissance including Raphael and Crivelli. In the tragic

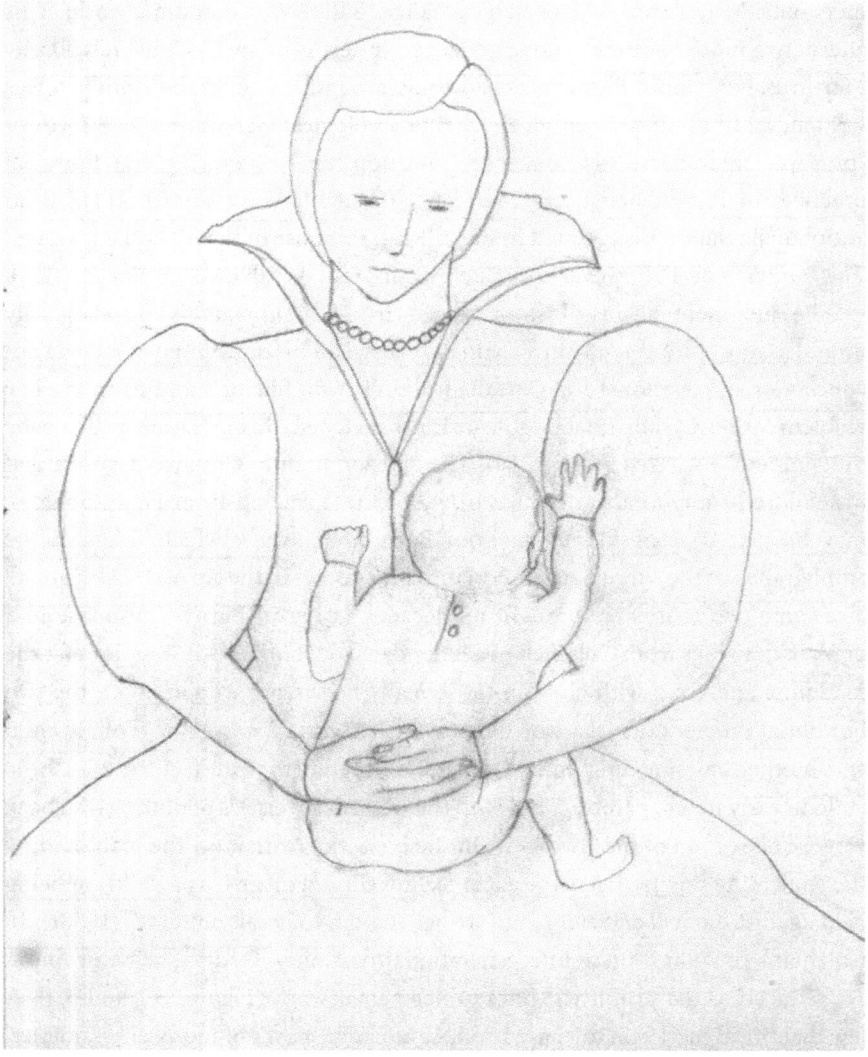

Figure 5.1 Emily Coleman, drawing from "Book of Drawings," undated. MSS 105, Emily Holmes Coleman papers, Special Collections, University of Delaware Library. Newark, Delaware. © by Estate of Emily Holmes Coleman.

Figure 5.2 Emily Coleman, drawing from "Book of Drawings," undated. MSS 105, Emily Holmes Coleman papers, Special Collections, University of Delaware Library. Newark, Delaware. © by Estate of Emily Holmes Coleman.

theater of the play, the mother ends up returning her enigmatic rodent of a child into her "belly full of thumbs" (*Selected Works*, 194). The sense here is of a negation that forecloses futurity.

In *The Antiphon*, the mother–daughter relation is conceptualized at the intersection of nativity and sin. Miranda is projected onto an allegorical screen in Augusta's imagination in Act Three, in the dense symbols of a black Mariology:

> My daughter is winged serpent, *and* the urn.
> Some damned dark Beatitude that sits
> In her heart's core, mewling like an idiot,
> Cribs her out of eminence and profit;
> Sweeps her from the kingdom and the general world—
> And she sits by, and strokes its bloody head.
>
> (*Selected Works*, 203)

Miranda, now an Isaian reptile (Isaiah 14:29; 30:6) and a vessel for the dead, is devotionally bound—not to the Virgin Mother—but the "mewling idiot" entombed in her, a cryptogram for "[s]ome damned dark Beatitude" draining her attachments to the socio-economic order ("eminence and profit"; "the kingdom and the general world") with a reverse investment in a vampiric nursling, who "cribs" her in a double operation: *nesting within* and *pilfering from* her. The "rodent" Christ child now morphs into some demonic presence with a "bloody head," eating away at "her heart's core," leeching her of herself. This ontological theft, implicated in the genealogical bond, begins already with Augusta, who incriminates Miranda as the "Magpie" of her being: "In what pocket have you my identity?/ I so disoccur in every quarter of myself/ I cannot find me" (*Selected Works*, 213). In *The Antiphon*, such genealogical decline is framed within a larger cosmic theater: gestating, suckling,[3] and birthing death rather than life,[4] the distortion of the Madonna into a prosopopoeia of tragedy accompanies the consignment of Creation itself to the "hour of the uncreate." The world enclosed in Barnes's play is one bound to an *end* without relief, an ultimate horizon of finitude.

Barnes's eschatological concerns seem to have resurfaced with renewed intensity in her later years, as is suggested by her reading around this time, which includes Paul Tillich's *The Courage to Be* (1952), as well as Josef Pieper's *The Silence of St. Thomas* (1957) and *The End of Time* (1954).[5] This last, opening with "*[t]he question of the end of history*," reads the Christ event as the inauguration of historical time proper: "a directed happening [...] a process with a beginning and an end," headed "irreversibl[y]" toward its "*end-state*" (1954, 15–16). *The Antiphon* sets up this eschatological tension while, however, replacing the conventional eschaton of Christianity in the arrival of the Kingdom of Heaven with something more similar to a tragic going-under of "the Christian aeon"

---

[3] "I still dangle for the cockatrice/ My unsucked eggs" (*Selected Works*, 213).
[4] "[S]ome women have no breasts/ Till they have buried children" (*Selected Works*, 173).
[5] Barnes requests a copy of *The End of Time* from Eliot in a letter on July 15, 1954, having sent him a draft of *The Antiphon*.

itself (1954, 15). Instead of the final parousia of the Kingdom, the apocalyptic negation of the created world terminates in the radical finitude of non-being; and the body, quite apart from any manner of resurrection, reverses into an aborted zygote, a "balking embryo" (*Selected Works,* 194).

Jacques Maritain's appreciation of *The Antiphon,* after *Nightwood,* appears to be founded on this grounding of tragedy in eschatology. In a letter to Barnes on November 12, 1958, he singles out Jack Blow's concluding lines back to her: "Say I was a man, of home so utterly bereft/ I dug me one, and pushed my terror in." Read within the eschatological perspective inaugurated by the Christ event, this displacement of humanity's ultimate "home" from history to the Kingdom unites tragedy and redemption, referring the suffering of the world to the transcendental horizon of its overcoming. Yet such a Christian overcoding of the tragic theater of *The Antiphon* once again subsumes the particular ontology of the artwork within the general ontology of an extrinsic metaphysics, as I have noted in my introduction. Resisting this temptation to read Barnes's tragedy within the terms of a divine comedy requires us to remain in the drama of history set up in the play itself. The eschatological perspective of *The Antiphon* is directed rather toward a focused negation of any form of salvation or continuity, enclosing all of Creation within the unbroken borders of radical finitude. Tillich's "dialectical" understanding of negation in *The Courage to Be* can thus only serve to show up, by way of contrast, the *totalizing* gesture of Barnes's tragedy. For Tillich, negation and tragedy embed a "No" within the heart of the eternal "Yes," and are overcome in the "self-affirmation of being-itself": courage "participates in the power of being which prevails against nonbeing" (1952, 166). Against this comic ontology, the opening proclamation of *The Antiphon* resounds almost as a direct riposte: "The very fad of being's stopped" (*Selected Works,* 82). The *end* that the play drives us to is one without any afterlife in or beyond time itself. I move on here to *The Antiphon's* de-authentication of history.

Sublimation and Its Discontents

In a letter to Coleman on June 6, 1939, the year of *The Antiphon's* setting, Barnes launches another of her formidable rants on the futility of love:

> Love is so horrible, its [*sic*] bloody, it's the most awful and evil thing in the world, and all books, poems, pictures to the contrary are LIES! LIES! LIES! and we are stuffed on them from the cradle, and go into the grave crying for that "pacifier" (in case you dont [*sic*] know what that is, its [*sic*] a rubber nipple on a bone ring flung to the baby when mother is tired!)

This conception of love as "evil" recalls the "Satanic" litanies of Baudelaire, Lautréamont, and de Sade, a point that is underscored several lines on in Barnes's letter by being appended to original sin: "Adam and Eve found out 'love' and lost Eden, thats [sic] the truth and everyone has been making out its [sic] only sex that lay in the heart of that apple!" Placing "love" beyond mere or "only sex" directs us beyond the immediacy of the physical acts of genital copulation. The constitutive insatiability of "love," raised beyond the purely physical dimension of inseminative intercourse, is coordinated with the decisive expulsion from Eden, condemning one to a lifetime of lack and substitute objects. From "cradle" to "grave," the oral cavity remains a site of absence, a psychosomatic recess where returning demands cancel out all customary dole—compensatory at best, if not downright false. The edifice of culture, conjured as the fanciful arabesques of "books, poems, pictures," turns out to be a compendium of "LIES! LIES! LIES!"— so much insubstantial feed with which "we are stuffed," a monumental "pacifier" for a history of pining souls. As an ersatz "nipple" of "rubber" and "bone," the "pacifier" names the ghosted teat of the retiring "mother," as much forcemeat as false meat. Weaning and individuation thus form the basis of a human history of dissatisfactions and lies, the "deal and dole," that is, of "man's despairs."

This association of culture and dissatisfaction is in fact a central feature of the many Freudo-Marxisms of the postwar era, including those of Herbert Marcuse's *Eros and Civilisation* (1956) and Norman Brown's *Life Against Death* (1959), both of which Barnes would later encounter in Susan Sontag's review of them in an essay collected in the volume *Against Interpretation* (1966). History in these accounts is conceptualized as a timeline of "sublimation" and "sublation," over the course of which the human body and civilization develop and co-adapt. The sequence of drive objects, from nipple to genitalia and books, are, Ricoeur explains, the "noematic correlates to sublimation" which culture provides, synchronizing, to a degree, the historical sequences of body and society (1977, 519). Freud's own accounts in the late 1920s in *The Future of an Illusion* and *Civilisation and Its Discontents* baptize the respective problems of physical need and resource scarcity with the names of Eros and the Greek goddess of necessity, Ananke—a prominent fixture of Attic tragedy. On the other hand, "our god Logos"—that is, reason and rational history—is said to ease the pressures of love and necessity by redirecting desire to its store of cultural objects, symbolic substitutes for the primitive needs of the body (*SE* XXI, 139, 54). The conjunction of Logos and Eros, which Freud reads in the "divine Plato" (*SE* VII, 134), thus opens up the possibility of "sublimation," which names, as Joel Whitebook puts it, "the mutability of Eros [...] to cathect nonempirical objects." What is made available here is an "immanent 'ladder' within the empirical domain [...] by means of which one can pull oneself out of the pure immanence of the totality of empirical determination" (Whitebook 1996, 245). When paired with Logos, love leads us up the ladder from "mother" to "books, poems, pictures."

Barnes's rejection of "sublimation" as so many "lies," however, is more in line with the Enlightenment critiques of Brown and Marcuse. Instead of the successful adaptation of the body to the objects of culture, enabling Eros to be conjoined to Logos, a profound dissatisfaction ends up exposing the falsity of the historical world. As Sontag points out, Brown's reading of this neo-Platonic body as, in the last instance, stunted with abnegation, leads him to place his hopes instead in "the resurrected body" of the theologians, replacing acculturation with "Christian eschatology" (1966, 261). The ultimate "real," disclosed to the embodied subject, is to be found no longer in time, but at the end of time. Sontag quotes Brown: "*The speciality of Christian eschatology lies precisely in its rejection of the Platonic hostility to the human body and to 'matter,' its refusal to identify the Platonic path of sublimation with ultimate salvation [...] Luther's break with the doctrine of sublimation (good works) is decisive*" (1966, 261). On this account, the "ladder" of desiderata that sublimation produces can only hollow out into a string of pacifiers, libidinal falsities that make up the history of human civilization, characterized by Brown as nothing less than a history of "neurotic compromise." "Historical process" and "neurotic process" are mutually implicated (Brown 1985, 11, 232). This forms the "deepest psychoanalytical insight of Lutheran Protestantism": the "massive withdrawal of Eros from sublimations and therefore from life in this world" results in the derealization of contemporary culture and its chronological—or indeed, *chronic*—progress (Brown 1985, 232).

Lutheranism, for Brown, constitutes a critique of the desiderata of *this world*—a critique, hence, of love and gold. Barnes here seems to share certain elements of Brown's reading of Luther, likely provoked further by her interest, following Eliot, in the Lutheran Protestant Tillich. By the end of March 1940, pressured into the sanatorium by the parsimony of her family, she writes again to Coleman. Referencing her poverty ("I starve"), she nonetheless refuses the palliatives afforded by the job market, and writes of her alienation from the socioeconomic order of capitalist modernity:

> Anyone who leaves the scene and goes abroad (for any length of time) is sunk financially. You become something that is no longer palatable to the New Yorker; you become terribly homeless; you begin to see through that dark glass ... you

see the hocum [*sic*] of nearly everything they do, including (and especially) these psychiatrists and all the other isms.

(1940b)

Money, psychiatry, civilization, the new world: all are cast aside universally as the "ho[k]um" that time has dredged up. The subject dislocated from the socioeconomic order is thus "homeless." Of these modern "isms," she notes in another letter: "Mother a Christian Scientist, living on New Thought etc—everyone I've seen hanging onto some ism—Mad!" (1939j). The things of the world and its systems of value, now de-authenticated, retreat behind the "dark glass" (1 Corinthians 13:12). "Hokum" indicates this spectrality on the one hand while gesturing to another kind of substance, set in relief by Barnes's spelling. Etymologically, the term probably derives from the Latin of the Roman Catholic liturgy: *Hoc est corpus meum* ("This is my body").[6] A logic of profanation comes to the fore. The sublimated objects of the historical and spiritual world here are desacralized: the Eucharistic *res* of Catholic-ism, as much as its modern rivals of Christian Science, psychiatry, and economy, are de-substantialized into fatuities behind a turbid pall. The very body of Christ, in Miranda's depiction in *The Antiphon*, is reduced to bestial provender: "I've seen my people set the canine tooth/ Into the Host" (*Selected Works*, 216).

Such a de-sacralization of the world is often coordinated historically with Lutheranism and the Reformation. As Tillich puts it: "the Protestant principle cannot admit any identification of grace with a visible reality" (cited in Brown 1985, 224). Tina Beattie's more recent account of the "making of modernity" similarly relates Lutheran doctrine to the "dis-gracing" of the material world: by dismissing the "value of all human works" and insisting on "salvation by faith alone," Luther effectively relocates the "real" from the public world to a private relation—"in radical solitude"—with God, leaving "all natural human existence in the grip of the satanic," as the "soul stands bereft" of a graced cosmos (Beattie 2013, 169–72). The historical world is spiritually and libidinally drained: the "bleeding dry of the sacramental imagination [...] herald[s] the emergence of a symbolic order in which matter mutates from graced organic life to meaningless and inaccessible otherness" (2013, 171–2). This "dis-gracing" of material life underlies the Lutheran judgment on the world as a desecrated heap: *scatet totus orbis* (Brown 1985, 226). Something of this sense of "dis-grace" appears to account for Barnes's characterization of Europe in a letter to Coleman in 1938.

[6] Wallenfang notes the derivation of "hocus-pocus" from this liturgical formula (2017, 1).

France, Canterbury, or "any old town" is presented simultaneously in the light of its informing architectural genius, and the converse aspect of its scatological desublimation. Contrasting her inability to find straightforward solace in the natural world with Coleman, she writes:

> its [sic] why I love France more than you do, France being covered with the guano of fitful (imaginative minds), here too of course if one goes to Canterbury, or any old town, what I seem to be in love with are the droppings of genius!! <u>you with what they eat, me with what they void</u>, its just a different destination.
>
> (1938h)

In Barnes's formulation, Coleman inhabits a world in which the supervenience of grace sanctifies the natural relation between organisms and the food they ingest; for herself, however, it is rather the "droppings of genius" processed out of the corrupted spirit of humanity that captivates. Yet even the allure of the city's architecture begins to fade. Where the French capital is now a "morgue" to her, the American is "less" even than that "nothing" (Barnes 1939b; 1939g). In the midst of a tirade against Peggy Guggenheim, we find the following Lutheran sentiment: "anyone who loves the world or things of the world is not of the Father" (Barnes 1939e).

In *The Antiphon*, this general "dis-grace" of the historical and material world sets up an economy of perpetual loss in which time, money, and the wastage of the flesh circulate as so many fungible units the self defends against. Augusta's vitriol, directed most acutely at her daughter, but also toward her sons, contrasts retention with flow and loss:

> But I know women, son. Before I'm cold
> They'll have me off the sheets [...]
> Before you can say "Knife!" take pot and pan;
> Snatch my very pediment; and from my poke,
> (With finger-tips like greedy Florentines
> Compounding mischief with the hurricane)
> Take all, clasping my hand, for sorrow's seal,
> Though in truth but cunning's gyve, to grapple
> The finger-rings from hungry *rigor mortis*.
>
> (*Selected Writings*, 172)

The daughter will unseat the mother, "snatch[ing]" the "pediment" on which she stands. "Poke," lexically condensing monetary and reproductive stores, is situated before a bracketed clause across which a gruesome process of excretion, effusion, and plunder draws out, as the body, broken into, breaks forth into so much stolen loot and blood. The 1958 edition, in fact, reads: "Compounding pledge against the 'Hemorrhage of time,'" recalling Barnes's 1939 self-diagnosis with her "hemmorhage for a menstruation" (*The Antiphon*, 132). The "finger-tips" of "greedy Florentines" point us to the merchants of the time of the Medici as well as surgical entry, turning flesh, coin, and time, into the analogues of loss. Temporal flow, bodily erosion, and monetary drain are conjoined here as the circulating liquidities in a universal exchange economy, with cannibalistic implication. Even in death, this oral drive remains insatiable: the daughter dresses up in "sorrow's seal," her "finger-tips" formerly busy in her mother's "poke" now "grappl[ing]" for her "finger-rings," which the dead fingers still clutch in "hungry *rigor mortis*." All sublimated objects in *The Antiphon* become insubstantial even as they are hunted down, and everyone is reduced to hunger: "Starving, sir," Jeremy, disguised as Jack Blow, claims at the play's outset—"as all the world is" (*Selected Works*, 97). It is the daughter, however, who receives the brunt of her mother's contempt. Unable to provide, she is the parasite in an economic order inhabited by men, a "female-vetch" vermicular, vinous, vulvar, vampiric, and venomous all at once:

> See how the bind-weed hauls against the ground
> And on the winch of autumn puts out hooks,
> To clamber greatness down. How like the vine,
> The female-vetch, that low perfidious crawl,
> That winding thief with estuary mouth
> That nibbles at the root, and topples boys,
> And thinks by climbing to the privet of the head
> To be the glory that she fattens on.
>
> (*Selected Writings*, 171)

The "low perfidious crawl" of a serpentine "bind-weed" recalls *Nightwood*'s "snarl of the groin," which Barnes glosses as a "curse on the female sex." This vaginal opening turns "thief," foaming "with estuary mouth" in a mixture of hunger and abject lust to "topple" the "boys" it feeds and foists itself on, "nibbling" them at the "root," and slithering up their erect posture or phallus to "the privet of the head" where it "fattens" itself into "glory." "Haul[ing]" and "hook[ing]" her way to the top, she "clamber[s] greatness down," reversing the usual prepositional direction of "clamber"—that is, *up*—and perverting it, in the process, into a transitive verb cleaving to its direct object: man. On these terms, Miranda is synecdochally reduced to "[her] starving puss," an "abominable slug of vengeance" (*Selected Works*, 178).

If the brothers Elisha and Dudley, integrated into the economic world, still stand, with their financial turnovers, as worthy investments in Augusta's eyes, in the form of an exchange of maternal flesh for filial coin, Miranda the wandering artist is merely wasted matter. Within such a world, the daughter is reversed from a symbol of futurity and generation into dung, that is, the substance robbed from the body of the mother. Augusta's repeated complaints of "starving" throughout the play are partially explained by Miranda's existence as "that part of me I can't afford" (*Selected Works*, 131). Miranda is manure, as she declares:

> Of that sprawl, three sons she leaned to fairly:
> On me she cast the privy look of dogs
> Who turn to quiz their droppings.
>
> (*Selected Works*, 87)

Dislodged from the financial order of modernity, the daughter, excreted onto the scene of life, remains at the level of valueless substance. Barnes's association here of daughter and dung recalls Luther's scatological representation of humanity. In Žižek's reading of this Lutheran paradigm, the subject's withdrawal from the order of Creation is embedded within a scatological tropology. From one angle, the secular world is reduced to excrement since the subject's relation to God is now the sole "real" (*sola fide*); from another angle, the subject itself is taken to be the excrement at odds with the order of the world:

> Modern subjectivity has nothing to do with the notion of man as the highest creature in the 'Great Chain of Being', as the final point of the evolution of the universe: modern subjectivity emerges when the subject perceives himself as 'out of joint,' as *excluded* from the 'order of things,' from the positive order of entities. For that reason, the ontic equivalent of the modern subject is inherently *excremental*: there is no subjectivity proper without the notion that at a different level, from another perspective, I am a piece of shit.
>
> (Žižek 2000, 157)

Where the "isms" of the world—or the "positive order of entities"—hold, the daughter is looked on as absolute alterity: "Without Protector,/ Husband, son or bank-account," she is, effectively, shit (*Selected Works*, 168). Reversing perspectives, however, it is Creation itself that is monumental dung: "And still dung-beetle Atlas carried on" (*Selected Works*, 165). As in Barnes's phrase—"the droppings of genius"—human subjectivity is that exalted portion of the universe it destabilizes, and which hence, seen from the latter's side, is figured more accurately as its excreta.

Barnes's transposition of the Sisyphean myth into the meaningless labor of an insect-Atlas desublimates Creation into so much "hokum" and linear time into eternal recurrence. A general crisis of sublimation informs *The Antiphon*, collapsing the ladder of elevating substitutions and, as a result, entrapping the subject in an eternal labor of recompense. Entry into existence itself names a grounding debt—of the subject to its progenitors, or, more generally, of each unit of being to non-being—payable, ultimately, only upon the strict equivalence of a return in kind. In *The Antiphon*, this lock-joint economy is indicated by an accounting discourse that comes to dominate all relations of exchange, turning each transaction between persons or entities into another incurrence of debt without remission. This founds the transcendental law of being and time in *The Antiphon* and constitutes its tragic principle—one that is in fact coded in a line jotted down in Barnes's *Notebook*: "Time was first divided into hours 293-B.C."

Ostensibly, the specific date of 293 BC would refer to Pliny's *Natural History*, which cites it as the time of the installation of the first sundial in Rome (Hannah 2009, 134). The "theory of shadows and the science called gnomonics," however, is attributed by Pliny to "Anaximenes of Miletus, the pupil of Anaximander" (Pliny 1938-93, 2.187), whereas Diogenes Laertius associates it directly with Anaximander (Hannah 2009, 68). The Anaximander Fragment, said to be the one surviving line of his writing, is cited in Simone Weil's *The Need for Roots*, which reads as follows in the English translation of Barnes's copy:

> It is out of indeterminateness that things take their birth; and destruction is a return to indeterminateness, which is accomplished by virtue of necessity. For things are subject to chastisement and expiation at one another's hands, because of their injustice, according to the ordering of time.
>
> (Weil 1952, 274)[7]

Things emerge and pass away according to the law of "necessity." Their very "birth" is a mark of an existential guilt atoned for ("expiated") only by a corresponding "destruction." This forms the very "ordering of time": justice (*díkē*) and injustice (*adikía*), becoming and perishing, credit and debt, are bound together in systematic barter, whose basic unit, *qua* aboriginal medium

---

[7] The term "indeterminateness" here may be misleading in its over-specification. The Greek *ex hōn* has a plural relative pronoun in the genitive case. Glenn Most and André Laks give this as "the things out of which" in the Loeb edition (2016, 283); Hermann Diels has "Woraus" (1912, 15). Compare this with Nietzsche's translation of this indeterminate origin with "Woher," or "whence": "Woher die Dinge ihre Entstehung haben, dahin müssen sie auch zu Grunde gehen, nach der Notwendigkeit; denn sie müssen Buße zahlen und für ihre Ungerechtigkeiten gerichtet werden, gemäß der Ordnung der Zeit" (Nietzsche 2009-, eKGWB/PHG-4). My gratitude goes to Eli Aizikowitz for his clarification here.

of exchange, is time—or, more precisely, the positing or ordinance (*táxis*) of time—a unit that can only be substituted in strict equivalence and never sublimated. This, as Werner Hamacher explains, constitutes "the time of the *quid pro quo*," "a guilt- and debt-continuum, continually advancing without a gap in its eternal recurrences":

> Its measure is a justice that represents itself as a *táxis* and thereby as the positing and the law of all becoming and vanishing, the law of *physis* and its demise as an onto-economic law. This taxiological order of time places every realm of the natural and human world under a law of substitution without exception; this also allows ethical, juridical, and economic concepts to substitute for one another within this order. [...] The time of history, ethical time, is thus interpreted in Anaximander's sentence as a normative time of inculpation and expiation.
>
> (2002, 82)

"Provenance" and "guilt" are united in the Greek *aítion*: the logic of causation—etiology—thus traces existence back to its ontological debt (2002, 83). The "cause" of my being, in other words, is also my "guilt" incurred upon entry into existence. The *táxis* of time is also a taxation on being. The Anaximander Fragment which codes the transcendental law of being and time in *The Antiphon* sets up a lock-joint economy of creation in guilt and "uncreat[ion]" in restitution. By the end of the play, Miranda's words at the outset resound as prophesy:

> If, say, this afternoon the earth should quake
> Sending a thousand flaggings stark upright,
> Would not the canted beetle stick his mark?
> [...]
> And on the dial's dislocated time
> Wind up his purpose?
>
> (*Selected Works*, 85–6)

What would have been the raising of the dead, imaged here in the overturned flagstones of a shaken earth, leads to naught. And "dung-beetle Atlas," presumably overturned ("canted"), would "wind up his purpose" with a fixing of the cosmic "dial," folding over "dislocated time" into a return to nonbeing. Augusta's words toward the end of the play thus refer to this "taxiological order" or "arrangement" of time: "The excellent arrangement of catastrophe./ The nice matter of the closed account!" (*Selected Works*, 219).

The numerous references to time and various timepieces that open the play gesture toward this transcendental postulate in *The Antiphon* of a cosmos that is—after *Hamlet*—"out-of-joint." Miranda refers to Augusta's marriage to Titus as her falling "victim to a dial without hours" (*Selected Works*, 85). The brothers Dudley and Elisha in particular appear to represent this deterministic temporality of inculpation and debtorship, explaining hence Miranda's redoubled exclamation: "I fear merchants"; "I fear brothers" (*Selected Works*, 89–90). Dudley is first introduced holding "*a large gold watch, chain dangling*," alongside Elisha, "*diligently strewing almond shells*" as though marking time (*Selected Works*, 97). The latter, inquiring about Dudley's watch, initiates the following repartee:

> Elisha: Why are you holding up that tell-tale watch?
> [...]
> Dudley: Timing.
> Elisha: Timing? What time have you?
> Dudley: Borrowed.
>
> (*Selected Works*, 100–1)

The characters of *The Antiphon* all live on "borrowed" time, their existence thieved from the void to which they return as guilty entities brought to justice. Time's commencement, in this scheme, signals the Fall:

> The salt spilled, the bread broke. Unmuzzled bone
> Drew on the hood of flesh, entombing laughter:
> Tongues came forth, and forth the hissing milk
> Its lashing noose, and snared the gaping mouth.
> A door slammed on Eden, and the Second Gate,
> And I walked down your leg.
>
> (*Selected Works*, 194–5)

Here, Miranda depicts her own birth with an allusion to the Biblical covenant of salt, now a profane contracture of nutritive substance between mother and daughter. Intercourse and gestation fold over in an overdetermined phrase: raw bone without flesh or face ("unmuzzled") is vested with body, in a line that simultaneously runs through the inseminative act as an "unmuzzled" pistol-penis with its foreskin ("hood of flesh") "dr[awn]," its barrel primed, perverting life into death. Laughter, "entomb[ed]" in the flesh, recalls us to its association with the Fall. Creation and procreation are synchronized here in the simultaneous exit of the daughter from Eden's door and the "Second Gate" of the mother. Miranda's theatrical entry onto the scene of life, in a quick recovery of the poise of her homunculus-self—"I walked down your leg"—is suspended in a lukewarm limbo between the comic and the tragic. The mother's milk is henceforth the "noose" by which the daughter is bound, eternally indebted to the maternal body. The conclusion to all this is the tragic inception: "And time commenced" (*Selected Works*, 194).

At this stage the "onto-economic" law of exchange that Hamacher reads in the Anaximander Fragment may be referred to the psychic structure of the nexus of guilt. It is perhaps in Melanie Klein's record of the "sexual development of the girl" that the link between "oral frustration" and the theater of guilt and foiled restitution is most concretely depicted (1997, 203). The child's ambivalent relation to its parents is dramatized in a series of attacks, "fear of being counter-attacked," attempts at reparation, in turn countered "by the fear of not being able to make restitution" (1997, 214, 218). Luther's theological stage over which the battle between the soul and the devil unfolds finds an analogue here in a psychic theater in which the charged negotiations between the child and its parents play out, the arsenal on both sides taking the form of "urine, faeces and flatus," "based upon the magic of excrements" (1997, 214–15).

For Klein, morphological similarities between daughter and mother render the process of individuation more difficult to sustain, more fraught with the sense of rapine and the threat of recrimination. If, in the girl's "phantasy," the mother's body features as the "store-house" of desired objects, the act of drawing satisfaction from her becomes "equated [...] with the complete demolition of that reservoir," leading to the "impulsion to make restitution" (1997, 217). Daughter and mother, in their anatomical kinship, become vessels of unknown quantities whose transactions are marked by gain on the one side and depletion on the other. If "numerous sublimations" are offered as reparative gestures—for instance, "little stars or crosses, which signify faeces and children," presented to the "mother's reconstituted body"—the "fear of not being able to make restitution" may lead to the more vitiating forms of exchange noted in "obsessional neurosis." In this case, "the girl is governed by a compulsion both to take away and to give back" (1997, 217–18). *Disrupted sublimation* thus forms an "obstacle to all constructive trends," paring down the transactions between mother and daughter to the stringent economics of close barter: "will the things she gives back to her mother be 'good,' and can she give them back correctly as regards quality and quantity and even as regards the order in which they should be arranged inside?" (1997, 218). In *The Antiphon*, the attempted recompense of the children is directed toward Victoria, Augusta's mother. The "children's votive offerings," however, including "[m]arbles, ribbons, pebbles, broken dolls/ And all such things that frightened children leave/ In tigers' dens," are desublimated in the "staggered sanctuary" of the Hobbs family, reduced to so much insufficient feed for parents transformed into predators (*Selected Works*, 156).

If, in the Kleinian narrative of individuation, the "phantasy" is on the side of the developing girl, *The Antiphon* returns the aging Augusta to a second childhood, often inverting the genealogical precedence of the mother. This explains Augusta's address to her daughter: "You who should have been the first born of the two" (*Selected Works*, 203). The economy of the "obsessional neurotic" is solidified in this shared theater of primitive barter, daughter and mother exchanging roles in plunder and recompense, bound to each other in a mythic cycle of vengeance. Miranda, Augusta repeatedly claims, is "that part of me/ I can't afford." Alternately, she slips into the role of daughter and cries to Miranda, now mother: "Unpack your purse—afford me" (*Selected Works*, 214). Instead of individuation, the two are noosed to each other: "[Miranda]'s all Augusta laid up in Miranda;/ Born again to be my new account—" (*Selected Works*, 146). As Miranda later claims: "Every mother, in extortion for her milk—/ With the keyhole iris of the cat—draws blood" (*Selected Works*, 210). In a world where sublimation is defunct, flesh can only be restored in kind: the daughter who takes her mother's milk has robbed the living substance of a cat-eyed miser. Revenge ("draw[ing] blood") and restitution are one. Such a return, however, will never be possible, bar the total reabsorption of the daughter into the mother. So Augusta claims:

> My hoard of me, remission, recompense.
> See how she darkens; how compounds me.
> But does she not breathe short of ransom?
>
> (*Selected Works*, 190)

Miranda may "compound" her mother, accumulating more life as it were, yet her "breath," in monetary terms, still runs "short of ransom." In the economy of the obsessional neurotic, a *lex talionis* as fateful on "Hobbs Ark" as on the House of Atreus comes to exhaust the filial relation wherein each molecule of milk is titrated against another. The gift of life, in this tragic enchainment, is rendered as the *guilt of life*, measuring out the length of the mother's gestation as the temporal debt whose restitution is to be undertaken by the daughter's own repetition—without difference—of the mother—that is, via her own insemination, gestation, and parturition. Each ounce of substance demands a similar return. Anything less is debt: "You're the terrier runs back without the bone" (*Selected Works*, 212).

I move on in the next section to consider a form of renewal suggested in the alternative temporality of the antiphon, one that charts a course away from the economic world the brothers embody. This will be unfolded from the "prosopic intercourse" given in the latter half of Barnes's citation from Corinthians: "For now we see through a glass, darkly; but then face to face: now I know in part; but then shall I know even as also I am known" (1 Corinthians 13:12). If hope is intimated here, however, we will come to witness its final foreclosure.

Play and Repining

Let's jump the Day of Wrath. Let us pretend.
The play is over and the boys are put to bed.
Let's play at being Miranda and Augusta.

(*Selected Works*, 197)

In these lines voiced by Augusta in the final third act of the play, a temporal logic distinct from the time of guilt is raised. The "Day of Wrath," Augusta suggests, can be overleapt. Instead of being run to the ground by a fatalistic settling of ontological accounts, another time unfolds: *playtime*. The time of guilt that the men represent is now at an end ("The boys asleep, and we are girls again"— *Selected Works*, 193). Mother and daughter are free to resume their game.

The ambiguity of this "play at being" works on several levels. First, the suggestion that both Miranda and Augusta have never been or are not quite themselves is made, both of them only ever partially existing in a masculine symbolic order from which they are at the same time partially withdrawn (they could therefore, now that the time of the boys is over, "play" themselves). Yet, if they are only "playing" themselves then it is not so much a return to authenticity that is suggested here than a histrionic staging or restaging of themselves. Furthermore, it is not quite clear who gets to play Miranda and who Augusta. As the rest of *The Antiphon* plays out, this impression that mother and daughter are swapping roles is to some degree corroborated. Where Augusta once had Miranda "wear my belly," she now wears her clothes: "*Without asking permission*, AUGUSTA *takes off* MIRANDA'S *shoes, puts them on her own feet, and in exchange puts her slippers on* MIRANDA." The desire to be delivered from the time of tragic enchainment produces a manic array of place-names, a psychic geography of Edens brought to earth: "Let's go to Ostend, Monte Carlo, Brighton;/ The Lido, Palm Beach, Breisgau, Carcassonne—" (*Selected Works*, 197). The list goes on: Vauxhall, Fontainebleau, the Trianon, Longchamp, Ascot, Aintree, Epsom—in short—"Anything" (*Selected Works*, 198). Historical implausibilities multiply: "I'll sit in a supper box with Richelieu—";

"I am Empress Josephine [...] Or no, Lily Langtry [...] Waiting on the inert Prince of Somewhere." These truncated vignettes of a life elsewhere carve out an opening from linear temporality: "*Did I sleep a hundred years?*" Augusta whispers, wondering—"Was I ever a princess in a legend?"—soon to wake up from the nightmare of history into the fulfilment of love (*Selected Works*, 199). Playtime, here, appears to offer a redemptive opening out of history.

In *The Antiphon*, playtime offers a way out from the timeline of sublimations of linear history. Donald Winnicott, the object-relations psychoanalyst associated with the notion of the "transitional space" opened up by "play," conceptualizes this "*potential space* between the baby and the mother" as an alternative to the Freudian account of sublimation (2005, 143–4). The transitional space of play enables a negotiation of individuation and merger without trauma, permitting explorative ways in and out of the omnipotence of inner fantasy and external resistance. It is where subject and object entwine, the "*intermediate area* [...] *allowed to the infant between primary creativity and objective perception based on reality-testing*" (2005, 15). Navigation through this "interplay between separateness and union" facilitates transitional, rather than traumatic passage from "me-extensions" to the "not-me," "*continuity*" to "*contiguity*" (2005, 134–6). While partially a developmental model, this "*third area*," sustained through life, also relates the adult to the child *structurally*: the adult does not merely grow out of the child once and for all, but coexists with its inner child (2005, 138). Even in adulthood, play is able to renew the time of historical necessity.

Winnicott's notion of the "in-between" has been linked to Martin Buber's notion of "*das Zwischenmenschliche* [the between-human]" for good reason, particularly since Buber himself explicitly associates the I-Thou relation with the "ante-natal life of the child" of "bodily interaction and flowing from the one to the other" (1958, 25). Barnes appears to have been reading Buber extensively probably around the time of *The Antiphon*'s publication, which would have provided yet another source for her thoughts on the theological corollaries of the mother-daughter relation. The "sphere of 'between,'" Buber writes, is "the real place and bearer of what happens between men"—or women—"ever and again re-constituted in accordance with men's meetings with one another" (2002, 241). As with Winnicott's "play," this intermediate region names an eternal beginning, an aperture out of a history that has been absorbed into tragic necessity. In *The Antiphon*, the I-Thou relation is raised with a reference to a kind of prelapsarian love, although eventually collapsed. In response to Augusta's plea—"Come, play me daughter" (*Selected Works*, 193)—Miranda responds with the "lost endearment" of a "thee":

> There was a time when we were not related.
> When I first loved thee—I say "thee" as if
> It were to use a lost endearment
> That in the loss has lost the losing world—
> When I first loved thee, thou wert grazing:
> Carrion Eve, in the green stool, wading,
> In the coarse lilies and the sombre wood;
> Before the tree was in the cross, the cradle, and the coffin,
> [...]
> When yet the salt unspilt, the bread unbroken,
> The milk unquested, unwept for, and unsprung,
> [...]
> The cock crew, the spur struck, and Titus Adam
> Had at you with his raping-hook
> And you reared back, a belly fully of thumbs.
>
> (*Selected Works*, 193–4)

The topography of a lost world is disclosed here. Prior to their individuated forms as mother and daughter ("when we were not related"), within the primordial I-Thou fold, Miranda and Augusta are said to have dwelt together in some Edenic region of love. Reference to paradise as "the losing world," however, suggests that the Fall is already under way, an omen thickened with the thorny theological question of nature in its prelapsarian aspect. Here it is depicted with a scavenging "Carrion Eve" and "green stool"—that is, tree stumps, but also animal dung—where the "lilies of the field" of Matthew 5:28 are now "coarse" and the woods "sombre." Creation and procreation are once again compressed into a single Fall whose consequences—suffering, birth, and death ("cross," "cradle," "coffin")—are aurally implicated with daybreak itself ("The cock crew"). This suggestion of a pre-masculine pastoral, however fragile, is interrupted by a "Titus Adam"—a father on earth and in Eden—who, as first man and first cause (*proton aition*) initiates the Fall into the time of guilt. With his "raping-hook" ("that breeding inch; it was the cause"—*Selected Works*, 184), he commits the first sin against eternal nonbeing: (pro)creation. Barnes's negative prefixes once again strive for a place prior to existence itself: "unspilt," "unquested," "unwept," and "unsprung."

In Barnes's haunting, necrophilic revision of paradise, mother and daughter are presented in a distant union beyond the covenantal terms of salt, bread, and milk (Numbers 18:19; Luke 22:19). The "play" that Augusta attempts to initiate hearkens back to a world outside of time, strangely in seed yet gone to seed.

"How do we thaw from history"—she remarks, reassessing her life with Titus (*Selected Works*, 183). Playtime, understood thus, suspends Ananke. In the antiphony between I and Thou, a time out of the time subsumed into the law of stringent substitutions might be found: "On the far side of the subjective, on this side of the objective, on the narrow ridge, where *I* and *Thou* meet, there is the realm of 'between'" (Buber 2002, 243). Buber's words appear to be recapitulated in *The Antiphon* in the only passage where its key term is discussed. Its very syntactic structure appears to be carried over: we are first apprized of the psychic topography of renewal ("On the far side … "; "on this side … "; "where … "), before it is anchored onto a conceptual map ("there … "). This structure is reproduced in a series of anaphoras in *The Antiphon*:

> Where the martyr'd wild fowl fly the portal
> High in the honey of cathedral walls,
> There is the purchase, governance and mercy.
> Where careful sorrow and observed compline
> Sweat their gums and mastics to the hive
> Of whatsoever stall the head's heaved in—
> There is the amber. As the high plucked banks
> Of the viola rend out the unplucked strings below—
> There is the antiphon.
> I've seen loves so eat each other's mouth
> Till that the common clamour, co-intwined,
> Wrung out the hidden singing in the tongue
> Its chaste economy—there is the adoration.
> So the day, day fit for dying in
> Is the plucked accord.
>
> (*Selected Works*, 214)

The only three topics Barnes professes interest in—"beauty, art and religion"—are woven together here in an esoteric portrayal of the antiphon and its redemptive potential. Even so, the dissonant compression of natural and sacred registers does not merely embed unredeemed life within a larger tapestry whose theme is fulfilment and harmony, but, in weighing salvation down and keeping it tethered to the secular world, installs the potential—or even propensity—for the antiphon to be diverted toward its own profanation. *Nightwood*'s "angel on all fours" may be said to make a reappearance here as angels turned, not to beasts, but this time to birds and bees. "Redemption" here, in its uneasy appearance in the natural world, makes precarious passage across incommensurable settings and images, each time coding and recoding it with an alternate sense till it sounds its final cadence in the manner of a contrived picardy third, forcing a "plucked accord" out of "dying," and a "chaste economy" out of "co-twined" tongues. If the "martyr'd wild fowl" find "purchase, governance, and mercy" through the Biblical motif of "honey," this promised desideratum, already uneasily close to the market, sheds its sacred provenance when redoubled as "amber," inset as it is within the redoubling of the entire image sequence: birds roosting on honeyed cathedrals morph into bees producing amber in their cells.

Thus, while the fulfilment intimated in these passages is given its salvific sense with its religious lexicon, the manner of its combination is strained, densely collagistic rather than integrated, working by force of dreamlike condensation and syntactical correspondence rather than a traceable logic. The progression into the less esoteric musical figure of sympathetic strings (recalling the music of the spheres) disperses the lexical density accumulated in the previous lines, but, to the extent that it clarifies it also reduces, leaving the relations between "honey" (or "purchase, governance and mercy"), "amber," and "antiphon" both *overdetermined* (reducible to the *musica universalis*) and *underdetermined* (logically loose) all at once. The next two terms introduced in this sequence of syntactic parallels—"adoration" and "accord"—continue the alliterative slide begun with "amber" as assonant overtones to its redemptive note, but, conversely, work to compress the call-response structure of protasis ("where ... ") and apodosis ("there ... ") into the very taxiological order of tragic time itself—the "excellent arrangement of catastrophe" that answers *emergence* into life with *merger* in death. If love, here as elsewhere in Barnes's writings, contains a soteriology in seed, it is one that is caught two ways between the gastronomic law of "eat[ing] each other's mouth" and its sublimated double of the "singing" of "tongue[s]," tending toward a "chaste economy" that at the same time threatens to slide back into the cannibalistic. Uncanny plosive *pizzicati* steadily profane the "compline" into a "common clamour, co-intwined" and an uncertain "economy" of grace. By the time the "plucked accord" is sounded, the final rearticulated "c" comes accompanied with two terminal "d"s, which, doubling those of the line before, drive through the semantic coagulate, and wind up the "day" with "dying." Buber's "sphere of the between" here implodes between call and response, protasis and apodosis. Or, in more Winnicottian terms, the intermediate zone of play shuts down when the logic of the sentence catches up. Or, once more, to modulate to a key more fitting to the musical reference of the play, the *rubato*—or "robbed time"—enabling the imagistic latitude ranging from angels to amber-production, violas to wild fowl, succumbs to the syntactic *stringendo* that pushes the "day" to its "dying." Each *da capo* of the "antiphon" theme, that is, alters its meaning in the direction of the conventional till the final cadence sounds, clinching meaning, with a cliché. The "[k]ey-gone generation" is thus resolved on a tonal chord, bringing disharmony into "accord." The "antiphon," tucked into the center of the entire passage, ends up as the pivot on which redemption as "mercy" lapses back into redemption as the restoration of the onto-economic tally.

Resurrection here turns into a "tussle in that trench," a battle over the units of grace left to the dead, and a continuation of this-worldly plaints and prejudices to a sham "justice" ("bootless [...] vindication") in the afterlife. Augusta, Miranda claims, would redistribute life from her daughter to one of the men of the family:

> You who would un-breath my dying breath
> From off the tell-tale mirror plate
> To blow into the famine of my brother's mouth,
> Haggling in a market place.
>
> (*Selected Works*, 217)

An unrelenting Mrs. Lear, unfazed by her Cordelia's death, she would sabotage the revival of her daughter, or at best continue her hair-splitting into the next world:

> Why, at the first trump of impending Doom
> You'll come roaring up the galleys of the dead,—
> [...]
> Crying "*J'accuse!*" and hale me by the browse
> And in alarm bark out "Not this arouse!
> Guilt has her, let guilt haul her house!"
> [...]
> Counting which of my hairs be summoned at the root.
>
> (*Selected Works*, 217)

The time of guilt is summed up here toward the play's end, with "guilt" as conditional ("Guilt has her") bound to "guilt" as consequence ("let guilt haul her house!"). The nursery reference of Act Two ("The king was in his counting house"— *Selected Works*, 120) is completed now by an accountant queen parsing graced follicle from damned.

In a recent phenomenological study of the Eucharist and its structural relation with Mariology, Donald Wallenfang proposes that a "prosopic intercourse" is involved in liturgical worship. He explains it in terms of a "dialectical relationship between logos and *fiat*"—that is, of the word given and its meaning received (2017, 209). In comparing it to the I-Thou relation, he considers it to involve an "antiphony of the gift," whose "partners" are "engaged in lively dialogical play around the object of truth." Noting its difference from the Hegelian dialectic,

Wallenfang associates this "dialectical relationship" of the liturgy with a form of "difference in proximate play": "the interplay" or "perpetual play of polarities between questions, assertions and meanings" at the heart of "communicative wonder" (2017, 42–3). The significance of the Eucharist, in short, is opened up in the "interplay" between communicant and host. The "boundless fecundity of the Eucharist" is ascribed to "the interrogative play around the symbolic phenomenality" that arises insofar as "Christ prototypically absents himself to the senses," necessitating thereby the "inversion" in the "subjective intentionality of faith" (2017, 207–9). Simply put, the withdrawal of Christ from empirical perception prompts the interrogative attention of the devotee, who receives a provisional response from the host in the form of symbols. The "prosopic intercourse" thus opens up the transitional space of intersubjective renewal.

Such a non-Hegelian "dialectic" derived from the sacramental relation would have been familiar to Barnes, who marks out in her copy of Maritain's *Art and Poetry* passages situating the Gregorian antiphonal chants next to the music of Arthur Lourié (Maritain 1943, 103). For Maritain, Lourié's *Dialectical Symphony*, after his *Liturgical Sonata*, bears no "reference to any logical play at all of thesis and antithesis," but relates rather to "that inner dialogue by which we converse continually with ourselves or with God" (1943, 98). In a somewhat tendentious claim, the twentieth-century composer is likened to "Mozart, angel of the word," one of the two composers of Marian hymns whose music Barnes imagines *The Antiphon* to be scored with (1943, 98).[8]

In *The Antiphon*, the "prosopic intercourse" appears to be explicitly raised in the face-to-face encounter Miranda alludes to in Act Two.[9] In Barnes's cryptic formulation, two bared faces appear to extend toward each other with the parting or "listing of the veil," under which, "[e]ither other head, empalmed, incline" (*Selected Writings*, 167). The I-Thou relation once again seems to be set up here. Yet, as Wallenfang also notes, this "dialectical relationship" has to be kept open with a differential zone between the "giver" and "givee" (2017, 201). Without this, he writes of "the danger for the gratuitousness even of grace to become sinister," reducing the "authentic human subject" into a "frozen receptacle or pawn of the repressive power of the gift"—"trapped," in his words, "in a lock-joint economy of exchange" (2017, 201–2). The antiphonal relation can collapse

---

[8] "I wonder what The Antiphon would sound like? What would it be like as an Opera (music, naturally, by Monteverdi, or Mozart!)'" (Barnes 1968d). The references to Mozart's "Queen of the Night" (from *Die Zauberflöte*, K.620) and the "Queen of Heaven" (from the Latin Marian antiphon, *Regina Coeli*, K.276) within the play underscore this connection (*Selected Writings*, 131, 212).

[9] Barnes was also likely influenced by the devotion to the Holy Face of Jesus of Thérèse de Lisieux, whose biography is held in the Archive.

given the "closing up" of "every fissure between body and word" (2017, 207–9). The meaning of the gift, in such a scenario, is not an imaginative return, but an identical substitute. In the filiative relation of *The Antiphon*, the gift of life ends up turning into an existential debt to be settled only in the return of life, that is, as ontological expiation: milk for milk; flesh for flesh. The prosopic encounter, in such a scenario, turns cannibal: more than a meeting of faces, it intussuscepts into a meeting of mouths ("I've seen loves so eat each other's mouth").

In the tragic theater of *The Antiphon*, the redemptive hope embedded in the prosopic intercourse ultimately proves itself ineffective against the force of necessity. The encounter of unveiled faces is most notably perverted by Dudley and Elisha's donning of animal masks (pig and ass), bestializing not only themselves but also their mother and sister with their sexual taunting. The description of Titus's first "dead bastard child" similarly focalizes on its collapsed prosopon: its "Face shut, foreclosed" (*Selected Writings*, 165). Further on, it is the visage of Christ himself on the Veil of Veronica that is profaned.[10] This veil, which Saint Veronica uses to wipe the sweat and blood off Christ's face on his way to Golgotha, is said to be impressed with his true (*vera*) image (*icon*). In a blasphemous pun, however, Barnes drains it of its sacred reference and reduces it to the red "veronica" used in bullfighting. It becomes the final defense of a flightless bird, presenting "a moor-hen, watching a hawk heel in,—/ Draw 'round in dust the broken wing/ Its last veronica" (*Selected Works*, 222). In *The Antiphon*, the prosopic intercourse is finally absorbed into the time of guilt, a "clocked encounter": "we are face to face/ With this the fadged up ends of discontent" (*Selected Works*, 189, 213).

In this foreclosure of all hope, the anti-theodicy enclosed in the tragic theater of *The Antiphon* reveals its foundations in a form of "negation" that is ultimately inassimilable to the dialectical continuities of history proposed in Tillich and Freud, as well as the intersubjective dialectics of the I-Thou relation. Set in 1939 at the outbreak of the Second World War, with the departure of the last ships out of Europe leaving the remaining residents stranded, *The Antiphon*, it would seem, encloses the long history of human existence leading up to it as so much "borrowed" time—the time, that is, of the contraction of ontological guilt: "The worlds [*sic*] history (to date) A beastly time for beasts" (1968b). Negation, here, is conceived in terms of a return of this stolen time, the expiation of existence itself. Bracketing out all of human history in this totalizing gesture, Miranda's tragic judgment on the time that has been is issued ultimately in a statement of radical finitude: "Mother, there's no more time. All's done" (*Selected Works*, 199).

---

[10] See also 2 Corinthians 4:6.

Conclusion: Life or Death?

To greet you back to springtimeconce [sic] again—and in the same domain, all furbished fresh, but long since the trotting horses gone, but then what price our glory, all who yet remain?

(Barnes to Natalie Barney, April 12, 1969)

Having lived through nearly eighty seasons of spring, Barnes greets the Dame Evangeline Musset of her Paris years from four decades ago with a reference to the yearly renewal of life. Characteristic of her letters to Barney is yet another allusion here to Proust. The time of year may be somewhat out of sync, given the late autumn setting that concludes the first volume of the *Recherche*. Yet something asynchronous is also introduced in Proust's narrative, with "the first awakening of this maytime of leaves" conjured forth of the Bois de Boulogne (Proust 1988, 414). The passage of years, however, has drained the woods of its cherished resemblance with the images of the narrator's youth. Apart from the dryadic appearance of the women and their elegant wear, swapped now for prodigally garnished hats and Graeco-Saxon tunics, one chief source of the narrator's plaint lands on the loss of "the trotting horses": "the cruel steeds of Diomedes" are now no more, replaced by "motor-cars driven by moustachioed mechanics" (1988, 417). The narrator's earlier belief in the immanent magic of the woods, making it seem "*le Jardin élyséen de la Femme,*" can no longer be sustained. Just as the women—now "terrible shadows of what they had been"—have "long since fled," the disenchantment of the woods appears to relay "the death of the Gods" (1988, 417–19).

Spring 1969—"furbished fresh"—recalls the senescent Barnes to the "glory" of Creation, breaking again as a gift upon those "who yet remain." Spring 1969—Patchin Place—the walls pushed back to expose the expiring "Virgilian groves" of turn-of-the-century Paris, is also pulled apart by an anamorphosis (1988, 419). The glorious present prompts one to an adoration of the time that yet remains;

the longer perspective of history, however, deposits the "price" of tarrying in this "same domain." A *memento mori* seems to emerge: "Spring Again!"—to recall—ushers in the "Grim Raper." Is the "price" of such "glory"—the existential toll levied on life—ultimately *worth it*? Is melancholy after all held in the hand of a *good enough* theodicy, and suffering and evil worked into the stronger light of a reconciling constellation—however minimally so?

In my reading of melancholy as a soteriological crisis, I have situated it in a zone of arrest between fallen existence and the court of judgment to which the subject is interpellated, stranded before the question of theodicy. In this liminal interface that cuts across the *status corruptionis* of divided being and the prospect of redemption—between denaturalization (from Animal-being) and divinization (into Christological Man)—the melancholic subject is ultimately brought before an existential either/or: to be or not to be. Throughout this book we have seen how Barnes's aesthetic creations each enclose a unique *aesthetic judgment* on the question, each in turn offering a sending in reverse to the Creator and His work in the manner of a co-responding antiphon. Might it be worth asking here, as a concluding gesture, if a final *existential judgment* is ever sealed in life itself? If the aesthetic last judgment enclosed in each of Barnes's works finds itself overturned or confirmed in the next, might it be possible to pose the question of a *last* last judgment? Does Barnes finally commit herself to life (in the light of the Resurrection) or death (as a decision against Creation)?

Barnes's self-sabotaged suicide attempt in 1981 does not, in the end, reveal much. Nor does the incomplete account of her earlier 1939 attempt. Another among modernism's most prominent figures, however, seals his judgment against life in Portbou, Catalonia, 1940, backed against the wall as the Nazi persecution of Jews intensifies—just six months before Virginia Woolf drowns herself in the River Ouse. It is in this very same year of 1940 that Walter Benjamin completes his seminal *Theses on the Philosophy of History*, scarcely more than a decade after he had proclaimed life in postwar Europe to be once again "worth living [*lebenswert*]."[1] Here we find his celebrated statement on the "*weak* messianic power" that binds the living to the "generations of the past" in a "secret appointment [*Verabredung*]": "For we have been expected upon this earth. For it has been given us to know, just like every generation before us, a *weak* messianic power, on which the past has a claim" (2003, 390). We are all burdened, it seems, with the power of a minor resurrection: "The past carries a secret index with

---

[1] See Ng 2020a, 382.

it, by which it is referred to its resurrection." A distorted representation of this orientation toward the resurrection is in fact found in Augusta's desire in *The Antiphon* to be put "on the index of The Book" (*Selected Works*, 206). For *all* to be put in God's "Book of Life,"[2] however, Benjamin suggests, a *strong* messianic power that may—or may not—be effective only at the Last Judgment is required: "only a redeemed mankind is granted the fullness of its past—which is to say, only for a redeemed mankind has its past become citable in all its moments. Each moment it has lived becomes a citation *à l'ordre du jour*. And that day is Judgment Day" (2003, 390). A weak messianic power, however, can only restore portions of lost existence by bringing these into dialectical constellation with the living present, differentially repeating the broken past from the eschatological perspective of a now-point—in the fullness, that is, of "now-time [*Jetztzeit*]." In recognizing ourselves *intended* in the very "image of the past," we seize it in a "tiger's leap," and *realize* our spiritual assignation with the melancholic dead (2003, 390, 395). As Hamacher notes, this messianic power bequeathed to us enables a redemption of "unfinished time," the fulfillment of "the missed or the distorted—hunchbacked—possibilities" of history. Benjamin's understanding of salvation history hence retains a "*weak* possibility of theology"—otherwise put, an "anatheology" (2005, 40-3).

A tragic note remains, however—perhaps too tragic even for criticism to come to terms with so far. Having spoken of this "*weak* messianic power," Benjamin goes on to suggest that we might after all be *too weak* to seize even this weak power:

> The Messiah comes not only as the redeemer; he comes as the victor over the Antichrist. The only historian capable of fanning the spark of hope in the past is the one who is firmly convinced that *even the dead* will not be safe from the enemy if he is victorious. And this enemy has never ceased to be victorious.
> (2003, 391)

Messiah and Antichrist are put into the agon of salvation history here. The terms of life and death splinter into finer ones: more than just the physical markers of sentience, they reference the notion of something like a *second life* and a *second death*.[3] Though death comes to all mortal bodies, the "historian" *strong* enough to make the tiger's leap to seize the image of the past in which she is intended achieves its *weak* resurrection in the long narrative of the

---

[2] Revelation 3:5; Daniel 12:1.
[3] Note also the "second death" of Revelation 21:8.

spiritual community. That she might fail in her task, however, is not only possible but perhaps inevitable: "*even the dead*"—in their first death as mortal beings—"will not be safe from the enemy if he is victorious." The strident qualifier—*if*—is soon fulfilled: the Antichrist, it turns out, "has never ceased to be victorious." A portion of humanity has already been delivered over to this *second death*.

It is possible to read this as a final consignment to total oblivion, an unrelieved, eternal exclusion from the sight of God and those created in His image. Two scenarios might hold in this victory of "the enemy": (i) when the "indolence of the heart" causes us to break our spiritual contract with the past, and melancholic time is never regained (2003, 391); and (ii) *when there are none left to look to the past*. No remembrance of past time is possible in a world *after humanity*. What Rowan Williams has termed the "showing of the sacred, that excess of unearned, unexpected life that sustains us in going on speaking and thinking" may after all present a sacred excess of time that—finally—expires (2016, 27). Facing the irreducible evil looming on the horizon of the Holocaust, Benjamin ultimately suggests that humanity's final decision to affiliate itself with life or death may not necessarily be what we expect. This *existential judgment* will be made in the actions of the species as a whole.

I conclude here with this question, manifestly too large for any book to answer. In rounding off the "weak theodicy" with which I began this book in a discussion of a "weak messianic power," however, one of the underlying motivations for undertaking this project may be registered here. Among other more mundane reasons, this book was also written as a struggle to fulfil the spiritual appointment between one melancholic woman of today and another of yesterday—and with, additionally, those who, like O'Connor, have thought that the best they could ever hope for in life is to "Be humble like the dust, as God intended, and crawl [...] crawl to the end of the gutter and not be missed and not much remembered" (*Nightwood*, 133). This spiritual appointment has brought me to a strange communion in melancholy with the radically unfulfilled, brought low, in the manner of beasts, by "the water hole of the damned":

> I'm an angel on all fours, with a child's feet behind me, seeking my people that have never been made, going down face foremost, drinking the waters of night at the water hole of the damned, and I go into the waters, up to my heart, the terrible waters!
>
> (*Nightwood*, 85)

It is my hope then, with O'Connor, to have fished among "my people that have never been made," and brought some of these forth of the baptismal waters of melancholy to be re-clothed in the garment of life, and perhaps even to have made the case for—at the very least—a *weak* justification for abiding in the time that remains.

Bibliography

Adamowicz, Elza. 1998. *Surrealist Collage in Text and Image: Dissecting the Exquisite Corpse*. Cambridge: Cambridge University Press.

Adorno, Theodor Wiesengrund. 2013. *Aesthetic Theory*, ed. and trans. Robert Hullot-Kentor. London: Bloomsbury Academic.

Adorno, Theodor Wiesengrund. 2005. *Minima Moralia: Reflections from Damaged Life*, trans. E.F.N. Jephcott. London: Verso Books.

Adorno, Theodor Wiesengrund. 2016. *Philosophy of Modern Music*, trans. Anne G. Mitchell and Wesley V. Blomster. London: Bloomsbury Academic.

Adorno, Theodor Wiesengrund. 2002. *Quasi Una Fantasia: Essays on Modern Music*, trans. Rodney Livingstone. London: Routledge.

Agamben, Giorgio. 1993. *Infancy and History: The Destruction of Experience*, trans. Liz Heron. London: Verso Books.

Agamben, Giorgio. 2011b. *Nudities*, trans. David Kishik and Stefan Pedatella. Stanford: Stanford University Press.

Agamben, Giorgio. 2011a. *The Kingdom and the Glory: For a Theological Genealogy of Economy and Government*, trans. Lorenzo Chiesa, with Matteo Mandarini. Stanford: Stanford University Press.

Agamben, Giorgio. 2005. *The Time That Remains: A Commentary on the Letter to the Romans*, trans. Patricia Dailey. Stanford: Stanford University Press.

Agamben, Giorgio. 1997. "Vocation and Voice." *Qui Parle* 10, no. 2 (Spring/Summer): 89–100.

Aragon, Louis. 1980. *Paris Peasant*, trans. Simon Watson-Taylor. Cambridge. MA: Exact Change.

Augustine, Saint, Bishop of Hippo. 1912. *St. Augustine's Confessions*, trans. William Watts. 2 vols. London: William Heinemann.

Augustine, Saint, Bishop of Hippo. 2008. *Homilies on the First Epistle of John (In epistolam Joannis ad Parthos)*, ed. Boniface Ramsey, Daniel E. Doyle, and Thomas Martin, trans. Boniface Ramsey. Hyde Park, NY: New York City Press.

Bahun, Sanja. 2013. *Modernism and Melancholia: Writing as Countermourning*. Oxford: Oxford University Press.

Balsamo, Gian. 2004. *Joyce's Messianism: Dante, Negative Existence, and the Messianic Self*. Columbia, South Carolina: University of South Carolina.

Barnes, Djuna. 1913. "The Joke in the Tragedy of the Other Man's Life." From "Types found in Odd Corners about Brooklyn." *Brooklyn Daily Eagle*, September 1, 1913. Djuna Barnes Papers, Special Collections, University of Maryland Libraries. Series VIII, Box 9, Folder 1.

Barnes, Djuna. 1916. "Becoming Intimate with the Bohemians." *New York Morning Telegraph Sunday Magazine*, November 19, 1916. DBP. Series III, Box 17, Folder 4.

Barnes, Djuna. 1922. "Against Nature: In Which Everything That Is Young, Inadequate and Tiresome Is Included in the Term Natural." In *Vanity Fair* 18, August 1922. DBP. Series III, Box 12, Folder 5.

Barnes, Djuna. 1923. "What Is Good Form in Dying: In Which a Dozen Dainty Deaths Are Suggested for Daring Damsels." *Vanity Fair*, June 1923. DBP. Series III, Box 13, Folder 25.

Barnes, Djuna. 1929. "Why Actors? Brother Sumac Searches for an Answer." *Theatre Guild Magazine*, December 1929. DBP. Series III, Box 13, Folder 27.

Barnes, Djuna. 1934. Letter to Charles Henri Ford. April 10, 1934. DBP. Series II, Box 7, Folder 14.

Barnes, Djuna. 1936. Letter to Emily Coleman. August 13, 1936. Emily Holmes Coleman Collection, University of Delaware Library Special Collections.

Barnes, Djuna. 1937. Letter to Emily Coleman. November 30, 1937. DBP. Series II, Box 3, Folder 10.

Barnes, Djuna. 1938a. Letter to Emily Coleman. May 21, 1938. DBP. Series II, Box 3, Folder 11.

Barnes, Djuna. 1938b. Letter to Emily Coleman. June 24, 1938. DBP. Series II, Box 3, Folder 11.

Barnes, Djuna. 1938c. Letter to Emily Coleman. July 25, 1938. DBP. Series II, Box 3, Folder 11.

Barnes, Djuna. 1938d. Letter to Emily Coleman. August 7, 1938. DBP. Series II, Box 3, Folder 12.

Barnes, Djuna. 1938e. Letter to Emily Coleman. August 11, 1938. DBP. Series II, Box 3, Folder 12.

Barnes, Djuna. 1938f. Letter to Emily Coleman. September 2, 1938. DBP. Series II, Box 3, Folder 12.

Barnes, Djuna. 1938g. Letter to Emily Coleman. October 13/16, 1938. DBP. Series II, Box 3, Folder 12.

Barnes, Djuna. 1938h. Letter to Emily Coleman. October 30, 1938. DBP. Series II, Box 3, Folder 12.

Barnes, Djuna. 1938i. Letter to Emily Coleman. November 13/19, 1938. DBP. Series II, Box 3, Folder 12.

Barnes, Djuna. 1938j. Letter to Emily Coleman. December 15, 1938. DBP. Series II, Box 3, Folder 12.

Barnes, Djuna. 1939a. Letter to Emily Coleman. January 5, 1939 DBP. Series II, Box 3, Folder 13.

Barnes, Djuna. 1939b. Letter to Emily Coleman. February 4, 1939. DBP. Series II, Box 3, Folder 13.

Barnes, Djuna. 1939c. Letter to Emily Coleman. February 28, 1939. DBP. Series II, Box 3, Folder 13.

Barnes, Djuna. 1939d. Letter to Emily Coleman. March 3, 1939. DBP. Series II, Box 3, Folder 13.

Barnes, Djuna. 1939e. Letter to Emily Coleman. March 20-23, 1939. DBP. Series II, Box 3, Folder 13.

Barnes, Djuna. 1939f. Letter to Emily Coleman. June 6, 1939. DBP. Series II, Box 3, Folder 13.

Barnes, Djuna. 1939g. Letter to Emily Coleman. June 28, 1939. DBP. Series II, Box 3, Folder 13.

Barnes, Djuna. 1939h. Letter to Emily Coleman. July 11, 1939. DBP. Series II, Box 3, Folder 14.

Barnes, Djuna. 1939i. Letter to Emily Coleman. November 12, 1939. DBP. Series II, Box 3, Folder 14.

Barnes, Djuna. 1939j. Letter to Emily Coleman. November 27, 1939. DBP. Series II, Box 3, Folder 14.

Barnes, Djuna. 1939-40. Letter to Emily Coleman. December 30/January 1, 1940. DBP. Series II, Box 3, Folder 14.

Barnes, Djuna. 1940a. Letter to Emily Coleman. February 17, 1940. DBP. Series II, Box 3, Folder 15.

Barnes, Djuna. 1940b. Letter to Emily Coleman. March 30/April 1, 1940. DBP. Series II, Box 3, Folder 15.

Barnes, Djuna. 1940c. Letter to Emily Coleman. April 8, 1940. DBP. Series II, Box 3, Folder 15.

Barnes, Djuna. 1940d. Letter to Emily Coleman. August 3, 1940. DBP. Series II, Box 3, Folder 16.

Barnes, Djuna. 1941a. Letter to Emily Coleman, April 19, 1941. DBP. Series II, Box 3, Folder 17.

Barnes, Djuna. 1941b. Letter to Emily Coleman. June 6, 1941. DBP. Series II, Box 3, Folder 17.

Barnes, Djuna. 1942a. Letter to Emily Coleman. September 24, 1942. DBP. Series II, Box 3, Folder 18.

Barnes, Djuna. 1942b. Letter to Emily Coleman. October 28, 1942. DBP. Series II, Box 3, Folder 18.

Barnes, Djuna. 1948. Letter to Agenzia Litteraria Internazional. October 8, 1948. DBP. Series II, Box 1, Folder 5.

Barnes, Djuna. 1954. Letter to T. S. Eliot. July 15, 1954. DBP. Series II, Box 4, Folder 62.

Barnes, Djuna. 1957. Letter to Edwin Muir. October 26, 1957. DBP. Series II, Box 12, Folder 24.

Barnes, Djuna. 1958a. Letter to Peggy Guggenheim. March 18, 1958. DBP. Series II, Box 8, Folder 28.

Barnes, Djuna. 1958b. Letter to Dan Mahoney. November 14, 1958. DBP. Series II, Box 11, Folder 31.

Barnes, Djuna. 1959. Letter to Wolfgang Hildesheimer. June 5, 1959. DBP. Series II, Box 9, Folder 27.

Barnes, Djuna. Circa 1950. "Notes Toward a Definition of *The Antiphon*." DBP. Series III, Box 5, Folder 7.

Barnes, Djuna. 1961. Letter to Emily Coleman. October 22, 1961. DBP. Series II, Box 3, Folder 20.

Barnes, Djuna. 1962. *Selected Works*. London and Boston: Faber & Faber.

Barnes, Djuna. 1968a. Letter to Natalie Clifford Barney. February 29, 1968. DBP. Series II, Box 1, Folder 46.

Barnes, Djuna. 1968b. Letter to Natalie Clifford Barney. April 12, 1968. DBP. Series II, Box 1, Folder 46.

Barnes, Djuna. 1968c. Letter to Natalie Clifford Barney. August 14, 1968. DBP. Series II, Box 1, Folder 46.

Barnes, Djuna. 1968d. Letter to Cristina Campo. October 2, 1963. DBP. Series II, Box 2, Folder 43.

Barnes, Djuna. 1968e. Letter to Elémire Zolla. April 23, 1968. DBP. Series II, Box 16, Folder 62.

Barnes, Djuna. 1969a. Letter to Natalie Clifford Barney. April 12, 1969. DBP. Series II, Box 1, Folder 46.

Barnes, Djuna. 1969b. Letter to Christine Koschel. April 15, 1969. DBP Series II, Box 10, Folder 47.

Barnes, Djuna. 1971a. Letter to Cristina Campo. May 20, 1971. DBP. Series II, Box 2, Folder 43.

Barnes, Djuna. 1971b. Letter to James Scott. April 15, 1971. DBP. Series II, Box 14, Folder 57.

Barnes, Djuna. 1972. Letter to James Scott April 1, 1972. DBP. Series II, Box 14, Folder 58.

Barnes, Djuna. 1974. *Vagaries Malicieux: Two Stories by Djuna Barnes*. New York: F. Hallman.

Barnes, Djuna. 1978. Letter to Silas Glossop. February 15, 1978. DBP. Series II, Box 8, Folder 3.

Barnes, Djuna. 1982. *Creatures in an Alphabet*. Design by Francesca Belanger. New York: The Dial Press.

Barnes, Djuna. 1985. *Interviews*, ed. Alyce Barry. Foreword by Douglas Messerli. Washington, DC: Sun & Moon Press.

Barnes, Djuna. 1987. *Smoke and Other Early Stories*, ed. Douglas Messerli. Los Angeles: Sun & Moon Press.

Barnes, Djuna. 1990. *New York*, ed. Alyce Barry. Foreword by Douglas Messerli. London: Virago Press

Barnes, Djuna. 1990 [1928]. *Ryder*. Afterword by Paul West. Normal, IL: Dalkey Archive Press.

Barnes, Djuna. 1995. *Nightwood: The Original Version and Related Drafts*, ed. Cheryl J. Plumb. Normal, IL: Dalkey Archive Press.

Barnes, Djuna. 1996. *Collected Stories*, ed. Phillip Herring. Los Angeles: Son & Moon Press.
Barnes, Djuna. 2000 [1958]. *The Antiphon*. Kobenhavn & Los Angeles: Green Integer.
Barnes, Djuna. 2001 [1936]. *Nightwood*. Preface by T. S. Eliot. London: Faber & Faber.
Barnes, Djuna. 2005. *Collected Poems, With Notes toward the Memoirs*, ed. Phillip Herring and Osías Stutman. Madison, WI: University of Wisconsin Press.
Barnes, Djuna. 2006 [1928]. *Ladies Almanack*. Afterword by Daniela Caselli. Manchester: Carcanet.
Barnes, Djuna. Undated. *Notebook*. DBP. Series I, Box 4, Folder 7.
Barnes, Djuna. Undated. Response to Emily Coleman's unpublished essay on *Nightwood*. DBP. Series II, Box 3, Folder 24.
Bataille, Georges. 2012 [1957]. *Literature and Evil*, trans. Alastair Hamilton. London: Penguin.
Baudelaire, Charles. 1981. *Selected Writings on Art and Artists*, trans. P.E. Charvet. Cambridge: Cambridge University Press.
Beattie, Tina. 2013. *Theology after Postmodernity: Divining the Void – A Lacanian Reading of Thomas Aquinas*. Oxford: Oxford University Press.
Béhar, Henri, Marieke Dubbelboer et Jean-Paul Morel. 2009. *Commentaires pour servir à la lecture de l'Almanach du Père Ubu, illustré, 1899*. Paris: Société des amis d'Alfred Jarry.
Benjamin, Walter. 2003. "On the Concept of History." In *Selected Writings, Volume 4, 1938-1940*, ed. Howard Eiland and Michael W. Jennings, trans. Edmund Jephcott et al., 390–400. Cambridge, MA: Harvard University Press.
Benstock, Shari. 1986. *Women of the Left Bank: Paris, 1900-1940*. Austin: University of Texas Press.
Bersani, Leo. 1990. *The Culture of Redemption*. Cambridge, MA: Harvard University Press.
Bersani, Leo. 2010. "Psychoanalysis and the Aesthetic Subject." In *Is the Rectum a Grave?: and Other Essays*. Chicago: University of Chicago Press.
Biles, Jeremy and Kent L. Brintnall, eds. 2015. *Negative Ecstasies: Georges Bataille and the Study of Religion*. New York: Fordham University Press.
Blanton, Charles Daniel. 2015. *Epic Negation: The Dialectical Poetics of Late Modernism*. Oxford: Oxford University Press.
Boone, Joseph Allen. 1998. *Libidinal Currents: Sexuality and the Shaping of Modernism*. Chicago: University of Chicago Press.
Booth, Wayne. 1974. *A Rhetoric of Irony*. Chicago: University of Chicago Press.
Breton, André. 1972. *Manifestoes of Surrealism*, trans. Richard Seaver and Helen R. Lane. Ann Arbor: University of Michigan Press.
Breton, André, and Louis Aragon. 1928. "La cinquantenaire de l'hystérie (1878-1928)." *La Révolution surréaliste* 11, no. 15 (March): 20-2.
Broe, Mary Lynn, ed. 1991. *Silence and Power: A Reevaluation of Djuna Barnes*. Carbondale and Edwardsville, IL: Southern Illinois University Press.

Brown, Norman O. 1985 [1959]. *Life Against Death: The Psychoanalytical Meaning of History*. Middletown: Wesleyan University Press.
Buber, Martin. 2002 [1947]. *Between Man and Man*, trans. Ronald Gregor Smith. Abingdon: Routledge.
Buber, Martin. 1958 [1923]. *I and Thou*, trans. Ronald Gregor Smith. New York: Charles Scribner's Sons.
Burke, Kenneth. 1945. *A Grammar of Motives*. New York: Prentice-Hall Inc.
Burke, Kenneth. 1957. "The Rhetoric of Hitler's 'Battle'." In *The Philosophy of Literary Form: Studies in Symbolic Action*, 164–89. New York: Vintage Books.
Burke, Kenneth. 1992. "Version, Con-, Per-, and In- (Thoughts on Djuna Barnes's Novel *Nightwood*)." In *Language as Symbolic Action: Essays on Life, Literature, and Method*, 240–53. Berkeley: University of California Press.
Burton, Robert. 1989–2000. *The Anatomy of Melancholy*, ed. Thomas C. Faulkner, Nicolas K. Kiessling, and Rhonda L. Blair. Introduction by J.B. Bamborough and Martin Dodsworth. 6 vols. Oxford: Clarendon Press.
Butler, Judith. 1993. *Bodies That Matter*. London: Routledge.
Campo, Christina. 1969. Letter to Djuna Barnes, November 1969. DBP. Series II, Box 2, Folder 43.
Carlston, Erin G. 1998. *Thinking Fascism: Sapphic Modernism and Fascist Modernity*. Stanford: Stanford University Press.
Caselli, Daniela. 2009. *Improper Modernism: Djuna Barnes's Bewildering Corpus*. Farnham and Burlington, VT: Ashgate.
Chaucer, Geoffrey. 2008. "The Knight's Tale." In *The Riverside Chaucer*, ed. F. N. Robinson. Oxford: Oxford University Press.
Chiesa, Lorenzo. 2016. *The Not-Two: Logic and God in Lacan*. Cambridge, MA: MIT Press.
Coakley, Sarah. 2000. "The Eschatological Body: Gender, Transformation, and God." *Modern Theology* 16, no. 1: 61–73.
Coleman, Emily. 1935a. Letter to Djuna Barnes. August 27, 1935. DBP. Series II, Box 3, Folder 6.
Coleman, Emily. 1935b. Letter to Djuna Barnes. December 19, 1935. DBP. Series II, Box 3, Folder 7.
Coleman, Emily. 1947. Letter to Djuna Barnes. December 4, 1947. DBP. Series II, Box 3, Folder 18.
Connor, Steven. 2000. *Dumbstruck: A Cultural History of Ventriloquism*. Oxford: Oxford University Press.
Curley, Michael J., ed. 1979. *Physiologus*. Introduction by Michael Curley. Chicago: University of Chicago Press.
Dalton, Anne B. 1993. "Escaping from Eden: Djuna Barnes' Revision of Psychoanalytic Theory and Her Treatment of Father-Daughter Incest in *Ryder*." *Women's Studies* 22, no. 2: 163–79.

Daniel, Drew. 2013. *The Melancholy Assemblage: Affect and Epistemology in the English Renaissance*. New York: Fordham University Press.
De Man, Paul. 1996. "The Concept of Irony." In *Aesthetic Ideology*, ed. Andrzej Warminski. Minneapolis: University of Minnesota Press.
Deleuze, Gilles. 1997. *Essays Critical and Clinical*, trans. Daniel W. Smith and Michael A. Greco. Introduction by Daniel Smith. Minneapolis: University of Minnesota Press.
Deleuze, Gilles. 2013. *The Logic of Sense*, ed. Constantin V. Boundas, trans. Mark Lester, with Charles Stivale. London and New York: Bloomsbury Academic.
Deleuze, Gilles and Félix Guattari. 1983. *Anti-Oedipus: Capitalism and Schizophrenia*, trans. Robert Hurley, Mark Seem, and Helen R. Lane. Minneapolis: University of Minnesota Press.
Deleuze, Gilles and Félix Guattari. 2013. *A Thousand Plateaus*, trans. Brian Massumi. London and New York: Bloomsbury Academic.
Deleuze, Gilles and Félix Guattari. 1994. *What Is Philosophy?* trans. Graham Burchill and Hugh Tomlinson. London: Verso.
Diels, Hermann. 1912. *Die Fragmente der Vorsokratiker*. Berlin: Weidmannsche Buchhandlung.
Dostoevsky, Fyodor. 2004 [1880]. *The Brothers Karamazov*, trans. Richard Pevear and Larissa Volokhonsky. London: Vintage Books.
Dostoevsky, Fyodor. 2008 [1872]. *Devils*, trans. Michael R. Katz. Oxford: Oxford University Press.
Douglas, Mary. 1975. "Jokes." In *Implicit Meanings: Essays in Anthropology*. Abingdon: Routledge.
Duchartre, Pierre-Louis and René Saulnier. 1925. *L'imagerie populaire: les images de toutes les provinces françaises du XVe siècle au Second Empire. Les complaintes, contes, chansons, légendes qui ont inspiré les imagiers*. Paris: Librairie de France.
Dunning, Benjamin. 2014. *Christ without Adam: Subjectivity and Sexual Difference in the Philosophers' Paul*. New York: Columbia University Press.
Edmunds, Susan. 1997. "Narratives of a Virgin's Violation: The Critique of Middle-Class Reformism in Djuna Barnes's *Ryder*." *Novel: A Forum on Fiction* 30, no. 2: 218–36.
Eliade, Mircea. 1969. *Le mythe de l'éternel retour*. Paris: Gallimard.
Eliot, T. S. 1975. *Selected Prose*, ed. Frank Kermode. London: Faber & Faber.
Eliot, T. S. 2004. *The Complete Poems and Plays*. London: Faber & Faber.
Esposito, Roberto. 2013. *Terms of the Political: Community, Immunity, Biopolitics*, trans. Rhiannon Noel Welch. New York: Fordham University Press.
Ferber, Ilit. 2013. *Philosophy and Melancholy: Benjamin's Early Reflections on Theater and Language*. Stanford: Stanford University Press.
Fiddes, Paul S. 1991. *Freedom and Limit: A Dialogue between Literature and Christian Doctrine*. Basingstoke: Palgrave Macmillan.
Fiddes, Paul S. 2000. *The Promised End: Eschatology in Theology and Literature*. Oxford: Blackwell Publishers.

Fiddes, Paul S. 2013. "Suffering In Theology and Modern European Thought." In *The Oxford Handbook of Theology and Modern European Thought*, ed. Nicholas Adams, George Pattison, and Graham Ward, 169–92. Oxford: Oxford University Press.

Fitzthum, Gerhard. 1992. *Das Ende der Menschheit und die Philosophie: Zum Spannungsverhaltnis von Ethik und Theodizee*. Gießen: Focus-Verlag.

Flatley, Jonathan. 2008. *Affective Mapping: Melancholia and the Politics of Modernism*. Cambridge, MA: Harvard University Press.

Freeman, Elizabeth. 2014. "Sacra/Mentality in Djuna Barnes's *Nightwood*." *American Literature* 86, no. 4 (December): 737–65.

Freud, Sigmund. 2001. *The Standard Edition of the Complete Psychological Works of Sigmund Freud*, trans. James Strachey, Anna Freud, Alix Strachey, Alan Tyson, and Angela Richards. 24 vols. London: Vintage Books.

Freud, Sigmund. 1905. *Three Essays on the Theory of Sexuality*. SE VII: 125–248.

Freud, Sigmund. 1913. *Totem and Taboo: Some Points of Agreement between the Mental Lives of Savages and Neurotics*. SE XIII: 1–161.

Freud, Sigmund. 1914. "On Narcissism." *SE* XIV: 69–102.

Freud, Sigmund. 1915. "Instincts and Their Vicissitudes." *SE* XIV: 117–40.

Freud, Sigmund. 1917. "Mourning and Melancholia." *SE* XIV: 237–58.

Freud, Sigmund. 1923. *The Ego and the Id*. *SE* XIX: 3–66.

Freud, Sigmund. 1925. "Negation." *SE* XIX: 235–9.

Freud, Sigmund. 1927. *The Future of an Illusion*. *SE* XXI: 3–58.

Freud, Sigmund. 1930. *Civilisation and Its Discontents*. *SE* XXI: 64–145.

Friedländer, Saul. 2003. "Ideology and Extermination: The Immediate Origins of the 'Final Solution.'" In *Catastrophe and Meaning: The Holocaust and the Twentieth Century*, ed. Moishe Postone and Eric Santner, 17–33. Chicago: University of Chicago Press.

Frye, Northrop. 1990. *Anatomy of Criticism: Four Essays*. London: Penguin Books.

Frye, Northrop. 1983. *The Great Code: The Bible and Literature*. London and New York: Harcourt Brace.

Geuss, Raymond. 1999. "Art and Theodicy." In *Morality, Culture, and History: Essays on German philosophy*, 78–115. Cambridge: Cambridge University Press.

Geyer, Carl-Friedrich. 1992. *Die Theodizee: Diskurs, Dokumentation, Transformation*. Stuttgart: Franz Steiner Verlag.

Gherovici, Patricia. 2017. *Transgender Psychoanalysis: A Lacanian Perspective on Sexual Difference*. Abingdon: Routledge.

Glassco, John. 2007 [1970]. *Memoirs of Montparnasse*. New York: New York Review of Books.

Glavey, Brian. 2016. *The Wallflower Avant-Garde: Modernism, Sexuality, and Queer Ekphrasis*. Oxford: Oxford University Press.

Glossop, Silas. 1965. Letter to Djuna Barnes. June 14, 1965. DBP. Series II, Box 8, Folder 1.

Goody, Alex. 2007. *Modernist Articulations: A Cultural Study of Djuna Barnes, Mina Loy, and Gertrude Stein*. Basingstoke: Palgrave Macmillan.

Greenberg, Jonathan. 2011. *Modernism, Satire, and the Novel*. Cambridge: Cambridge University Press.

Guarnieri, Romana and Paul Verdeyen, ed. 1986. *Corpus Christianorum: Continuatio Medievalis*, Volume 69. Turnholt: Brepols.

Guégan, Bertrand et al., ed. 1919. *L'almanach de cocagne pour l'an 1920: Dédié aux vrais Gourmands et aux Francs Buveurs*. Paris: Sirène.

Guégan, Bertrand et al., ed. 1920. *L'almanach de cocagne pour l'an 1921: Dédié aux vrais Gourmands et aux Francs Buveurs*. Paris: Sirène.

Guégan, Bertrand et al., ed. 1921. *L'almanach de cocagne pour l'an 1922: Dédié aux vrais Gourmands et aux Francs Buveurs*. Paris: Sirène.

Guirl-Stearley, G. C., ed. 1999. "The Letters of Djuna Barnes and Emily Holmes Coleman (1935-1936)." *The Missouri Review* 22, no. 3: 105–46.

Hallward, Peter. 2006. *Out of This World: Deleuze and the Philosophy of Creation*. London: Verso.

Hamacher, Werner. 2002. "Guilt History: Benjamin's Sketch 'Capitalism as Religion,'" trans. Kirk Wetter. *Diacritics* 32, no. 3/4: 81–106.

Hamacher, Werner. 2005. "'Now': Walter Benjamin on Historical Time." In *Walter Benjamin and History*, ed. Andrew Benjamin, 38–68. London: Continuum.

Hannah, Robert. 2009. *Time in Antiquity*. Abingdon: Routledge.

Hanson, Ellis. 1997. *Decadence and Catholicism*. Cambridge MA: Harvard University Press.

Hayot, Eric. 2012. *On Literary Worlds*. Oxford: Oxford University Press.

Heaney, Emma. 2017. *The New Woman: Literary Modernism, Queer Theory, and the Trans Feminine Allegory*. Evanston, IL: Northwestern University Press.

Hegel, G. W. F. 2010. *Hegel's Aesthetics: Lectures on Fine Art. Volume 2*, trans. T. M. Knox. Oxford: Clarendon Press.

Hegel, G. W. F. 2012. *Lectures on Natural Right and Political Science*, trans. Michael J. Stewart and Peter C. Hodgson. Oxford: Oxford University Press.

Heidegger, Martin. 2010. *Being and Time*, trans. Joan Stambaugh, revised by Dennis J. Schmidt. Albany: State University of New York Press.

Heidegger, Martin. 2001a. *Poetry, Language, Thought*, trans. Albert Hofstadter. New York: HarperCollins.

Heidegger, Martin. 2001b. *Sein und Zeit*. Tübingen: Max Niemeyer Verlag.

Herf, Jeffrey. 1984. *Reactionary Modernism: Technology, Culture, and Politics in Weimar and the Third Reich*. Cambridge: Cambridge University Press.

Herring, Phillip. 1995. *Djuna: The Life and Work of Djuna Barnes*. New York: Penguin Press.

Herring, Scott. 2007. *Queering the Underworld: Slumming, Literature, and the Undoing of Lesbian and Gay History*. Chicago: University of Chicago Press.

Hewitt, Andrew. 1996. *Political Inversions: Homosexuality, Fascism, and the Modernist Imaginary*. Stanford: Stanford University Press.

Hick, John. 2010. *Evil and the God of Love*. Basingstoke: Palgrave Macmillan.

Hobson, Suzanne. 2011. *Angels of Modernism: Religion, Culture, Aesthetics 1910-1960*. London: Palgrave.

Hollywood, Amy. 2016. *Acute Melancholia and Other Essays: Mysticism, History, and the Study of Religion*. New York: Columbia University Press.

Hollywood, Amy. 2001. "Suffering Transformed: Marguerite Porete, Meister Eckhart, and the Problem of Women's Spirituality." In *Meister Eckhart and the Beguine Mystics: Hadewijch of Brabant, Mechthild of Magdeburg, and Marguerite Porete*, ed. Barnard McGinn, 87–113. New York: Continuum.

Hopkins, Gerard Manley. 1931. *Poems of Gerard Manley Hopkins*, ed. Robert Bridges. London: Humphrey Milford.

James, William. 1982. *The Varieties of Religious Experience*, ed. Martin E. Marty. New York: Penguin.

Joyce, James. 1986 [1922]. *Ulysses*, ed. Hans Walter Gabler, with Wolfhard Steppe and Claus Melchior. Preface by Richard Ellmann. Afterword by Michael Groden. New York: Vintage Books.

Justaert, Kristien. 2012. *Theology after Deleuze*. London and New York: Continuum.

Kannenstine, Louis. 1977. *The Art of Djuna Barnes: Duality and Damnation*. New York: New York University Press.

Keats, John. 1982. *John Keats: Complete Poems*, ed. Jack Stillinger. Cambridge, MA: Harvard University Press.

Keats, John. 1820. "Ode on Melancholy." 283–4.

Keats, John. 1935. *The Letters of John Keats*, ed. Maurice Buxton Forman. New York: Oxford University Press.

Kermode, Frank. 2000. *The Sense of an Ending: Studies in the Theory of Fiction*. Oxford and New York: Oxford University Press.

Kirchberger, Clare, ed. 1927. *The Mirror of Simple Souls, by an Unknown French Mystic of the Thirteenth Century: Translated into English by M.N.* New York: Benziger Brothers.

Klein, Melanie. 1997. *The Psycho-Analysis of Children*, trans. Alix Strachey, revised H. A. Thorner. London: Vintage.

Kristeva, Julia. 1992. *Black Sun: Depression and Melancholia*, trans. Leon S. Roudiez. New York: Columbia University Press.

Lacan, Jacques. 2007a. *Écrits*, trans. Bruce Fink, with Héloïse Fink and Russell Grigg. New York and London: W.W. Norton and Company.

Lacan, Jacques. 2015. *The Seminar of Jacques Lacan, Book VIII: Transference*, trans. Bruce Fink, ed. Jacques-Alain Miller. Cambridge: Polity Press.

Lacan, Jacques. 1998. *The Seminar of Jacques Lacan, Book XX: Encore, On Female Sexuality, The Limits of Love and Knowledge*, trans. Bruce Fink. New York and London: W.W. Norton and Company.

Lacan, Jacques. 2007b. *The Seminar of Jacques Lacan, Book XVII: The Other Side of Psychoanalysis*, trans. Russell Grigg. New York and London: W.W. Norton and Company.

Laks, André and Glenn W. Most, ed. and trans. 2016. *Early Greek Philosophy, Volume II: Beginnings and Early Ionian Thinkers, Part 1*. Loeb Classical Library 525. Cambridge, MA: Harvard University Press.

Larrimore, Mark, ed. 2001. *The Problem of Evil: A Reader*. Oxford: Blackwell.

Lautréamont, Comte de. 1924. *The Lay of Maldoror*, trans. John Rodker. Introduction by Remy De Gourmont. Plates after Odilon Redon. London: The Casanova Society.

Leader, Darian. 2016. "Hysteria today." In *Hysteria Today*, ed. Anouchka Grose, 27–34. London: Karnac Books.

Lewis, Pericles. 2010. *Religious Experience and the Modernist Novel*. Cambridge: Cambridge University Press.

Lewis, Wyndham. 1931. *Hitler*. London: Chatto & Windus.

Lewis, Wyndham. 1939. *The Hitler Cult*. London: Dent.

Loughlin, Gerard, ed. 2007. *Queer Theology: Rethinking the Western Body*. Malden, MA: Blackwell.

Loy, Mina. 1997. "Auto-Facial-Construction." In *The Lost Lunar Baedeker*, ed. Roger L. Conover. Manchester: Carcanet Press.

Lukács, György. 1963. *The Meaning of Contemporary Realism*, trans. John and Necke Mander. London: Merlin Press.

MacDougall, Allan Ross. 1931. *The Gourmets Almanac*. London: D. Harmsworth.

Magnus, Bernd, Jean-Pierre Mileur, and Stanley Stewart. 1993. *Nietzsche's Case: Philosophy as/and Literature*. Abingdon: Routledge.

Mâle, Émile. 1961 [1913]. *The Gothic Image: Religious Art in France of the Thirteenth Century*, trans. Dora Nussey. London & Glasgow: Collins Clear-Type Press.

Marcuse, Herbert. 1998 [1956]. *Eros and Civilisation: A Philosophical Inquiry into Freud*. Abingdon: Routledge.

Marcuse, Herbert. 2007. "The Affirmative Character of Culture (1937)." In *Art and Liberation: Collected Papers of Herbert Marcuse*, ed. Douglas Kellner. Volume 4. Trans. Jeremy J. Shapiro. Abingdon: Routledge.

Marin, Louis. 1976. "Les corps utopiques rabelaisiens." *Littérature* 21 (Février): 35–51.

Maritain, Jacques. 1943. *Art and Poetry*, trans. Elva de Pue Matthews. New York: The Philosophical Library.

Maritain, Jacques. 1958. Letter to Djuna Barnes. November 12, 1958. DBP. Series II, Box 11, Folder 39.

McHale, Brian. 1987. *Postmodernist Fiction*. London and New York: Routledge.

Miller, Tyrus. 1999. *Late Modernism: Politics, Fiction, and the Arts between the World Wars*. Berkeley and London: University of California Press.

Milne, Drew. 2019. "The Critique of Modernist Wit: Djuna Barnes's *Nightwood*." In *Shattered Objects: Djuna Barnes's Modernism*, ed. Elizabeth Pender and Cathryn Setz, 114–29. University Park, PA: Pennsylvania State University Press.

Morfee, Adrian. 2005. *Antonin Artaud's Writing Bodies*. Oxford: Oxford University Press.

Muir, Edwin. 1939. *The Present Age from 1914*. London: Cresset Press.

Mutter, Matthew. 2017. *Restless Secularism: Modernism and the Religious Inheritance*. New Haven, Yale University Press.

Nadler, Steven. 2010. *The Best of All Possible Worlds: A Story of Philosophers, God, and Evil in the Age of Reason*. Princeton and Oxford: Princeton University Press.

Neiman, Susan. 2015. *Evil in Modern Thought: An Alternative History of Philosophy*. Princeton, NJ: Princeton University Press.

Ng, Zhao. 2021. "After *Physiologus*: Post-Medieval Subjectivity and the Modernist Bestiaries of Guillaume Apollinaire and Djuna Barnes." *symplokē* 29: 1–2.

Ng, Zhao. 2020a. "Mad Love: Surrealism and Soteriological Desire." *Literature & Theology* 34, no. 3: 363–85.

Ng, Zhao. 2020b. "Of Beasts Blond and Damned: Fascist and Hysterical Bodies and Djuna Barnes's *Nightwood*." *Twentieth-Century Literature* 66, no. 1: 79–102.

Nieland, Justus. 2008. *Feeling Modern: The Eccentricities of Public Life*. Champaign, IL: University of Illinois Press.

Nietzsche, Friedrich. 1914. *Beyond Good and Evil: Prelude to a Philosophy of the Future*, trans. Helen Zimmern. New York: Macmillan.

Nietzsche, Friedrich. 2009–. *Digitale Kritische Gesamtausgabe Werke und Briefe*. Under the direction of Paolo d'Iorio. Paris: Nietzsche Source. www.nietzschesource.org/eKGWB.

Nietzsche, Friedrich. 2006. *Thus Spoke Zarathustra*, ed. Adrian Del Caro and Robert Pippin, trans. Adrian del Caro. Cambridge: Cambridge University Press.

O'Neal, Hank. 1990. *"Life Is Painful, Nasty and Short … in My Case It Has Only Been Painful and Nasty." Djuna Barnes 1978-1981*. New York: Paragon House.

Parsons, Deborah. 2003. *Djuna Barnes*. Tavistock: Northcote House Publishers.

Pender, Elizabeth and Cathryn Setz, ed. *Shattered Objects: Djuna Barnes's Modernism*. University Park, PA: Pennsylvania State University Press.

Pickstock, Catherine. 2013. *Repetition and Identity*. Oxford: Oxford University Press.

Pieper, Josef. 1954. *The End of Time. A Meditation on the Philosophy of History*, trans. Michael Bullock. London: Faber and Faber.

Pieper, Josef. 1957. *The Silence of St. Thomas: Three Essays*, trans. John Murray and Daniel O'Connor. New York: Pantheon Books.

Pinkerton, Steve. 2017. *Blasphemous Modernism: The 20th-Century Word Made Flesh*. Oxford: Oxford University Press.

Pleij, Herman. 2001. *Dreaming of Cockaigne: Medieval Fantasies of the Perfect Life*, trans. Diane Webb. New York: Columbia University Press.

Plessner, Helmuth. 2003 [1941]. *Lachen und Weinen: Eine Untersuchung der Grenzen menschlichen Verhaltens*. In *Ausdruck und menschliche Natur*. Frankfurt: Suhrkamp Verlag.

Pliny the Elder. 1938-93. *Natural History*, trans. H. Rackham, W.H.S. Jones. 10 vols. Cambridge, MA: Harvard University Press.

Porete, Marguerite. 1993. *The Mirror of Simple Souls*, trans. Ellen Babinsky. New York: Paulist Press.

Proust, Marcel. 1973. *À l'ombre des jeunes filles en fleurs*. Paris: Gallimard.

Proust, Marcel. 1988. *Du côté de chez Swann*, ed. Antoine Compagnon. Paris: Gallimard.

Proust, Marcel. 1990. *Le Temps retrouvé*, ed. Pierre-Louis Rey, Pierre-Edmond Robert, Jacques Robichez, and Brian G. Rogers. Paris: Gallimard.

Proust, Marcel. 1934. *Remembrance of Things Past*, trans. C. K. Scott Moncrieff. 4 vols. New York: Random House.

Rabelais, François. 1973. *Œuvres complètes*, ed. Guy Demerson. Paris: Seuil.

Rabelais, François. 1892. *Five Books of the Lives, Heroic Deeds and Sayings of Gargantua and His Son Pantagruel*, trans. Sir Thomas Urquhart of Cromarty and Peter Anthony Motteux. Illustrated by Louis Chalon. London: Bullen.

Rabelais, François. 2006. *Gargantua and Pantagruel*, ed. and trans. M.A. Screech. London: Penguin Press.

Radden, Jennifer, ed. 2002. *The Nature of Melancholy: From Aristotle to Kristeva*. Oxford: Oxford University Press.

Ragland-Sullivan, Ellie. 1988. "The Limits of Discourse Structure: The Hysteric and the Analyst." *Prose Studies* 11, no. 3: 61–83.

Rascoe, Burton. 1923. "The Books of Christmas Time." *Vanity Fair*, December 1923.

Raschke, Carl. 2014. "Subjectification, Salvation, and the Real in Luther and Lacan." In *Theology after Lacan: The Passion for the Real*, ed. Creston Davis, Marcus Pound, and Clayton Crockett, 58–70. Eugene, OR: Cascade Books.

Reik, Theodor. 1929. *Lust und Leid im Witz: Sechs Psychoanalytische Studien*. Wien, Leipzig, and Zürich: Internationaler Psychoanalytischer Verlag.

Renard, Jules. 1965. *Journal, 1887-1910*, ed. Léon Guichard and Gilbert Sigaux. Paris: Gallimard.

The Revelation of Saint John The Divine. 1926. Foreword by Ernest H. Short. Plates by Albrecht Dürer. London: P. Allen.

Ricoeur, Paul. 1974. *The Conflict of Interpretations: Essays in Hermeneutics*, ed. Don Ihde, trans. Kathleen McLaughlin et al. Evanston: Northwestern University Press.

Ricoeur, Paul. 1977. *Freud and Philosophy: An Essay on Interpretation*, trans. Denis Savage. New Haven: Yale University Press.

Ricoeur, Paul. 2004. *Le mal: Un défi à la philosophie et à la théologie*. Genève: Labor et Fides.

Ricoeur, Paul. 1985. *Time and Narrative, Volume 2*, trans. Kathleen McLaughlin and David Pellauer. Chicago: University of Chicago Press.

Robinson, Joanne Maguire. 2001. *Nobility and Annihilation in Marguerite Porete's Mirror of Simple Souls*. Albany: State University of New York Press.

Ronen, Ruth. 1994. *Possible Worlds in Literary Theory*. Cambridge: Cambridge University Press.

Rupprecht, Caroline. 2006. *Subject to Delusions: Narcissism, Modernism, Gender*. Evanston: Northwestern University Press.

Rushworth, Jennifer. 2016. *Discourses of Mourning in Dante, Petrarch, and Proust*. Oxford: Oxford University Press.

Sacerdoti, Giorgio. 1992. *Irony through Psychoanalysis*, trans. Geraldine Ludbrook. London: Karnac Books.

Saint-Amour, Paul. "Weak Theory, Weak Modernism." *Modernism/modernity* 25, no. 3: 437–59.

Sanchez-Párdo, Esther. 2003. *Cultures of the Death Drive: Melanie Klein and Modernist Melancholia*. Durham: Duke University Press.

Schults, F. LeRon. 2014. *Iconoclastic Theology: Gilles Deleuze and the Secretion of Atheism*. Edinburgh: Edinburgh University Press.

Scott, Bonnie Kime. 1995. *Refiguring Modernism: Postmodern Feminist Readings of Woolf, West, and Barnes*. Bloomington: Indiana University Press.

Seidel, Michael. 1979. *Satiric Inheritance: Rabelais to Sterne*. Princeton: Princeton University Press.

Smith, Paul J. 2014. "Rereading Dürer's Representations of the Fall of Man." In *Zoology in Early Modern Culture: Intersections of Science, Theology, Philology, and Political and Religious Education*, ed. Karl A. E. Enenkel and Paul J. Smith, 301–23. Leiden: Brill.

Sontag, Susan. 1966. *Against Interpretation and Other Essays*. New York: Penguin Press.

Späth, Eberhard. 2004. "'Did He Smile His Work to See?': Blake and the History of Theodicy." In *But Vindicate the Ways of God to Man: Literature and Theodicy*, ed. Rudolf Freiburg and Susanne Gruss, 261–78. Tübingen: Stauffenburg Verlag, 2004.

Steiner, George. 1963 [1961]. *The Death of Tragedy*. New York: Hill & Wang.

Steiner, George. 2008. "'Tragedy,' Reconsidered." In *Rethinking Tragedy*, ed. Rita Felski, 29–44. Baltimore: Johns Hopkins University Press.

Stratton, Matthew. 2014. *The Politics of Irony in American Modernism*. New York: Fordham University Press.

Targoff, Ramie. 2014. *Posthumous Love: Eros and the Afterlife in Renaissance England*. Chicago: University of Chicago Press.

Taylor, Charles. 1989. *Sources of the Self: the Making of the Modern Identity*. Cambridge, MA: Harvard University Press.

Taylor, Julie. 2012. *Djuna Barnes and Affective Modernism*. Edinburgh: Edinburgh University Press.

Tillich, Paul. 1952. *The Courage to Be*. New Haven: Yale University Press.

Trubowitz, Lara. 2005. "In Search of 'The Jew' in Djuna Barnes's *Nightwood*: Jewishness, Antisemitism, Structure, and Style." *Modern Fiction Studies* 51, no. 2: 311–34.

Wallenfang, Donald. 2017. *Dialectical Anatomy of the Eucharist: An Étude in Phenomenology*. Foreword by Jean-Luc Marion. Eugene, OR: Cascade Books.

Walter, Christina. 2014. *Optical Impersonality: Sciences, Images, and Literary Modernism*. Baltimore: Johns Hopkins University Press.

Warren, Diane. 2008. *Djuna Barnes' Consuming Fictions*. Aldershot: Ashgate.

Weber, Samuel. 2015. "Tragedy and Trauerspiel: Too Alike?" In *Tragedy and the Idea of Modernity*, ed. Joshua Billings and Miriam Leonard, 88–114. Oxford: Oxford University Press.

Weil, Simone. 1952. *The Need for Roots: Prelude to a Declaration of Duties Towards Mankind*, trans. A. F. Wills. Preface by T. S. Eliot. London: Routledge.

White, Hayden. 2010a. "Ideology and Counterideology in Northrop Frye's *Anatomy of Criticism*." In *The Fiction of Narrative: Essays on History, Literature, and Theory 1957-2007*, ed. Robert Doran, 247–54. Baltimore: Johns Hopkins University Press.

White, Hayden. 2010b. "Northrop Frye's Place in Contemporary Cultural Studies." In *The Fiction of Narrative: Essays on History, Literature, and Theory 1957-2007*, ed. Robert Doran, 263–72. Baltimore: Johns Hopkins University Press.

Whitebook, Joel. 1996. *Perversion and Utopia: Study in Psychoanalysis and Critical Theory*. Cambridge, MA: MIT Press.

Wilde, Alan. 1981. *Horizons of Assent: Modernism, Postmodernism, and the Ironic Imagination*. Baltimore: Johns Hopkins University Press.

Williams, Robert R. 2012. *Tragedy, Recognition, and the Death of God: Studies in Hegel and Nietzsche*. Oxford: Oxford University Press.

Williams, Rowan. 2017. *God with Us: The Meaning of the Cross and Resurrection – Then and Now*. London: SPCK Publishing.

Williams, Rowan. 2016. *The Tragic Imagination*. Oxford: Oxford University Press.

Winnicott, D. W. 2005. *Playing and Reality*. Abingdon: Routledge.

Winning, Joanne. 2013. "Dreams of a Lost Modernist: A Reevaluation of Thelma Wood." *Modernist Cultures* 8, no. 2: 288–322.

Wolfe, Judith. 2013. "Messianism." In *The Oxford Handbook of Theology and Modern European Thought*, ed. Nicholas Adams et al. Oxford: Oxford University Press.

Wolfe, Judith. 2017. "Eschatology." In *The Oxford Handbook of Nineteenth-Century Christian Thought*, ed. Joel D.S. Rasmussen, Judith Wolfe, Johannes Zachhuber. Oxford: Oxford University Press.

Wordsworth, William. 2008. *The Major Works*, ed. Stephen Gill. Oxford: Oxford University Press.

Wordsworth, William.1807. "Ode." 297–302.

Wordsworth, William.1819. Peter Bell. 91–128.

Young, Julian. 1992. *Nietzsche's Philosophy of Art*. Cambridge: Cambridge University Press.

Žižek, Slavoj. 2009. "The Fear of Four Words: A Modest Plea for the Hegelian Reading of Christianity." In *The Monstrosity of Christ: Paradox or Dialectic?* ed. Creston Davis, 24–109. London and Cambridge, MA: MIT Press.

Žižek, Slavoj. 2000. *The Ticklish Subject: The Absent Centre of Political Ontology*. London: Verso Books.

Index

Addison, Joseph 101
Adorno, Theodor 66, 81, 86, 101–2
affects ix, 108, 153
    affect theory 8, 66
    affective conversion 74–7, 85, 96, 138–43
    affective mapping 4
    amalgamated 38, 43, 93, 105, 112
    in Deleuze and Guattari 55–7, 66, 73–7, 80
    as ontological premise 3, 5, 21, 25, 28, 42–3, 87 (*see also* mood)
    phenomenology of 6–8, 12, 31, 136–7
Agamben, Giorgio 5, 25, 30–1, 63, 119 n.4
almanacs. *See also* Jarry
    Almanach Hachette 63
    L'almanach de cocagne 59
amor fati 86, 96–7, 100–1, 103
Ananke 158, 172
Anaximander 164–5, 167
Anaximenes of Miletus 164
angels 8 n.8, 40, 43, 125, 172–3, 175
    Angel of Death 146
    in the Bible 121
    fallen 11, 13, 35, 132–3, 172–3, 180
    l'être-ange 134–5, 138–9, 143–4
    and sexual indifference 121, 133–6, 139
Antichrist 127, 179–80
antiphon 24–5, 29, 137, 151–3, 168, 172–5, 178
    Gregorian 175
    Marian 152, 175
anti-Semitism. *See also* Judaism
antitype 24–5, 151. *See also* typology
apocalypse 24, 46, 118–19, 131, 134, 146–7, 157
Aquinas, Saint Thomas 9–10, 119 n.4, 149
Aragon, Louis 134
    Le Paysan de Paris 142–3
archetype 90, 100–1, 107, 120, 144
Arendt, Hannah 129
Aristophanes 95

Aristotle 3, 80
Arnauld, Antoine 14
ars moriendi 118
Artaud, Antonin 81
Aryan 126, 129–31, 142
atheism xi, 86, 97, 113
attunement 28, 30. *See also* mood
Augustine, Saint 9–11, 17 n.17, 65, 120
    Confessions 42, 59 n.5
avant-garde 7–8, 58, 150

Backhaus, Wilhelm 2
Barker, George 131
Barnes, Djuna
    birth 2–3
    correspondence ix–x, 1, 9 n.9, 9 n.10, 11, 15–16, 17 n.17, 19, 21, 33–4, 42, 45–6, 49 n.11, 55 n.2, 97, 112, 118 n.2, 120–1, 123 n.10, 124 n.11, 126, 128, 132, 139–40, 145, 146 n.25, 149–50, 152–3, 157, 159–61, 177
    death 100
    family 114
        Elizabeth Chappell Barnes 3, 19, 97, 128, 160
        Wald Barnes 3, 113–4
        Zadel Barnes Gustafson 40
    illness 1–2, 20
    journalism 36, 55, 93–4, 114, 118, 123, 129
    Notebook xi, 153, 164
    religious background xi, 15–16
    scholarship on 8
    sexual abuse 91–2, 92 n.1
    and suicide ix, 20, 178
    works
        The Antiphon 9 n.9, 15, 24, 32, 42, 44, 78, 149–76, 179
        "Becoming Intimate with the Bohemians" 55
        The Book of Repulsive Women 44, 119

Collected Poems 36 n.5, 38, 44
Creatures in an Alphabet 62
"Farewell Paris" 23 n.20, 58, 145
"How It Feels to Be Forcibly Fed" 114
Interviews 2, 19
Ladies Almanack 31, 53–81
Nightwood 2, 8 n.8, 9 n.9, 31, 36 n.3, 38, 40–3, 46, 50–2, 117–48, 151, 162, 172
"Rite of Spring" 100
Ryder 31, 36–7, 65, 68–9, 83–115, 142 n.22
Smoke 43
"A Sprinkle of Comedy" 43
"The Terrorists" 43
"Vagaries Malicieux" 59–60
"Vantage Ground" 22 n.19, 23, 38
"War in Paris" 36 n.3
"A Way of Life" 23
"What is Good Form in Dying?" 118
"Why Actors?" 123, 146
Barney, Natalie 59, 63, 149–51, 177
Barth, Karl 17, 66 n.10, 125
Bataille, Georges 34
Baudelaire, Charles 3–4, 30, 34, 44–5, 158
De l'essence de rire 38–41
Bauer, Bruno 2
Beach, Sylvia 149
Beethoven, Ludwig van 2, 112
Benjamin, Walter 7, 35, 178–80
Bible x, 24, 62, 95, 109–11, 120, 166, 173
  New Testament
    1 Corinthians 117–8, 160, 169
    2 Corinthians 122–3, 136, 176
    Daniel 179 n.2
    Ephesians xi
    Galatians xi n.1
    Luke 62, 171
    Mark 62
    Matthew 61–2, 66, 121, 171
    Revelation 51, 137 n.20, 140, 146, 179 n.2–3
    Romans 111, 122
  Old Testament 10, 23
    Genesis 56, 146, 151
    Isaiah 156
    Job x, 23, 81, 111 n.7
    Numbers 171

Song of Songs 62, 137
Blake, William 10, 34
blasphemy 8, 13, 16, 113, 121, 137, 151–2, 176
Bloch, Ernst 81, 102
Boyle, Kay 55 n.2
Breton, André 134, 142
  Nadja 134 n.17
Broch, Hermann 32
Brontë, Emily 34, 121
Brooklyn Daily Eagle 93–4
Brown, Norman 158–9
Browne, Thomas 63
Buber, Martin 9, 152, 170, 172–3
Burke, Kenneth 8, 129
Burton, Robert 1, 3, 14, 76

Calvinism 15 n.15
Catholicism 9, 15–16, 51, 137–8, 146
Cellini, Benvenuto 144
Chaucer, Geoffrey 97, 109
Chesterton, Gilbert Keith 23, 151
Children's Crusade 128 n.14
Christ 35, 36 n.3, 47–8, 50, 56–7, 114, 120, 127, 146, 176
  arma christi 142
  body of x–xi, 138–42, 175–6
  Christ child 153–6
  Christ event 156–7
  Christological Man 118, 122–3, 125, 146, 178
  imitatio Christi 138
Christianity 38, 41, 60, 118, 122, 151
  Christian eschatology (*see* eschatology)
  Christian salvation history (*see also* history)
  Christian Science 160
  early Christianity 10, 51
church 13, 36, 51 n.13, 64, 136–8, 151
  Church of England 15
Cockaigne, land of 59–60, 79
Cocteau, Jean 38
Coleman, Emily 1, 8, 11–12, 15–16, 17 n.17, 21, 33–4, 45–6, 55 n.2, 112, 120–1, 126, 128 n.15, 131–3, 139, 146, 150, 157, 159–61
  drawings 153–5
  and the Maritains 9
Colette 59

collage 142, 144–5, 173
comedy 30, 38, 81, 83, 92–3. *See also* literary worlds
  divine comedy 10, 29–30, 57, 157
  as mediated laughter 45, 52, 105
  and reconciliation 31, 56, 65, 79, 83, 85–7
  and tragedy (*see also* judgment)
communion 40, 42–3, 105, 110, 180
  Holy Communion 78
Crivelli, Carlo 154
Cronus 153

Dada 8 n.6, 58 n.4
Dali, Salvador 121 n.6
damnation xi, 1, 25, 30, 118–19, 121, 155–6, 174
  and beasts 123–48, 180
  and laughter 41–3
  and women 39, 76, 80, 92
D'Annunzio, Gabriele 126
Dante Alighieri 120–2
Dasein 28, 42, 44
de Sade, Marquis 34, 126–7, 158
death 20, 85, 106, 121, 162,
  in allegory 42 n.9, 101, 145–8, 153
    Dance of Death ix–x
    Death and the Maiden 118
    Grim Raper 84, 91, 178
  Barnes's (*see also* Barnes)
  being-toward x, 117–19, 123, 127, 150
  and birth 96–7, 151, 153–6, 166, 171–4
  of God (*see also* God)
  and love ix–xi, 140, 171
  and resurrection x, 3, 32, 95, 122–3, 176–81
Decadence 7, 126, 138
decreation 56–7, 64–7
Deleuze, Gilles and Félix Guattari 4, 66, 69, 81 *See also* affects
  iconoclastic theology 56–8, 63–4
  ontology of art 71–3
  percepts 73–4, 76, 80
  schizophrenia 72 (*see also* God)
  sensation 71, 73, 75–8
devil 33–5, 39–41, 125, 127, 167
  Lucifer 35
  Satan 38–9, 114, 158, 160

dialectic 30, 65, 117, 128, 133, 135
  body and image 55, 117, 121, 131
  dialectical constellation 5–6, 10, 25–8, 47, 52, 179
  and history 66 n.10, 71–2, 152–3, 157
  liturgical 174–6
  melancholy and theodicy 1–32, 52
Dickens, Charles 71
Diogenes Laertius 164
Divine Economy 11, 23, 45, 50–1, 132, 173
divinization 10–12, 51, 57, 123, 178
doll 125, 133–4, 144, 167
Dostoevsky, Fyodor 10, 23–4, 97–8, 112, 138
Dürer, Albrecht 46–9, 146–7
Durkheim, Émile 13

Eckhart, Meister 57, 64
Eden 36, 58 n.4, 59, 73, 158, 166, 169, 171
Einstein, Albert 35
ek-centricity 37, 44. *See also ek-stasis*
ek-stasis 38, 40, 50–2, 123, 143, 148
Eliade, Mircea 86, 89–90, 100, 102
Eliot, T. S. 8, 119 n.3, 140, 151, 156 n.5, 159
Éluard, Paul 135
engraving 46–9, 140–1, 146–7
Enlightenment 10, 14, 159
Episcopalian 15
eschatology 10, 30, 46, 179. *See also* death. *See also* Kingdom of Heaven
  and art 21–2, 25, 29
  and the body x–xi, 57, 117–29, 131–48, 159 (*see also* resurrection)
  Christian xi, 156–9
  Nazi 128, 130–1
  projective 66, 81
  realized 65–6, 77–8, 86
eternal recurrence 35–6, 92–7, 100, 102, 164–5
evil 33–5, 157–8. *See also* reconciliation
  and good 12, 17 n.17, 35, 39, 113
  mystery of 12, 14, 35, 52
  natural 11, 33
  necessary 12
  the problem of 10 n.11, 10 n.13, 11–12, 33
  radical 17, 180
  and suffering 9–14, 17, 21, 35, 52, 150, 178

Fall, the 2–3, 57, 63, 67, 81, 121. *See also* angels. *See also* melancholy
   and Creation 166, 171
   fallen existence 6, 10, 17, 26, 36, 178
   symptoms of (*See also* laughing and crying)
fascism 126–7, 130–1. *See also* Nazism
felix culpa 40, 50, 132
Ficino, Marsilio 3
First World War 66 n.10
Flanner, Janet 114
Fratellini brothers 38
Frazer, James 105
Freud, Sigmund 2–6, 13, 37, 57, 60, 68, 71, 121 n.6, 125, 170, 176
   Civilisation and Its Discontents 158
   The Ego and the Id ix, 104, 112
   The Future of an Illusion 158
   "Mourning and Melancholia" ix, 35, 36 n.1, 41, 104
   "Negation" 105–6
   Three Essays on the Theory of Sexuality 128–9, 143, 158
   Totem and Taboo 105–6
Freytag-Loringhoven, Baroness Elsa von 58 n.4

Galen 3
Gauguin, Paul 126
Girard, René 89
God 9–19, 36, 51, 62, 68, 99–100, 120–3, 148, 151, 153, 163
   and artist 24–5, 31, 34, 81, 178
   in Baudelaire 38–9
   in Benjamin 179–80
   in Dostoevsky 97–8
   death of 14, 19, 99, 177
   fascist 126–7, 131
   in Freud 158
   Goddess 58, 77, 158
   Gods 93–5, 177
   and the hysteric 135–8
   Kingdom of (*See also* heaven)
   in Porete 64–6
   queer xi, 63–6, 81
   relationship with 5, 29–31, 160, 163, 175
   schizophrenic 57, 64–6, 72
   vindication of (*see* theodicy)
   in Wordsworth 33–4
Goethe, Johann Wolfgang von 2

Gogol, Nikolai 112
Goya, Francisco 153
grace xi, 25, 43, 51, 57, 65, 67, 81, 124, 146, 173–5
   and *sola fide* 36 n.3, 160–1
Grand Inquisitor 23–4, 30–1
Greenwich Village 97
Gregory of Nyssa 132
Guggenheim, Peggy 112, 152, 161

Hades 84
Hammarskjöld, Dag 9 n.10
Handel, George Frideric 78, 118
heaven 11–13, 34–5, 38, 65, 118, 121, 132, 137, 145–8, 175 n.8
   Kingdom of Heaven 58, 61–2, 66, 80, 129, 156–7
Hegel, Georg Wilhelm Friedrich 2, 10, 16–18, 56, 66 n.10, 69, 72, 153, 174–5
Heidegger, Martin x, 5, 26, 28–9, 35, 37, 118
hell 34, 80
Hildegard von Bingen 130
Hitler, Adolf 2 n.1, 126–9, 131, 135
Hobbes, Thomas 20
Holy Community 43, 122
homosexual 56, 121, 145 n.23. *See also* lesbian
Hopkins, Gerard Manley 25
humor 41, 43, 75, 108. *See also* laughing and crying
   Barnes's 2
   forms of 84–7, 97, 100–1, 104, 108, 115. *See also* irony
   de-sublimating humor 88, 91
   sublimating humor 92–3
   and repetition 83–5
hybrid bodies xii, 37, 45–52, 58, 69–71, 78–9
   sexual difference 31, 45–6, 68, 118 n.1, 121, 126, 131–5, 139
   species difference x, 31, 45–52, 68, 100, 104, 107, 126
hyperbole 95–6, 110
hysteria 127–8, 131, 133–9, 143–5

Ignatius of Loyola, Saint 138
immanence 64–6, 81, 101–3, 106–8, 110–2, 120, 153, 159, 177
Incarnation 56
Irenaeus of Lyon 10–12. *See also* theodicy

irony 83, 85–8, 100–5, 108, 110, 136, 149
    and spitting 104–5, 110, 112, 114

Jack the Ripper 126
James, William 10, 13
    Varieties of Religious Experience 14, 16–7, 19
Jarry, Alfred 65
    Almanach de Père Ubu 63
Jesus. *See* Christ
    Jesus Mundane 103, 108, 110–12, 114
Joachim de Fiore 66 n.10
jouissance 67, 133, 135
Joyce, James 22–3, 25, 63
Judaism 9, 13, 16. *See also* anti-Semitism
    16, 127 n.12, 131
    Jew xi n.1, 1, 16, 126, 128, 178
Judas 34
judgment 19–20, 104–5, 153
    aesthetic 9–10, 17, 20–31, 45, 52 178
    comic 21, 31
    either/or 21, 25, 28, 52, 178
    existential 20, 178, 180
    and God 15, 17, 23–5, 101, 136, 160
    Last Judgment 21–2, 28–31, 66 n.10, 139 n.21, 169, 178–80
    and psychoanalysis 105–6
    tragic 21, 31–2, 148, 150, 153, 176

Kant, Immanuel 57 n.3
Keats, John 3, 10
    letters 2, 12, 101
    "Ode on Melancholy" 1
kenosis 56
Kierkegaard, Søren 24
Klein, Melanie 37, 104, 167–8
Kleist, Heinrich von 132
Kristeva, Julia 3, 6

La Dame à la Licorne 49
Lacan, Jacques 57, 122, 125, 130–2, 134–5, 143
    "The Signification of the Phallus" 68–9
laughing and crying xii, 3, 6, 15, 31, 37–45, 51–2, 135, 138, 145
    laughter 87, 148, 101, 104–5, 108, 110, 148, 166
        of the gods 93, 95
        soothlaugher 95
        will-to-laughter 85–6, 92

tears 12, 24, 44, 137, 144, 148
Lautréamont, Comte de 38–9, 41, 42 n.8, 158
Lazarus 118
Leibniz, Gottfried Wilhelm 10, 14, 16
lesbian 56, 58, 62, 66–7, 73–9, 81
    the lesbian phallus 69–71, 77
    Lesbos 59, 77
    Sappho 36, 55, 58–60, 67–8, 77
Lewis, Wyndham 129–31
literary worlds xi, 5, 7, 11, 21, 24–31, 45, 52, 157, 178
    comic 56, 81, 83, 86
    tragic 19, 119, 152, 154, 176
Logos 57, 68–9, 71, 158–9, 174
Lombroso, Cesare 126
Lourié, Arthur 175
Loy, Mina 54–5, 59
Lukács, György 37, 71–3
Luther, Martin 9, 36, 114, 159–61, 163, 167

MacDougall, Allan Ross 58
Madonna. *See* Mary
Mahoney, Dan 38, 121 n.7, 124 n.11, 145
Malebranche, Nicolas 14
Marcuse, Herbert 158–9
Maritain, Jacques 9, 146, 175
    and *The Antiphon* 9 n.9, 157
    and *Nightwood* 9 n.9
Maritain, Raïssa 9
Marx, Karl 18, 158
Mary, mother of Jesus 43, 124–5, 153–4.
    See also antiphon
    Mariology 152–3, 155–6, 174
medievalism 36, 55, 59, 62–3, 68–70, 142, 149
    art 49, 120, 139 n.21
    rhetoric 75
melancholy 31, 39–40, 72, 118, 131, 178–81. *See also* dialectic
    in allegory 46–52
    and the Fall 31–7
    in history 2–3, 36–7
    and ontology 1–10, 30, 35–7, 46
    and psychoanalysis ix, 4, 7, 104, 110, 112, 128
    subject ix, 9, 19, 31, 35–6, 43, 52, 56, 73, 108, 110, 112, 148, 178
    as structure of existence 3–7, 26, 31, 35–7, 45–6, 50, 56, 65, 73, 123

and suffering 7, 9–10, 14, 20
symptoms of xi, 1–3, 5–6, 35, 38–41, 43, 52
and theology 2–3, 5, 7, 14
memento mori 84, 122, 178
Memling, Hans 2, 42 n.9
menstruation 1, 39, 41, 161–2
messianism 30, 129
    messianic time 25
    weak messianic power 178–80
mode 24, 26–32
modernism xi, 18, 29, 71–2, 77, 81, 87, 104, 108, 149, 178
    French 2
    and the novel 7, 13
    and religion 7
Monteverdi, Claudio 175 n.8
mood 5–6, 21, 26–32, 35, 37, 42
    counter- 4–6, 25, 28, 37
Moore, George 126
motherhood 84–6, 91, 96–7, 103–5, 113, 153–8, 166–70
mourning x, 4, 30, 40–1, 43, 45, 111
Mozart, Wolfgang Amadeus 2, 175
Muir, Edwin 36, 140
Musée de Cluny 49
Mussolini, Benito 126
mystery 11–12, 15, 51, 62, 70, 132, 137. *See also* evil
mysticism 9, 63, 120, 129, 138
myth 13, 18, 24, 50–2, 60, 79, 81, 84, 104, 107, 118, 128–31, 135
    as cyclical time 86, 88–91, 101–3, 106–7, 111, 164, 168

Napoleon Bonaparte 126
narcissism 125, 127–31, 133–5
Nazism 128–31, 142, 178. *See also* fascism
Neagoe, Peter 113
Nietzsche, Friedrich 13, 18–19, 35, 86, 97–8, 100–2, 110, 115, 129, 164 n.7
    Beyond Good and Evil 93, 95
    Thus Spoke Zarathustra 95–6
Nordau, Max 126

Odin 131
Oedipus 57, 99, 153
Ontology. *See also* melancholy

archaic 90, 102
homo-ontology 56, 66–7, 78–80
onto-economy 156, 165, 167–9, 173–6
ontological exile 36, 40, 42, 45–6, 50–1, 124, 139
ontological incompletion of the body 10, 50, 123, 125, 127
ontological monism 56
ontological status of the hysteric. *See* hysteric
of history and virtuality 58, 72–3. *See also* Deleuze
of the virtual 58, 72
as structure of world 5–7, 20–1, 26–7, 30, 60, 65 (*see also* work of art)
(*See also* literary worlds)
as world-making 60, 72–3, 126
ontotheology 16–17, 19, 29–30
Origen 62, 119 n.4
Ottinger, Joseph 140–2

Paisiello, Giovanni 137
Pascal, Blaise 111
pastoral 36, 60–1, 78, 80, 171, 177
Paul, Saint 25, 57, 111, 122
Pearson's Magazine 19
Perse, Saint-John 9 n.10
Persephone 84, 90
Petronius 123
Pieper, Josef 9, 156
Plato 2, 24, 90, 132, 158–9
play 169–76
Plessner, Helmuth 44–5
Pliny the Elder 164
polyphony 103, 108–12
Pope, Alexander 10, 78
Porete, Marguerite 9, 57, 63–6
Pound, Ezra 149
prosopic intercourse 153, 169, 174–6
Protestantism 9, 15, 36 n.3, 140, 159–60. *See also* Luther. *See also* Tillich
Proust, Marcel 2, 23, 54–5, 126
    À la recherche du temps perdu ix, 4, 21–2, 53
    À l'ombre des jeunes filles en fleurs 53
    Du Côté de chez Swann 177
    Le Temps retrouvé 21–2
psychoanalysis 7–8, 56–7, 87, 107, 112, 122, 128 n.15, 159

queer theory x, 7–8, 69, 122

Rabelais, François 65, 67, 76, 79
Rachilde 59
Ragnarök 118
Raphael 154
reconciliation 21, 31, 97, 150, 178. *See also* comedy
   and evil 11, 17
   false 100, 115, 135, 139
redemption 29–30, 33, 37, 40–1, 47, 57, 59, 152, 157, 170–9. *See also* salvation
   in Eliade 86, 90
   false 101, 127
   in Nazism 129–31
   in Nietzsche 86, 95–100
Reformation 36, 66 n.10, 160
Renaissance 63, 121, 154
Renard, Jules 59
repetition x, 25, 92–3, 121–7. *See also* eternal recurrence. *See also* humor
   conservative 22, 24, 33–4, 89–90, 100, 107, 168
   differential 4, 22, 24–5, 27–8, 90
resurrection 77–8, 95, 101, 121, 152, 157, 159, 165, 174. *See also* death. *See also* eschatology
   of Christ xi, 29, 56, 118
   Resurrection history 30, 118–9
Ricoeur, Paul x, 10 n.11, 16–17, 22–3, 29, 118, 158
Rimbaud, Arthur 126
Romanticism 2, 10, 34, 36, 66 n.10
Rosenberg, Alfred 131
Rubens, Peter Paul 153
Rutebeuf 140

sacrament xi, 8 n.7, 36
   baptism xi, 122, 181
   Eucharist 77–8, 105, 152–3, 174–5
   sacramental bread 78, 105, 160
salvation 60, 102, 127, 152, 157, 159, 172–3
   in Deleuze and Guattari 57
   in Dostoevsky 98
   history 11, 18, 29, 50, 119, 132, 158, 179 (*see also* divine economy)
   reversal of 152–3
   in Porete 64 (*see also* redemption)
   sola fide 36 n.3, 160, 163

soteriology 40–7, 107, 114, 173
   soteriological crisis 36–7, 52, 125, 127, 133–4, 178
   soteriological desire 41, 124, 126
   soteriological indecision 31, 123
   soteriological relation 125, 128, 131, 134–6, 139
satire 60, 87–92, 97–8, 104, 109–10
   Mennipean 109
Saul, King 118
Schopenhauer, Arthur 19
Schreber, Daniel Paul 57
Schubert, Franz 137
Scotus, Duns 66
Second Coming, the 122
Second World War x, 152, 176
secularization 13–14
sex-relation 70
sexology 8 n.8, 68
sexual difference. *See also* hybrid bodies
Shakespeare, William 2, 38, 150–1, 166
silverpoint 46, 48
sin 38, 43, 59, 146, 155, 171
   original 10, 30, 63, 158
Sisyphus 102, 164
Sköll 118
Sontag, Susan 158–9
species difference. *See also* hybrid bodies
Stein, Gertrude 59, 63
Stephen of Cloyes. *See* Children's Crusade
Stimmung. *See* mood
Stoicism 96–7
Stravinsky, Igor 100–2
sublimation 158–60, 162, 164–5, 167–8, 170, 173
suffering 19, 28, 43, 119, 145, 157. *See also* evil. *See also* melancholy
suicide 97–9, 101, 178. *See also* Barnes
Surrealism 7, 8 n.6, 38, 58 n.4, 31, 135, 142
   La Révolution surréaliste 134
Symbolism 7, 38, 126
synderesis 31, 63, 65

teleology 11–12, 51
   autoteleology 54, 57
   of the drives 129, 143
   and Soul-making 12
theodicy 3, 22, 31, 48, 72, 86, 97, 102, 153
   anti-theodicy 17, 21, 176
   Augustinian 10–11

in history 10, 15
Irenaean 10–12
negative theodicy 86
the question of 9–16, 19–25, 29–31, 52, 87, 150, 178
rationalist 16–19
theodistical unconscious 9, 15, 17–18, 20
weak theodicy 9, 16–21, 152, 178, 180–1
Theognis 19
theology 8, 35, 40, 132, 136, 170–1. *See also* melancholy
crime of 86, 101
of immanence (*see* immanence)
and literature 6–7, 14–15
systematic theology 9, 12–16, 18–19
theological anthropology 7, 41, 118 n.1
and theory 6–7, 18–20, 56–8, 64, 122
weak theology 179
theophany 63, 81
theosis. *See* divinization
Theresa, Saint 3
Thérèse of Lisieux 175 n.9
Thoreau, Henry David 113–4
Tillich, Paul 9, 156–7, 159–60, 176
Tolstoy, Leo 112–3
Toulouse-Lautrec, Henri de 126
tragedy 29–32, 38, 83, 93, 127, 145–7, 150–8, 167–70, 179. *See also* judgment. *See also* literary worlds
as mediated tears 45
pan-tragism 17
tragic temporality 164, 173
tragicomic 43, 137, 145 n.24
trans 118, 123, 126, 132, 134, 137–8, 144

theory 8, 134, 135 n.18
transcendence 64–5, 101, 103, 114, 120, 124, 134
transference 124–5
Trappist 149
trauma 4, 9, 83, 92, 170
Turgenev, Ivan 112
typology 24–5, 28–30, 86, 118 n.1, 127, 151

utopia 56, 58, 60, 65–7, 71–3, 80–1

Vanity Fair 36
Veil of Veronica 176
Venus 68–9, 76, 123
   Cyprian 77
Verlaine, Paul 126
Voltaire 16

Wagner, Richard 129
Weber, Max 13
Weil, Simone 9, 57, 129, 164
White, Antonia 145
Whitman, Walt 113
Winnicott, Donald 170
Wisdom of Silenus 19
Wood, Thelma ix, 17 n.17, 46, 48
woodcut 46, 142 n.22, 146–7. *See also* engraving
Woolf, Virginia 178
Wordsworth, William 36
   "Intimations of Immortality" 33–4
   Peter Bell 33
work of art, the 6–7, 9, 12, 20–2, 24–32, 37
   the unconscious of 26–8, 45–6

www.ingramcontent.com/pod-product-compliance
Lightning Source LLC
Chambersburg PA
CBHW062228300426
44115CB00012BA/2262